CULTURAL HISTORIES OF CINEMA

This new book series examines the relationship between cinema and culture. It will feature interdisciplinary scholarship that focuses on the national and transnational trajectories of cinema as a network of institutions, representations, practices and technologies. Of primary concern is analysing cinema's expansive role in the complex social, economic and political dynamics of the twentieth and twenty-first centuries.

SERIES EDITORS
Lee Grieveson and Haidee Wasson

ALSO PUBLISHED

Arab Cinema Travels: Transnational Syria, Palestine, Dubai and Beyond, *Kay Dickinson*
Cinema Beyond Territory: Inflight Entertainment and
Atmospheres of Globalisation, *Stephen Groening*
Empire and Film, *edited by Lee Grieveson and Colin MacCabe*
Film and the End of Empire, *edited by Lee Grieveson and Colin MacCabe*
George Kleine and American Cinema: The Movie Business and Film Culture
in the Silent Era, *Joel Frykholm*
Global Mexican Cinema: Its Golden Age, *Robert McKee Irwin and Maricruz Castro
Ricalde (with Mónica Szurmuk, Inmaculada Álvarez and Dubravka Sužnjević)*
The Grierson Effect: Tracing Documentary's International Movement,
edited by Zoë Druick and Deane Williams
Making Movies into Art: Picture Craft from the Magic Lantern to Early Hollywood,
Kaveh Askari
Shadow Economies of Cinema: Mapping Informal Film Distribution, *Ramon Lobato*

Spanish Film Cultures

The Making and Unmaking of Spanish Cinema

Nuria Triana-Toribio

•

A BFI book published by Palgrave

First published in 2016 by
PALGRAVE

on behalf of the

BRITISH FILM INSTITUTE
21 Stephen Street, London W1T 1LN
www.bfi.org.uk

There's more to discover about film and television through the BFI. Our world-renowned archive, cinemas, festivals, films, publications and learning resources are here to inspire you.

PALGRAVE in the UK is an imprint of Macmillan Publishers Limited, registered in England, company number 785998, of 4 Crinan Street, London N1 9XW. Palgrave Macmillan in the US is a division of St Martin's Press LLC, 175 Fifth Avenue, New York, NY 10010. Palgrave is a global imprint of the above companies and is represented throughout the world. Palgrave® and Macmillan® are registered trademarks in the United States, the United Kingdom, Europe and other countries.

Cover design: Alex Connock

Images from *El bosque animado* (José Luís Cuerda, 1987), Classic Film Company/TVE Televisión Española; cartoon on p. 25, Manuel Summers, *Magazine Sábado Gráfico*, 20 July 1974

Typeset by Cambrian Typesetters, Camberley, Surrey
Printed and bound by CPI Group (UK) Ltd, Croydon, CR0 4YY

This book is printed on paper suitable for recycling and made from fully managed and sustained forest sources. Logging, pulping and manufacturing processes are expected to conform to the environmental regulations of the country of origin.
British Library Cataloguing-in-Publication Data
A catalogue record for this book is available from the British Library
A catalog record for this book is available from the Library of Congress

ISBN 978–1–84457–821–4 (pb)
ISBN 978–1–84457–822–1 (hb)

Contents

Acknowledgments

My editors at BFI Publishing/Palgrave and the Cultural Histories of Cinema series editors, Lee Grieveson and Haidee Wasson, have my deepest gratitude. Besides them, many interlocutors have guided me along the process of research and writing. Firstly, thanks to the two anonymous readers who made excellent suggestions. Sarah Barrow, Ann Davies, Stephanie Dennison, Marvin and Carol D'Lugo, Jo Evans, Sally Faulkner, Santi Fouz Fernández, Carmen Herrero, Dona Kercher, Jo Labanyi, Susan Martin-Márquez, Deborah Shaw, Paul Julian Smith, Rob Stone, Katie Vernon, Sarah Wright, Barbara Zecchi and many, many others have offered support and advice at different stages. Special thanks to my dear Belén Vidal, whose deep knowledge of and discernment about all matters cinematic, her kindness and friendship I treasure.

Spanish and Catalan family and friends have challenged and shared my views over good humour, good food and even better wine. Among them, Valeria Camporesi, Josetxo Cerdán, Ángel Quintana, Miguel Fernández Labayén, Marga Lobo and Marta Mateo. The Triana-Toribio, Amorín Triana, Triana Fernández and Pérez Daniel branches of my family provided focus groups, researchers and astute audience members. Chapter 4 is for Nacho and 5 for Carlos Triana Fernández, my budding film-maker nephew.

Patricia Viada at the Academia library was very helpful and so were Ana Arrieta and Rosa Vergés, Gracias/Gracies! Special thanks go to the amazingly knowledgeable and kind Fernando Lara and José Luis Cienfuegos.

To my colleagues at SECL in Kent, thanks for an intellectually stimulating environment! Thank you, Anna Katherina Schaffner, for our walks and chats about the editing process, and Shane Weller, for his wit, encouragement and friendship.

My students, particularly my doctoral students, teach me constantly. Jara Fernández Meneses shared much material with me and was willing to discuss my most protean ideas. I owe her a huge debt. Emilio Gómez Barranco's help was invaluable to source key articles. Film Studies at Kent has provided wonderful friends in the department. Thank you, Tamar Jeffers McDonald and Peter Stanfield. Thanks to my co-directors in the Centre for Film and Media Research.

From the northwest, I received encouragement from Ricardo Bermúdez-Otero, Anke Bernau, Dani Caselli, Diana Cullell, Cornerhouse/HOME/Viva, Rob and Leo Duggan, Matthew Frost, Jeff Geiger, Hal Gladfelder, Noelle Gallagher, Angela Keane, Par Kumaraswami, Emma Liggins, Scott McCracken, David Matthews, Hilary Owen, Chris Perriam, Lucía Sà, Andy Willis and other friends from the powerhouse that has always been Manchester. You know who you are.

From across the ocean, I am indebted to Melissa Jacques, Betsy de Vos, SR, and closer to home, to Elle Nathan, for keeping me going when the going was tough!

Mil gracias, a mi amiga Cecilia Sayad for her affectionate company, her intellectual generosity and to Antonio Lázaro-Reboll, my amazing *colega*, for excellent suggestions and for never closing his door. Thanks to his family too, particularly to Elsa for *Frozen*!

Peter Evans and Isabel Santaolalla, my love and gratitude for you knows no bounds.

Without Anastasia Valassopoulos, Marina Díaz López, Josep Lluís Fecé and Cristina Pujol Ozonas, this book would not exist.

This book is dedicated to Peter Buse, *que me hace vivir a tres metros sobre el cielo*.

NOTE ABOUT REFERENCING AND TRANSLATIONS

All translations are mine, unless stated in the text. For film titles, I have used the IMDb official title where available. I have used the English titles of films after first mention, to facilitate the flow of the text to non-Spanish-speaking readers. In tables, I have provided the Spanish title only due to space limitations.

The journal *Cahiers du Cinéma España* changed its name and numbering sequence in December 2011 to *Caimán Cuadernos de Cine*, but it continued with the same editorial line.

Introduction

The past four decades have seen a great flowering of Spanish film. An industry which was once barely known outside its national borders, or was represented by a single exiled film-maker, Luis Buñuel, now has broad international recognition, thanks to high-profile directors, actors and films. *Belle Époque* (Fernando Trueba, 1992) was awarded Best Foreign-Language Film in 1993, as was *Todo sobre mi madre/All About My Mother* (Pedro Almodóvar, 1999) in 1999 and *Mar adentro/The Sea Inside* (Alejandro Amenábar, 2004) in 2005. In 2008, Javier Bardem won the Academy Award for Best Supporting Actor for *No Country for Old Men* (Ethan and Joel Cohen, 2007), and in 2009 Penélope Cruz won Best Supporting Actress for *Vicky Cristina Barcelona* (Woody Allen, 2008). Almodóvar's *Hable con ella/Talk to Her* (2002) was the Academy Award-winning screenplay in 2004, a momentous event, as Marvin D'Lugo points out, since this was only the second time in the history of the Oscars that a non-American script had won (*Pedro Almodóvar*, p. 114). Other measures of success are the significant achievements at major film festivals in Europe. Almodóvar won Best Director at Cannes in 1999, Álex de la Iglesia was awarded the Silver Lion at Venice for Best Director in 2010 and Catalan Lluís Miñarro was producer of *Uncle Boonmee Who Can Recall His Past Lives* (Apichatpong Weerasethakul, 2010), winner of the Palme D'Or at Cannes in 2010.

These successes have not come about by chance, but are the result of deliberate strategies and legislation – mostly inspired and fashioned by members and sympathisers of the Spanish Socialist Party (Partido Socialista Obrero Español) from the advent of democracy in the mid-1970s until the Socialist Party's last period in power (2011). Key to this strategy was the establishment of the Academia de las Artes y las Ciencias Cinematográficas (AACC), the Spanish Film Academy. The Academia was created by key professionals of the Spanish film-making industry between 1986 and 1987, and it is, as it completes its third decade, the largest and most important association of film professionals working in Spain. Among its membership are recognised transnational professionals and also critically acclaimed younger directors such as Icíar Bollaín (*Te doy mis ojos/Take My Eyes* [2004]) and Juan A. Bayona *(El orfanato/The Orphanage* [2007]; *Lo imposible/The Impossible* [2012]*).* When national and international media seek and cite the 'opinion of Spanish cinema', it is the president of the Academia whose words are sought.

The Academia's role in shaping Spanish film did not derive from its media presence or the lobbying by its influential membership alone. Since 1987, Academia members have decided annually what constitute achievements in Spanish film-making, what practices should be encouraged, and which ones discouraged. Academicians make their judgment public through awarding prizes (the Goya awards) at a ceremony that is Spain's version of the Oscars ceremony and has become a major annual media event. And the same members are in charge of selecting Spain's yearly submission to the American Academy's foreign-language film award.

The Goya awards are the highest accolades to which a Spanish film or film-maker can aspire nationally, and the Academia's site in Calle de Zurbano, a renovated eighteenth-century palace in central Madrid, is the main physical home of Spanish cinema and its professionals. It is also a repository of Spain's filmic heritage, where events and screenings focusing on Spanish film productions of all eras are held and which receives significant donations from living members and legacies from those who have passed away. It is a key space where Spanish film-makers and film professionals can meet, network, and make use of library and screening resources. The Barcelona office in Passeig de Colom serves the same purpose for Catalan academicians.

In this book, I will argue not only that the Academia has shaped Spanish film cultures in democracy, but that it has created the idea of Spanish cinema as we know it. Spain's film culture – both the dominant or hegemonic and the emergent and the waning film cultures that have grown or withered in conflict or opposition to it between 1986 and 2011 – depended and depends on the Academia. The Academia, in its turn, was a direct product of a perceived need to protect film-making after Francoism by turning it into a democratic and reputable industry populated by professionals pursuing common objectives.

WHY ACADEMIES?

Spain is not the first or only country to have a film academy. If the background from which academies emerged is specific to each one, their tales of origins and basic functions are not. Therefore, reflecting on what they share is a good starting point to argue for their study, demonstrating how this particular analysis of the Spanish Academia will prove fruitful for the investigation of the attempts made by other national organisations to negotiate and harness the forces of film-making, which has always been such a transnational enterprise. I will be relying on comparison with the Academia's 'sisters' around the world, such as the Academia de las Artes y Ciencias Cinematográficas de la Argentina (first established in 1941 and disbanded by the military junta in 1955, later reopened in 2004), the Academia Mexicana de Artes y Ciencias Cinematográficas (AMACC) (established in 1946), the British Academy of Film and Television Arts (BAFTA) (formed in 1947), the French Académie des Arts et Techniques du Cinéma (AATC) (1979), the European Film Academy (EFA) (1988), the Deutsche Filmakademie (2003) and the Acadèmia del Cinema Català (2008).[1] Repeated reference will be made to their 'mother' as well: the American Academy of Motion Picture Arts and Sciences (AMPAS) (1927).

Film academies exist due to a combination of nationalism and the desire to generate what could be called the 'academy effect'. Andrew Higson has shown how nationalism in cinema has often translated itself into finding ways of 'asserting national autonomy in the face of (usually) Hollywood's international domination' (p. 37). The intervention of the state is key for the execution of this assertiveness, even after decades of speaking of a '"supersession" of the state under the forces of globalization', argues Crofts (p. 5). Often the state needs an interlocutor, a group from the industry that represents all the separate branches of film-making, and lobbies for their interests. In such instances, founding an academy became a tool of nationalism and protectionism, even if not every territory made use of it.

James English argues that the creation of academies and the prizes they awarded worked well from the late Renaissance and the Enlightenment in Europe as an instrument 'to bring cultural workers and their products under tighter supervision and discipline' (p. 37). He explains how in seventeenth-century Italy and France, the success of the academies in arts such as painting 'led to its widespread emulation and hastened the process by which the production of art and of artistic value was brought under the control of national bureaucracies' (ibid.).

By the time cinema was invented, academies already possessed a reputation for effectiveness and respectability, both very desirable qualities for a nascent 'art' or cultural industry aiming to lift itself from its origins as a fairground attraction in the late 1910s, to use the expression coined by Tom Gunning in 'The Cinema of Attractions' in 1986 (pp. 63–77). The status of cinema was changing on both sides of the Atlantic. France led the way in conferring on cinema the legitimacy that older arts possessed and in establishing their learned study in sites of knowledge such as the university and the museum. Susan Hayward argues that '[t]he genesis of film theory belongs to France and dates from around the 1910s' (p. 76). Alongside this transformation, the two rising ideologies of the early twentieth century, Communism and Fascism, saw in films essential instruments to reach the masses and sought control over cinema, something that is captured in telling remarks by Lenin and Mussolini respectively: 'The cinema is the most important of all the arts', and 'For us, the cinema is the most important weapon' (both cited in Nowell-Smith and Dupin, p. 23). The status of cinema was greatly enhanced by its utility for both.

Haidee Wasson (*Museum Movies: The Museum of Modern Art and the Birth of Art Cinema* [2005]) and Geoffrey Nowell-Smith and Christophe Dupin (*The British Film Institute, the Government and Film Culture 1933–2000* [2012]) are among the scholars who have explored cinema's formative years in the English-speaking contexts of the US and Britain, crucial for the transformation of films' social and cultural function. In the 1920s, small but influential groups in both countries legitimated film viewing as a cultural practice through the creation of national film libraries, associating cinema in this way with institutions such as museums, which possessed strong academic and cultural credentials (see *Museum Movies*). Acceptability came as well through the founding of film societies and institutes which pursued educational goals, such as the British Film Institute (Nowell-Smith and Dupin, pp. 17–24). All these efforts towards preservation, elevation, education – in short, towards the use of film for purposes other than entertainment – developed alongside the first film academy in Hollywood, which was pursuing comparable respectability for the main industry. After the interruption of World War II, the academy model arrived in Mexico and Britain and took hold there as well.

The rise of the late Renaissance and Enlightenment academy is a European phenomenon, but the first film industry to appropriate this tried and tested instrument of control and nationalist protectionism was the US industry located in Hollywood, followed by Mexico and Argentina a couple of decades later. Robert Osborne (p. 8) explains how the legendary producer Louis B. Mayer set out to create AMPAS in 1927 in order to 'benefit the entire industry', help solve technological problems, aid in arbitrating labour disputes and assist Will Hays in policing screen content (ibid.). Of all these aims, compliance with the Hays Code would secure respectability for the studios and the Academy. Seeking respectability and strength in numbers in order to 'bring cultural workers and their products under tighter supervision and discipline', in English's words, lies at the heart of all academies (p. 37). The statement that the organisation published on 20 June 1927 emphasised this aspiration to become one respectable voice by concluding with the following aim: 'In a word, the Academy proposes to do for the motion picture profession what other great national and international bodies have done for other arts and sciences and industries' (cited in Osborne, p. 9).

AMPAS became the interlocutor with the US government and the outside, since it had succeeded in becoming both a legitimate representative and a valid representative with the inside – the workforce in all its different branches. AMPAS was and still maintains, as an honorary organisation, the status from which to lobby for state protection, for instance. The award ceremony works as a sounding box for the demands of its professionals. Osborne reminds us how the industry-wide union, the Writers Guild of America, called for a strike in November 2007. The clock started ticking in the run-up to the ceremony, which focused the negotiations and ensured that all parties would work for a resolution. The strike was settled just before the eightieth award ceremony was due to take place (p. 378).

AMPAS, popularly known as the Hollywood Academy or even simply the Academy, expanded over the eighty-something years that have followed, attracting members (around 6,000 at the time of writing) and prestige, mostly due to the huge national and international significance of the prizes it created in 1929, two years after its foundation: the Oscars or Academy Awards. In most cases, when the history of AMPAS is related, it is normally as a preamble to the history of the Academy Awards themselves, as in the case of Osborne's study.

But what I call 'the academy effect' is generated not simply by the Academy keeping the industry together and having award-giving powers, although these are undoubtedly very strong elements. Crucially, academies endow respectability to film-making and its professionals ('honour and good repute', in the vocabulary used by AMPAS in 1927). For 'the academy effect' to work, the institutions have to succeed in fulfilling their principal agenda, which, as English explains, is academicism itself:

> The task of the academies, quite apart from their particular missions of aesthetic conservatism or reform … was that which faces all agents of cultural production, whether individual or institutional: to make themselves definitive authorities or certifiers of value across as large a portion of the cultural field as possible. (p. 38)

Academicism on its own does not make films, even if it influences the kinds of films that are made. What it does make is film cultures.

FILM CULTURES

Taking as its focus the period 1986–2011, this project examines the decisive effect the Academia had on Spain's films and film cultures. The Academia became the mouthpiece for the hegemonic film culture, while competing film cultures often articulated their identity in disagreements with the Academia.

Since the phrase 'film culture' has been used in many ways, it seems sensible to define the term from the outset. In this study, film cultures are the soil in which cinema grows: a whole array of events, institutions and practices which are not film but without which there would be no films. This understanding of film cultures draws on a number of sources.

In Nowell-Smith and Dupin's *The British Film Institute, the Government and Film Culture 1933–2000*, film culture is not explicitly defined, but their implicit understanding aligns closely with the definition I propose here. Nowell-Smith starts his Chapter 1 by describing two existing British film cultures and the building of a third in the 1920s – invoking 'the locus' of these cultures as the picture house and the museum – and continues by tracing the cultural practices they involved, even as he takes the concept of film cultures as read (p. 14).

A comparable understanding of film cultures is found in the work of two researchers in particular, Janet Harbord and Haidee Wasson. Harbord's *Film Cultures* (2002) brings contexts and methodologies of cultural theory to the study of film and trains the light on 'film as a practice embedded in special and psychological contexts of social hierarchy and distinction' (p. 2). She shows compellingly how to locate 'the sites where value of film is produced', while presenting how elusive those sites of distribution, exhibition and marketing of film have been to the scholar's scalpel (ibid.). From Harbord we learn to be attentive to the ways in which institutions distribute cultural capital, and for whose benefit. She helps us to see that there is something intangible at work behind the special status attached to certain films, film-makers and movements, something just as powerful, if not more powerful, than anything a close analysis of a film could reveal by itself. That something is inextricably connected with practices of exhibition and distribution, and with the cultural agents who implement them. Harbord also crucially demonstrates how the location of cinema-related events contributes to the construction of their value.

Wasson's *Museum Movies: The Museum of Modern Art and the Birth of Art Cinema* takes as a case study the Film Library at MoMA (Museum of Modern Art in New York), which was one of the first institutions to promote the then revolutionary idea that 'select films [could be made] more visible to an emergent public under the rubric of art and history' (p. 7). Her study traces the strategies undertaken by MoMA to turn films into cultural artifacts worthy of preservation and collection in a library for future generations. Wasson conceives film culture not only as knowledge about cinema, but cinema as a kind knowledge which resides in educational institutions, such as the museum and the library; she alerts us to how institutions have powers to make or break careers in film-making and are influential agents in canon formation, encouraging the research and curating of some films and documents and not others.

It is also productive to see film cultures as cultures in the microbiological sense, a notion that has long been embraced by sociologists. We can imagine Spanish film cultures as something growing inside a Petri or cell-culture dish, cultivating, instead of bacteria, a particular type of film or film-maker. This approach to film cultures is developed most distinctively in John Thornton Caldwell's *Production Culture: Industrial Reflexivity and Critical Practice in Film and Television* (2008). Caldwell explains that the world he studies – the world of people who make television and film in the US – 'function[s] on a microsocial level as local cultures and social communities in their own right' (p. 2). He provides a valuable model for a close reading of cultural practices, belief systems, self-narratives and rituals, all of which can also be detected in the methods Spanish cinema professionals find to make sense of themselves and their place in the wider culture.

In this book, then, I will be exploring the Academia, its strategies for generating film cultures and academicism, as well as the practices around it and against it. The study asks in what ways various aspects of film culture interacted under the auspices of the Academia, to what extent they were integrated and whether they changed over the period in question. Most importantly, this book seeks to understand and determine what kinds of film and film professionals the Academia nurtured, and what kinds found it to be sterile ground.

ACADEMICISM: AN AUTHORITY OVER FILM CULTURES

I frequently refer to film cultures in the plural, because at any given time there are many. As Thomas Elsaesser indicates, we could broadly map them into three camps that he argues make up the film industries of most European nations. As well as an 'art and auteur cinema', and the 'commercial productions facing Hollywood', there is 'another player, the avant-garde cinema whose filmmakers, however, have almost always refused the label national cinema, because they saw themselves as both international and anti-Hollywood' (p. 42). Spain's hegemonic film culture represents in general a combination of the first two camps, while sometimes includes elements from the third. The academicism of the Academia in essence can be defined as its authority over the first two areas.

A hegemonic or dominant film culture consists of the practices and strategies that have generated the most widely acclaimed canonical film movements and thematic trends. To make their preferred idea of cinema hegemonic, the Academia had to count on its academicism and express this power through prizes. 'Institutionally,' explains English, 'the prize functions as a claim to authority and an assertion of that authority' (p. 51). Film academicism, then, is a type of authority or entitlement of the cinema hegemonic group to confer cultural value on a number of films and professionals, and this authority is principally derived from the following elements:

1. Distinctiveness and achievements of the hegemonic group.
2. Rules that are democratically applied, consistently executed and externally examined.
3. Alignment with and approval of peers, already established academies, national and foreign film scholars and the patronage of the state or the monarchy (where relevant).

Distinctiveness and achievements of the hegemonic group

Some film academies are very large (AMPAS has more than 6,000 members), others are small, but seldom do you see a list of all the affiliates. A perfect occasion to identify at least the most salient ones is the time around the award ceremonies, when, as English states, the limelight is trained on the award winners but also on the conferring group, 'in particular, journalistic attention, which produces the specifically modern form of capital we call celebrity' (p. 51). Academies, like the winners themselves, need celebrity to survive.

Academies are formed when the territories' stakeholders feel the need for respectability and control of their film industry. Since the 1920s in Hollywood, when the membership is under scrutiny, this show of rigour and discipline has translated itself into adopting the formal evening dress that was the prerogative of the nobility and upper classes for such spectacles as the theatre or the opera, following the lead of other cultural academies like the Swedish Academy, which confers the Nobel prizes. The 'festive official banquet' at the Crystal Ballroom of the Biltmore Hotel in Los Angeles (Osborne, p. 9) that brought together the Hollywood Academy founders in their finest, even before the first Oscar ceremony was organised, is the source of all the red carpets of Hollywood and world cinemas (including the Spanish Academia awards), as well as film festivals, since, in many ways, these too emulated the Hollywood Academy public galas from the time Cannes was founded two decades after AMPAS in 1947.

But cassocks alone do not make monks, and members of the academy have to act as well as look the part. In the Hollywood Academy, '[q]ualification for membership is based on distinctive achievements in one of the branches of the motion pictures covered by the Academy' (Osborne, p. 9). Nowadays, it includes world cinema professionals whose work has met with the approval of American academicians, as well as American nationals, but there have never been any membership drives and admission has always been by invitation only (ibid.). As well as prestigious and elegant when the occasion demands it, membership has to be representative of all the branches of film-making to be convincing. Osborne explains that there were five such branches when AMPAS was founded: Producers, Actors, Directors, Writers and Technicians; and he adds, 'the number of branches has gradually been increased over the years to reflect the greater diversity of activity and specialization in the production of motion pictures' (ibid.).

In the case of the Spanish Academia, membership can be applied for even if the original founding group was selected by invitation (see Chapter 1). Any film-making professional of Spanish nationality may belong to the Academia after having worked on at least three films that have been premiered in Spain (Granado, p. 25). In Chapters 1 and 2, I will be introducing men and women who contributed to the early life of the association and created its rules (such as this one about membership).
Foreign nationals can apply for membership if they have clear links to the Spanish industry. There are two further categories in addition to the regular fee-paying membership: associate members and honorary members, for those who do not work on the making of films directly. Heads of the Spanish Film Institute (such as Fernando Méndez-Leite [1986–8]) and ministers of culture have been honorary members.

Associate members tend to be film festival programmers and journalists (see García Fernández, 'Los miembros', p. 52). There were fourteen branches, or *comisiones*, in 2011 (production, scriptwriting, direction, performance, photography, art direction, costume design, hair and make-up, music, editing, special effects, animation, sound and production direction), up from the initial eight in 1986.

Challenges to the authority of Academia members have been many, and this is something that affects all the academies. AMPAS, for instance, endures questioning on a regular basis. Articles published around the time of the announcement of Academy Award nominations (normally in January), and in the weeks leading up to the ceremony, sometimes query the choices and make predictions based on the ethnic and gender composition of AMPAS. It is usual to come across articles highlighting that the majority of the membership is WASP, male and over seventy and therefore, writers argue, hardly representative of mainstream film consumers who do not even engage with film in the old setting of the movie theatre. Writing in the *Guardian* in February 2011, Tom Shone argued that a 'generational warfare' has been taking place for decades, with the baby boomers in power in AMPAS far removed in audiovisual taste and habits from the younger generations who make up the bulk of cultural consumers. And yet, these baby boomers select the Academy Award winners year after year (n.p.).

Those who seek to wrest power from film academies do so, like Shone, by enquiring into the institutions' membership in terms of gender, age and ethnicity, and even arguing that there is an over-representation of certain professions (branches) within the industry. In the case of the Spanish Academia, it is often pointed out that it was founded by producers, and above all represents their interests, a claim I will explore in Chapter 1. In Chapter 5, I will in turn examine how avant-garde and experimental film-makers and producers who consider themselves transnational professionals rather than belonging within Spanish cinema have serious misgivings about the authority and academicism of the Academia.

Such challenges are effective enough that academies feel they have to make changes to their membership and other symbolic gestures, such as attempts at parity and visibility in gender (having a female president, vice-president or deputy in the Academia), and highlighting the representativeness of non-white members in their official documents. From 2013, the president of AMPAS's Board of Governors was an African-American woman, Cheryl Boone Isaacs, from the public relations' branch. The producers', actors' and directors' branches are the largest, and such an appointment helps to demonstrate a wider representation of the industry ('Board of Governors', n.p.). From these positions of power, governors can call for a greater diversity in the Oscars nominations, as Boone Isaacs did in 2015 (see 'Oscars Head Isaacs', n.p.). These changes are crucial to the preservation of academicism, to ensure that there are no reasons for splinter groups to be formed when their concerns are not addressed, which in turn maintains their hegemony as a group in the industry intact.

Rules that are democratically applied, consistently executed and externally examined

When you are in the business of conferring film awards, you have to surround yourself with credible and reputable examiners (in the case of the Academia and AMPAS, the prestigious esteemed membership), and you need consistent and clear rules that stand up to external validation. And for purposes of transparency, membership rules should be openly published and easily accessible. For this reason, the Academia's rules for voting for awards ('Bases para el premio', n.p.) are prominently displayed on its website, as are the criteria for membership. In addition, they are printed in the programme *Candidatos para las votaciones* that the Academia yearly provides for its members, which also contains information about the eligible films. There is also a carefully defined window for these. In 2008, for example, it was only films premiered between 1 December 2007 and 30 November 2008 that were eligible. The final voting deadline was 14:00 on 21 January 2009 and only a notary knew the identity of the winners until the awards were announced at the ceremony in February (Academia, *Candidatos*, p. 10). The presence of the notary as external validator at the site is crucial, since it is he or she who hands over the closed envelopes containing the winners' details in each category during the award ceremony (ibid.).

Alignment with and approval of peers, already established academies, national and foreign film scholars and the patronage of the state or the monarchy

Clear rules that are scrupulously followed are key to investing institutions with authority. Another strategy is peer validation. If other academies see you as an equal, and if you have the support of authoritative voices in scholarship – experts in the study of cinema – your status is confirmed. As we will see in Chapters 1 and 6, the Spanish Academia was recognised as the interlocutor of AMPAS from the outset, and since its creation has selected Spain's submission to the Oscars. This privilege belongs to the Argentine and Mexican academies as well. Each year, the selection of Argentina and Mexico's entries for the Goya award for the Best Hispano-American Film is made by these academies in the same manner. There will be further discussion of this pan-Hispanic award in Chapter 6.

As well as these international interlocutors, the Academia has collaborators in its academicism in the Communication Studies, Film Studies and Hispanic Studies departments of national and international universities. Particularly in the years between 1994 and 1998, when the producer and director José Luis Borau was president, the Academia embarked on a series of archival projects, conferences and publications in collaboration with members of the Spanish Association of Film Historians (Asociación Española de Historiadores del Cine) (AEHC) and with Spanish film scholars in the UK, the US and France. The role that these research and archival projects had in making the Spanish cinema 'a national cinema legitimated as an object of study and research' cannot be underestimated (Triana-Toribio, 'Residual Film Cultures', p. 74). But the consequences of these strategies for academicism cannot be dismissed either, as I have argued elsewhere:

> Inevitably, in overseeing these activities geared to the legitimating and cataloguing of film knowledge as key cultural knowledge for the nation, the Academia and its academic partners (in Spain and abroad) appointed themselves as arbiters of classification and canon creation and also, inevitably, aligned Spanish film culture with high culture. (ibid., pp. 74–5)

As Nowell-Smith explains, other academies such as BAFTA tried in their origins to 'encourage research' and had 'intellectual aspirations' which competed with those of the BFI, whose remit was more explicitly educational and academic, but were eventually curtailed by lack of funding (p. 27). The Academia too had to claw back costly scholarly activities (the most explicitly academic collaboration, the publication of *Cuadernos de la Academia*, was discontinued in 2005).

Finally, by elevating cinema to an appropriate object of consumption for the middle and upper classes, academies made cinema legitimate enough to attract the patronage of the nobility and royal families. So, respectable academies in countries ruled by monarchs had the endorsement of the ruler or of a royal house member who presided in an honorary capacity, a practice of reciprocal legitimation that continues to this day (see English, pp. 50–5). We will see in Chapter 1 how this mutual validation worked in the case of the Academia and the Spanish monarchy in the late 1980s.

WHAT DOES ACADEMICISM WANT?

If academicism is a type of authority held by a group, to what ends does it exercise that authority? Academicians have succeeded in becoming the 'certifiers of value across a large portion of the cultural field' (English, p. 38), ruling themselves by clear criteria that are externally validated and aligning themselves to peers and scholars. So, what are they equipped to value? The short answer is that academies are equipped to certify quality. And quality is interpreted differently depending on which film culture is charged with finding it.

In the case of the Spanish Academia between 1986 and 2011, hegemonic film culture identified quality in practices, products and professionals bolstering the European art cinema model. This model has been defined by Ginette Vincendeau, Tim Bergfelder and others, and takes in cinema that is 'aesthetically innovative, socially committed and humanist in outlook' (Vincendeau, p. 56). As we will see in Chapter 1, the auteurist tradition – the denomination used in scholarship for Spanish films inspired by European art cinema movements from the 1950s to the present – is embodied in auteurs such as Juan A. Bardem, José Luis Borau, Víctor Érice and Carlos Saura, as well as producers such as Elías Querejeta. It is continued in art auteurs and social realist auteurs such as Julio Medem, Icíar Bollaín and Fernando León de Aranoa, mentored by elders such as Borau (and in some cases Querejeta, as Tom Whittaker argues [p. 5]). This tradition is also found in the work of the avant-garde – for instance, in the films of José Luis Guerín and Isaki Lacuesta, who are clear inheritors of Érice and other European avant-gardists such as Chris Marker.

For the Academia, though, the European art cinema model on its own was not enough. Instead, the institution's ideal film was a compromise: a high cultural product, but one that was accessible, not *too* aesthetically innovative, socially committed but leavened by mainstream formulas. The awards and Galas discussed in Chapter 2 prove that claim. In Chapter 5, I will show how professionals in the avant-garde sections of the industry are often the most clear-sighted and candid when addressing this bias of the Academia towards the middlebrow, the accessible place where the mainstream meets auteur cinema, or what Thomas Elsaesser calls 'commercial cinema facing

Hollywood' (p. 42). For producer Miñarro, the Goyas, and by extension the Academia, simply confirm the box office. To a large extent, the Academia uses its prizes, Miñarro argues, 'to reinforce what is popular, what supports the industry by endorsing the financial investment that was made' (p. 63).

For an example of the type of process and film Miñarro alludes to, we need look no further than Alejandro Amenábar's *The Sea Inside*. *The Sea Inside* was awarded the three main awards – Best Film, Best Director, Best Original Screenplay – in 2005, during a ceremony attended by the Spanish Socialist Party prime minister, Rodríguez Zapatero. The film was also chosen by the Academia to represent the nation at the 2005 AMPAS awards and won Spain its fourth Oscar. Amenábar's film tells the story of Ramón Sampedro (Javier Bardem), a man from the Galician region in the northwest of Spain, who, after an accident that left him with tetraplegia, campaigned for almost thirty years in favour of euthanasia and the right to end his life with dignity. The film, which follows the conventions of melodrama and the biopic, has been praised for Bardem's moving and believable performance, but also for the fact that a film with such a sombre subject matter should be so life-affirming and even-handed (Smith, 'The Sea Inside', p. 72). I have called elsewhere these types of film 'genre films but with aspirations' (paraphrasing Spanish critics) ('Residual Film Cultures', p. 68). The aspirations of this film are political. Since regaining democracy, Spain has been a country living with the inheritance of the enormous role that the Catholic Church had as a ballast of Franco's dictatorship. While Spain is no longer a confessional state, the division between Church and State took place only relatively recently, in 1973 (Graham and Labanyi, p. 436), and the Church's doctrine still carries much weight in the public opinion, particularly in conservative sectors and for the older population. *The Sea Inside* was more than just a film that fascinated audiences in Spain and beyond; it was an intervention in public debate on the side of secular rights and expressed an attitude to life and death very much in tune with those of other modern European non-confessional states.

Does this mean that all 'genre films with aspirations' that have political overtones and the potential to succeed at the box office can expect to win the favour of the academicians, who would corroborate this success with prizes? That is not exactly the case. A less ideal film is perhaps Guillermo del Toro's *El laberinto del fauno/Pan's Labyrinth* (2006). This Goya winner (Best Screenplay, 2007) is a fantasy/horror film about Ofelia (Ivana Baquero), and her adventures in nightmarish worlds above and below the ground following the end of the Civil War, in 1944. Ofelia lives under the terrible oppression of one of Franco's captains, her stepfather Vidal (Sergi López). She also enters a mythical subterranean kingdom and is sent on quests by the title's Pan to prove her status as the long-lost princess, daughter of the king of the underworld (Federico Luppi). A CGI and Animatronics modern-day fairy tale, the film broke box-office records, not simply in Europe but in other major territories (see Lázaro-Reboll, *Spanish Horror Films*, pp. 256–7). The film was awarded only one of the three major prizes: the Goya for its screenplay. It failed to pick up Best Film and Best Director, but did win Best Cinematography, Best New Actress, Best Sound, Best Make-up and Hairstyles and Best Special Effects.

The Sea Inside and *Pan's Labyrinth* are unabashedly genre films, and yet the Academia as a rule shuns mainstream genre films when awarding the Goyas. Or rather, it does not mind genre films, as long as they are disguised as something else, or as long as genre is being used to sugar the pill of social or political commitment. And here is the secret of the great success of *The Sea Inside* and the more moderate one of *Pan's Labyrinth* with the academicians in 2005 and 2007. While it was the generic components that secured the films' popularity with transnational audiences, it was their combination with another element that attracted the Academia. As a director of highly commercial blockbusters, del Toro does not fit the Academia mould, but he has a dual career, including more personal projects associated with the strategies and traits of transnational auteurism (see Shaw, *The Three Amigos*, p. 20). For example, the Mexican director's first entry to the Spanish film industry was through *El espinazo del diablo/The Devil's Backbone* (2001), produced by the respected company El Deseo (run by the Almodóvar brothers and Esther García). Like *Pan's Labyrinth*, the earlier film has the quality indicators of a genre film with higher expectations, so the academicians could pick it without anxiety. Here again, by aspirations, we mean political aspirations. Lázaro-Reboll pinpoints the element attractive to the Academia when he argues:

> But it is with ... [*Pan's Labyrinth*] that del Toro has succeeded in speaking directly to the Spanish psyche, tapping in particular into current topicality with debates around the legacy of the Civil War and ... historical memory. These debates intensified following the excavation of mass graves and the exhumation of the victims of Fascist repression demanded by the ... [Association for the Recovery of Historical Memory], founded in 2000, ... as well as the controversial [Historical Memory Law], which acknowledges the memory of victims of the Spanish Civil War, passed by the Socialist government of José Luis Rodríguez Zapatero in 2007. (*Spanish Horror Films*, p. 256)

The Sea Inside is an ideal Academia film not because it is 'commercial cinema facing Hollywood' (as Elsaesser would have it) but because it is a film that succeeded with audiences while containing clear links to such public debates as the place of the Catholic Church and the role of Catholic doctrine about life in Spanish secular society. *Pan's Labyrinth* is less ideal, because although it too was a great success with audiences, it connects to the country's past from which lessons could be learned but whose remembrance still divides the country (see Smith, 'Pan's Labyrinth', pp. 4–8).

What is regarded as far from ideal is popular or local comedy. Such forms are almost never rewarded and those professionals involved in the genre are a challenge when not a vexation to the Academia – particularly Almodóvar (when he uses the genre), Álex de la Iglesia and Santiago Segura, whose work I defined elsewhere as part of the 'new vulgarities' (*Spanish National Cinema*, p. 151). In Chapter 4, therefore, I will address a tricky contradiction that besets the Academia. On the one hand, local comedies alone make it possible for national production to enjoy a healthy share of the market, but on the other hand, the Academia finds it nearly impossible to reward any aspect of them as representative of best practice; they cannot be redeemed by having 'aspirations'.[2]

Finally, the Academia is keen not to stifle, but at the same time does not want to give too much weight to, those film cultures that generate films that are too experimental, a topic I will explore in more detail in Chapter 5. The Academia has a problem with the existence of film-makers who do not want to be part of the industry, preferring exhibition platforms such as the internet, museums and film festivals. Principally, their refusal to abide by industrial imperatives is counterproductive for an organisation that serves as a lobby for the industry, but their film-making in the margins may generate professionals who could be absorbed by the industry.

Examples of this process are numerous. Almodóvar, whose complex relationship with the Academia will be examined in Chapter 3, started out as an experimental and avant-garde film-maker who moved to the mainstream very productively at the end of the 1980s (Smith, *Desire Unlimited*, pp. 2–6). Side by side with the defenders of the dominant film culture who have become part of the Academia we find several emerging professionals and films, defining themselves in opposition to the hegemonic and negotiating their existence as the true inheritors of the auteurist tradition, the same auteurism that the Academia purports to represent in many cases. For instance, film-makers such as Guerín and Jaime Rosales have been distinguished with awards, but continue to inhabit the margins, never truly assimilated. These emerging or contesting film cultures, their main representatives and what lies behind their posture are addressed principally in Chapters 4 and 5.

In short, what does the Academia's academicism want? Based on the numerous examples examined by Sally Faulkner in her superb *A History of Spanish Film* (2013), the answer is that Spain is a film-making nation resolutely seeking the middlebrow. Faulkner sometimes locates this middlebrow in 'accessible works of avant-garde experiments or accessible works which pass for avant-garde experiments' (Bourdieu, *Distinction*, p. 323), citing examples such as Pilar Miró's *El perro del hortelano/The Dog in the Manger* (1996), which connects with pan-European middlebrow trends such as the costume drama and heritage films of the 1980s and 90s (Faulkner, pp. 217–21). On other occasions, middlebrow takes in films like *Solas/Alone* (Benito Zambrano, 1999) that offer 'a middlebrow blurring of highbrow Italian Neorealism and lowbrow *paleto* (country bumpkin) cinema' (ibid., p. 202). Although Faulkner does not discuss *Pan's Labyrinth*, it is perfectly in line with her reading of Spanish cinema's progress as plotting a straight and successful middle course, but a course that could not have been followed between 1986 and 2011 without the consistent support and guidance of the Academia.

WHEN THE ACADEMIA?

One important characteristic that most academies share is that they have been created at times when the national industry feels strong, and that strength persuades producers, director, actors, screenwriters and critics that the moment is right to raise its profile, to stand up and be counted. In moments of strength, different national industries have seized the opportunity to occupy a space from which to fight perceived threats, whatever these may be. AMPAS was formed when the growing film industry saw on the horizon the unionisation of workers and the uncharted territories for cinema that the technologies of sound announced. The Argentinian Academia was formed at a buoyant time for the country's cinema, when it was second to none among Spanish-speaking nations. In Mexico, the AMACC was founded in 1946 – when the Mexican industry was in its 'Golden Age' and could face Hollywood – bringing together prominent Mexican producers and directors and launching its own film awards (see Irwin and Castro Ricalde, pp. 10–11).

Spanish Film Cultures: The Making and Unmaking of Spanish Cinema addresses the challenges that all film academies share, regardless of where and when they operate. However, the specific context in which the Spanish Academia was born accounts for much of its evolution and its role. Spain's early democratic years and the landslide election victory of the PSOE in 1982 paved the way for cultural stakeholders to affirm their position. The PSOE had long been announcing their intention to bolster culture, and cinema in particular, by putting it to the service of democracy, for instance in a key conference celebrated in 1979. This was the crucible in which the Academia was formed, and from which issued many of its actions, even when that original context had long faded away. Without knowing some key details about the Academia's backstory, particular events and actions that took place much later may seem either inexplicable or meaningless. Here is an example.

In the 1990s, a then young Álex de la Iglesia (b. 1965) set out on a course to become a 'popular auteur' by declaring with deeds and words his rejection of his particular *cinéma de papa*, vowing not to make films about the Civil War (1936–9) and the postwar period (1940s–60s). As Buse, Triana-Toribio and Willis argue, his first feature film, *Acción mutante/Mutant Action* (1993), was a deliberate intervention in his filmic context, 'an all-out assault ... on the hegemonic literary-political cinema of the 1980s' (p. 37). De la Iglesia's subsequent career continued along this path, and he was rewarded with large audiences, a youthful cult following and general neglect from official prize-givers in Spain. Then, in 2009, he was elected president of the Academia. His mandate was to use his status as a popular auteur with street credibility among young mainstream audiences to transform the institution. He declared: 'I want to open the Academia to the people, I want to show them how it works, to get them to see seasons of European and Spanish films and films no longer available [in the Academia's screening facilities]' (Rocío García, 'De la Iglesia', n.p.).

I will leave you in suspense, until Chapter 4, to find out what de la Iglesia did next at the Academia. I want to observe here only that the film he scripted and directed while president, *Balada triste de trompeta/The Last Circus* (2010), seems to turn its back on everything he had believed in as a young film-maker. It starts with the Civil War, telling a story of the bitter and violent rivalry between two circus clowns. As Andrés Romero-Jodar argues, it 'can easily be seen as a historical revenge movie ... in the same line as Quentin Tarantino's *Inglourious Basterds* (2009)' (n.p.). With its theme of retribution and its depiction of the Civil War as a conflict that needs to be addressed, the film is clearly political. The division of Spanish society into winners and losers that it depicts reaches into the present; the diegesis fits perfectly in the priorities of the literary-political hegemonic cinema of the 1980s. *The Last Circus*, de la Iglesia declared, was his most personal and most Spanish film (see Toni García, n.p.), quite an admission for a film-maker who lamented Spanish cinema's obsession with the past.

As president of the Academia, Álex de la Iglesia made a film whose subject matter and themes clashed with his previous oeuvre. I am suggesting that this is because the institution itself interpellates its members and officers because of when and who created it. The birth of the Academia in early democracy determined its mandate all the way to 2011. Álvarez Monzoncillo and Menor Sendra have argued that the hegemonic cinema culture was intent on 'transforming audiences rather than satisfying them' (p. 26). This idea will be developed in the next chapter, which starts by explaining who the first academicians were, and how they were socialised into specific ideas about cinema that resulted in the creation of the Academia.

The founders were cinephiles who came of age cinematically during Francoism and early democracy – that is, from the late 1940s to the early 80s. Once handed the reins of the film-making industry, this generation determined to use cinema to address the country's past, which is why we can call them the war generation. As I mentioned above, the generation who created the Academia is more or less contemporary with the baby boomers who, Shone argues, control AMPAS. Those born around the time of the Spanish Civil War and at the end of World War II – that is, 'the auteurist generation', following its use by Peter W. Evans in 1990 (see *Spanish Cinema*).

Considering the Academia as a product of its time and shaped by political and social changes, as I do in Chapter 1, will enable us to understand its priorities. Without that background, we cannot address the challenges to the organisation's representativeness and authority, and the expressed and unvoiced assumption that it may no longer be fit for purpose without substantial reform, bearing in mind that it was dreamed of at the end of Francoism and created in 1986.

In the late 1970s and early 80s, the hazardous change from dictatorship to democracy was by necessity gradual and full of compromises and pacts. These were essential, because what took precedence then, as Ignacio Echevarría states, was creating the possibility of living together again as a nation and not as two factions of winners and losers, 'after the deep scars left in Spanish society by the Civil War and Francoism' (p. 28). Politicians and trade union leaders sought consensus and it was taken for granted that sacrifices would be made. However, the concessions were greater on one side than on the other, in a transition 'directed by the successors of Franco, not their adversaries' (C. T. Powell cited in Hopewell, *Out of the Past*, p. 109).

Film-making bore the brunt of Francoist repression but it gave the regime a run for its money, as we will see in Chapters 1 and 2 particularly. The generation of the war that created the Academia contained many who were in the front line of the political fight to banish the traces of Francoism from Spain's culture, and the institution bore, and bears, the imprint of that positioning. Film professionals such as director Saura and producer Querejeta, at the forefront of the opposition against the dictatorship, became the cultural gatekeepers in the transition to democracy and in the democratic period.

Those who shaped democracy, who created the laws and institutions by which democratic Spain lives, such as the monarchy and the Academia, forged with them what I call the hegemonic Spanish film culture. This is an important detail to bear in mind, because the creation of the Academia is steeped in this need for consensus, which, as we will see, comes across in the way the institution represents itself and the ways in which critics engage with the Academia's self-representations.

Shone describes a generational warfare in AMPAS, and there is a similar conflict at work in Spain. There is a strong perception that those with an outmoded understanding of cinema are ruling over the new Spanish cinema, and, at the same time, that the political imperatives of the transition are dominating over a reluctant younger generation who are ruled by them unwillingly and want to move beyond them. If we use de la Iglesia's *The Last Circus* as an example, we could argue that, at least in 2010, the hegemonic literary-political priorities of the war generation were winning out in the generational war.

This is why, in this study, I will be engaging with what is known as 'The Culture of the Transition' (CT) and its contestation, either in a direct manner or by implication. This critique comes to the fore particularly in Chapter 5. 'The culture of the transition is the consequence of the country's cultural and intellectual class positioning themselves *en masse* behind [the political] project [of moving from dictatorship to democracy]' (Echevarría, pp. 28–9).

There is a deep lack of satisfaction with the instruments crafted in that momentous historical process – such as the constitution, the main basic law by which Spain is ruled, and the monarchy – as they come under the scrutiny of the generations who lived in democracy. There is also a desire by many of those involved in film-making to move beyond the hegemonic literary-political, and even to move beyond other traditional hegemonic ideas such as where cinema is consumed and how it reaches its audiences.

At the time of writing in 2015, King Juan Carlos has abdicated in favour of his son, Felipe, who came of age in democracy, and many of the main politicians and union leaders among the 'winners and losers' have passed away: for example, Adolfo Suárez, the dictatorship minister who ushered in democracy, and Marcelino Camacho, the Communist leader who negotiated the labour laws. Querejeta, the legendary producer who embodied the fight against the dictatorship in the 1970s and hegemonic film culture in the 80s and 90s, died in 2013. Whether the challenges and demands of emerging film cultures calling for a generation replacement are being met by the Academia, these pages will show.

Is the Academia part of the old and thus residual? This study ends in 2011, because this marks the end of the last period in power of the party that crafted the film culture that inspires the Academia, the Spanish Socialist Party. But even in jeopardy at the time of writing, the Academia lives on. Does it have a future? AMPAS continues to thrive but the challenges to it come thick and fast. Do academies have a future? Are national or supra-national instruments, in the case of AMPAS and the EFA, at odds with the workings of transnational cultural industries? A question I will be returning to at the end of this book is whether academies will survive in the context of transnational film industries and, if so, in what form.

The House Is Built of the Stones That Were Available[1]

The Academy of the Cinema Arts and Sciences of Spain, **founded on the 8th of January 1986**, is a private law institution, of **inclusive and democratic character**. According to its statutes it is a non-for-profit association of professionals involved in the different specialties of film creation, with its own juridical status, constituted for an indefinite period and ruled by the **principles of democracy, pluralism, transparency and participation**.[2]

THE VALUES AND THEIR ORIGINS

The Academia declares itself on its website to be an inclusive, transparent and democratic institution. This declaration departs from the boilerplate text of its Academia counterparts such as BAFTA and the French Académie des Arts et Techniques du Cinéma. Where the homepage of BAFTA satisfies itself with stating simply that its mission is to 'support, promote and defend' its nations' films, the Academia feels the need to provide details about its ethos that in most European professional organisations would be taken for granted. Some words are emphasised, most notably: *democratic, democracy, pluralism, participation*. Its style is somewhat outmoded. It reads like a text from the time when Spain was a very young democracy and these concepts needed to be spelled out.[3] Yet, this is the text that opens the Academia's online site forty years after Franco's death, and it reveals much about the institution's priorities. Foremost among these has been putting cinema at the service of the political process of democratisation, and educating audiences in a specific type of film culture.

This affirmation may appear polemical – is not the Spanish Academia, like all the other academies, preoccupied with film culture, beyond the political slant of the films themselves? The answer is that there is no outside of party politics when it comes to hegemonic Spanish culture. The cultural environment that was created in the transition principally by the two major parties, the Spanish Socialist Party and the Partido Popular (henceforth PP), monopolised the institutional discourse during the period of this study. The Academia emerged as part of a process of modernisation which started in the 1970s and was fully developed in the 80s, a process intended to transform the conditions of production, dissemination and exhibition of Spanish cinema to make it fit for the wider European democracy it was about to join. The existing cinema was the mainstream cinema, sometimes derisively called the Old

Spanish Cinema, paraphrasing critics Hernández and Revuelta, who named it thus in allusion to the New Spanish Cinema (*Nuevo Cine Español* [henceforth *NCE*]), Spain's answer to the New Cinemas movement of the 1960s. (p. 76). The Old Spanish Cinema consisted mainly of genre films, dramas, comedies and musicals of the 1960s and 70s, which transmitted the cultural backwardness and lack of freedom of expression fostered in the Franco era. Retrograde though it was, this was a strong and profitable cinema industry. 'From 1960,' explain José María Álvarez Monzoncillo and Juan Menor Sendra, 'between 120 and 150 feature films per year were made in Spain, a high quantity if we consider the size of the market. The market share for Spanish films was well over 20 per 100' (p. 24). That figure increased once more permissive legislation allowed some 'freedoms' and the possibility of embracing international models of film, and from 1977 the Old Spanish Cinema became an even greater source of embarrassment for choosing from among all the possible international models explicit horror and pornography.[4]

The men and women I will be introducing in this chapter had revisionist ambitions. In sum, that the 'bad' Old Cinema would be replaced with 'good' modern, auteur cinema or arthouse films of European standards. What is more, the modern films that the new system would produce would themselves be instruments for democracy and for educating audiences. Films would be vehicles for transmitting the all-important need for consensus, for accepting the position of the other side (pluralism) by teaching Spaniards about their past and showing them areas of the nation's heritage and history that had remained hidden from them: the point of view of those who lost the Civil War. But this had to be done without endangering the possibility of living together. In other words, certain divisive topics had to be put aside in the 1980s (and for much of the 90s), such as the legitimacy of the monarchy or the role of the armed forces in the violence against the urban and rural working class during the Civil War and beyond. Moreover, these films would be fit for exportation to democratic audiences in Spain's new partner countries. After all, Spain had been admitted to Europe in 1986. The films that would be created by the state and endorsed by the newly created Academia were destined to do all these jobs while remaining attractive as entertainment.[5]

Back in 1986, the emerging Academia fought to take everyone with it. Its actions were geared, to a great extent, towards being accepted as a large enough tent to house all cinema, and it fought to make Spanish film-making a concern of everyone, including those on the left and right of the political spectrum. Winning this battle was crucial if the Academia was going to function as the arbiter of taste, and endower of distinction and cultural value, a role enjoyed by its counterparts in other countries. Like everything else in the culture of the transition, institutions sought to be the embodiment of social and political consensus, of compromise. Consensus was the watchword of the 1980s, but it was an ongoing concern for the entire period studied here.

This chapter shows how the Academia developed its academicism, and became the key arbiter in matters of cinematic taste in Spain. It introduces the leading actors in the push to transform the 'bad' Old Cinema of the dictatorship into 'good' cinema for democracy, through their participation in an Academia that would police Spanish cinema.[6] It will also take into account the class and gender dynamics of this group that agitated for a specific model of cinema. Among the young cinephiles who became part of the 'emergent dissident intelligentsia' (Jordan, *Writing and Politics*, p. 245), there were many disaffected offspring of the upper-middle-class victors of the Civil War. Pursuing a university education in the 1950s and 60s was the privilege of their class, but there were also many lower-middle-class and some working-class young men who aspired to join the upper classes by cultivating their taste and modes of consumption.

Belonging to a particular generation dictated the taste of the first cinephiles, who were young men in the late 1950s and into the 60s. Growing up at the same time as the generation of the French *nouvelle vague* affected them greatly. The young Spanish men who were in their twenties during the 1950s connected with the experiences and aspirations of other European youth and became the intellectual pioneers of Spain's cinema, argues Cristina Pujol Ozonas (*Fans, cinéfilos*, p. 127). For them, as for their Scottish contemporary Peter Cowie, the period between 1958 and 1968 represents the golden years of European film-making (p. xvii).

They developed a long-standing attachment to a narrow conception of European cinema as *cinéma engagé*, based on films as a reflection on social reality (and passed this preference on to younger men and women in the 1990s and beyond). This preference directly connected them to the realist tradition of Italian neorealism (see, among others, Hernández and Revuelta, p. 74). But their attachment to this model put them out of step with their contemporaries in France and other European democracies, whose themes and styles had moved away from neorealism (Triana-Toribio, *Spanish National Cinema*, p. 57). Addressing reality was particularly pressing at a time when only part of the cultural production demonstrated engagement with society as a way of contesting Francoism. In one of their key public fora in the 1960s, the film magazine *Nuestro Cine*, members of this group declared that engaging with Spain's reality (as much as they could) prevented them from adopting more styles that were less conducive to realist representation (Ángel Fernández-Santos, 'Sobre un nuevo cine español', p. 12), such as those of the *nouvelle vague*. Making films according to that European realist and *engagé* model was still an aspiration when the Academia was created.

This continued attachment to a particular model of engaged cinema goes some way to explaining why particularly politically conservative film professionals, whether members of the PP or not, did not feel part of or were not included in the creation of the Academia, which is firmly associated with the Socialist Party. At the same time, the defence of auteurist cinema alienated the Academia from other film professionals for reasons that cannot be simply ascribed to political differences. The following sections will examine the role of this generation and the implications of their endeavours.

ACADEMIC FOUNDATIONS

On the way to the transition we need to stop first at Francoism. The regime is a constant, recurrent and uncomfortable backdrop against which the specific qualities of Spanish film cultures are constructed. And when the Academia expresses its commitment to the principles of democracy, plurality, transparency and free participation, it declares its intention to make up for the decades in which the Spanish film industry was closely watched by the dictatorship. Francoism feared the power of cinema – as a main entertainment for the masses – and for this reason, its watch over it was very close indeed, as has been demonstrated in various influential studies (see Gubern, *La censura*; Labanyi, pp. 207–14).

The oldest Academia members can surely recall when Franco's regime brought in legislation in 1942 forcing all cinema professionals to belong to vertical trade unions. These unions included everyone involved in making films, regardless of their role in the profession – whether they were studio set workers or powerful producers – or the fact that their interests often clashed. These *sindicatos verticales* (top-down trade unions) were ruled by regime-appointed civil servants, and were, obviously, undemocratic in their structure and aims. In order to access the film industry and be accepted as a member of the *sindicato vertical*, aspiring candidates served apprenticeships under experienced professionals who were already members, a further mechanism for screening and cultivating future generations. The men and women who eventually created the Academia were principally involved in the Sindicato Nacional del Espectáculo (National Entertainment Union) (SNE) and the Círculo de Escritores Cinematográficos (Circle of Writers for the Cinema) (CEC). The role of these non-unions of the dictatorship was crucial for the industry. Ramiro Gómez Bermúdez de Castro (pp. 24–5) has shown, for instance, how the SNE also controlled the financing of Spanish films, particularly until the end of the 1960s.

The Academia was born out of a desire to consign to oblivion the period in which every activity related to cinema was controlled by the dictatorship through these undemocratic non-unions. Censorship, another instrument of control in the hands of the regime, also had a central role in the inception of the Academia. Censorship was a constant backdrop but a protean one. As historian Román Gubern, witness of this time and member of this cinephile generation, explains, the censorship system evolved with the regime and was moulded differently by the different groups which were put in charge of the censorship apparatus: first Falange, and subsequently, the Church (*La censura*, pp. 91–171). A generation of film professionals developed in opposition to censorship and determined to banish it as soon as the time was right.

To understand, then, why the founding group of the Academia fought so hard to uphold democratic values, and why they felt that a narrow model of auteurist cinema was the best weapon to do this, requires looking into two aspects of their background. The first is how they came into contact with cinema and which type of cinema became their love object. The second is how all their experiences as spectators, as critics and as film-makers were mediated by censorship. These two things are intimately connected and constitute the formative experiences of the Academia.

The future academicians encountered censorship first as young cinephiles in the late 1950s when they were only permitted partial access to neorealism, along with other key European movements and discussions about cinema, initially through university film clubs and occasional special events such as those held at the Italian embassy in Madrid (see Hopewell, *Out of the Past*, p. 51; Monterde, 'Continuismo', pp. 278–81). Like their European counterparts (such as François Truffaut, Jean-Luc Godard and Michelangelo Antonioni), they were keen to read and write about films, and were doing so (under the watchful eye of the state) in cinema magazines affiliated to these film clubs (for instance, *Cinema Universitario*, *Índice* and *Film Ideal*).

The censors may have been watching these young men, but obviously not carefully enough. As Gubern admits, he never needed to resort to forging permits to show censored films in the Cine-club Universitario de Barcelona he ran (quoted in Gracia, p. 97). The curiosity of these privileged young men – mostly bourgeois sons of the victors – and their yearning to keep up with modern film trends and the European avant-garde perhaps did not rank as a high priority for the censors compared with ensuring that mainstream audiences were protected from watching the wrong films. As Jordan observes, 'penalties for student dissent were nothing compared to the punishment meted out to those clandestine opposition party workers and militants unfortunate enough to be arrested' (*Writing and Politics*, p. 254). Some did serve time in prison for their political affiliations, particularly around the mid-1950s when student culture became part of a significant wider culture of dissidence which the regime 'tolerated and repressed in turn' (Monterde, 'Continuismo', p. 241).

For instance, the producer and critic Ricardo Muñoz Suay, who, in the late 1960s, championed the New Cinemas movement in Catalonia, Escuela de Barcelona, spent time in prison (see Riambau and Torreiro, p. 69). So did Juan Antonio Bardem (see his memoir, *Y todavía sigue*, p. 104). Some future film-makers were fined for their transgressions, while others had their passports confiscated and were unable to travel, as in the case of the film student Pere Portabella, director and producer of some of the Escuela work. But their class and gender gave them access to special conditions within which their love of cinema took hold. For the Escuela film-makers, class and the benefits of a private education, including knowledge of French, coupled with the proximity of Catalonia to France, enabled them to travel to see banned films in easily accessible Perpignan, and thereby develop a taste for the foreign and cosmopolitan in their own cinema (see Riambau and Torreiro, p. 85). For those based in or around Madrid, for instance in the old university town of Salamanca nearby, the Sindicato de Estudiantes Universitarios (University Students' Union) (SEU) hosted a film club. Film clubs created the conditions for an enthusiastic kindling of cinephilia among university students.

Reflecting on the formative years of this generation of cultural actors in the Franco era, historian Jordi Gracia argues that the SEU film clubs made a significant contribution to the vibrancy of film cultures in the 1950s. These student-run organisations, he claims, were instrumental in disseminating knowledge of past and present cinema avant-gardes. Modern film culture came back to life through film clubs and film magazines and journals that supplemented the basic tuition of the Instituto de Investigaciones y Experiencias Cinematográficas (Institute of Cinema Research and Experience) (IIEC) (p. 96). This was the only centre authorised to train film-makers under Francoism. Gracia contends that without such a supplement, cinephilia would not have taken the hold it did among these university students of the 1950s. Their 'habitus', in other words, was of great consequence to their future aesthetic and thematic choices.[7]

The IIEC, located in Madrid along with the bulk of the film industry, was Spain's only official film school between 1947 and 1962, when its name was changed to Escuela Oficial de Cine (Official Film School) (EOC). The IIEC/EOC was an 'elitist [institution], island of tolerance' (Torreiro, p. 307), loosely monitored by the state, with specialisations such as direction, screenwriting, art direction, camera and acting.

This centre of training was operational for a total of twenty-nine years in different locations and under the aegis of several institutions, including Madrid's Universidad Complutense (from 1972). It was closed down in 1976 after a turbulent time in which Spain's universities became active in the fight for democracy. Many crucial founding members of the Academia are among its alumni (see Heredero, 'IIEC-EOC', p. 467).[8] Among its former students are, for example, Juan Antonio Bardem and Luis García Berlanga, Pablo García del Amo, Antón Eceiza, Ángel Fernández-Santos, Joaquín Jordà,[9] Elías Querejeta, Carlos Saura, while later graduates include José Luis Borau, Mario Camus, Julio Diamante, Basilio Martín Patino, Manuel Picazo, Manuel Summers, Angelino Fons, and others. Once it became known as the EOC, Víctor Érice, Pedro Olea, Claudio Guerín, Pere Portabella, Jesús (Jess) Franco, Helena Lumbreras and Fernando Méndez-Leite studied there, and were followed by Fernando Colomo, José María González Sinde, Pilar Miró, Josefina Molina, Iván Zulueta and Imanol Uribe.

Alongside lessons about film history, but mostly in classes on film technique, students developed a taste for the types of films that their contemporaries were making in Europe in the various New Cinemas movements, as far as this was possible. A political context characterised by a lack of freedom of expression determined the aesthetic and thematic choices of those who were anti-Franco dissidents, which turned out to be most of the alumni. Imbued with the responsibility to bear witness to their surrounding reality in the face of censorship, they continued to engage in the techniques and themes of neorealism. Being out of step with other film cultures left the Academia and hegemonic film culture with a determining legacy that will be addressed in the following chapters.

Through the IIEC and EOC, through film clubs and magazines, these men (joined eventually by a few women such as Cecilia Bartolomé, Miró, Molina and Ana Mariscal, as EOC instructor) learned how to be auteurs. They also learned that the cinema worth pursuing was certainly not genre cinema, which at the time was the territory of established and conformist directors and producers whose involvement in film-making either predated the creation of the school, or who had simply joined the industry directly (the Old Spanish Cinema, mentioned earlier). Cinéma engagé for these future auteurs was one that presented Spain's current and past reality from a dissident perspective. It should be pointed out here that this direct engagement with reality was the strategy pursued by Madrid-centred NCE graduates (called mesetarios [dwellers of the plain] by the Barcelona-based critics): Camus, Martín Patino and Saura among them. Other IIEC/EOC alumni like Jordà, Jacinto Esteva and Portabella (and Vicente Aranda, who tried but could not join the film school because he did not meet the entry requirements),[10] on seeing the censorship hurdles that the Madrid-based graduates battled with, decided to aim beyond realism (Riambau and Torreiro, pp. 60–8). But this chapter is concerned with the aesthetic and thematic choices of the film-makers based in Madrid, since it was they who formed the Academia and whose habitus impinged on hegemonic film culture and the policing of its borders in the 1980s and 90s.

The origins of the empowerment of this influential group can be traced to a key figure and a key meeting. The figure is a civil servant, José María García Escudero, who shared these young men's cinephilic taste and wrote in their film magazines; the meeting was with these young men in the Castilian university city of Salamanca. García Escudero was invited by their main university film club, led by Martín Patino, to speak at Las Conversaciones de Salamanca (The Salamanca Conversations), a much studied and well-documented gathering in May 1955 devoted to the state of Spanish cinema.[11] The conference was a momentous discussion, highly critical of the cinema of the time, in which film-makers, actors and critics – some known as active participants in the resistance movement, such as Muñoz Suay and Bardem (undercover members of the Communist Party) – talked with representatives of the regime. Bardem issued a manifesto declaring Spanish cinema '1. politically futile; 2. socially false; 3. intellectually worthless; 4. aesthetically valueless; 5. Industrially paralytic' (Hopewell, *Out of the Past*, p. 57). The talks concluded that the quality of Spanish films was inferior compared to European films, not due to scarcity of talent or an unwillingness to make better films, but because they did not engage with Spain's reality. Censorship and underfunding shackled Spanish cinema and unless these two areas were tackled, Spanish cinema would never be prestigious internationally.

The participants in Salamanca were prescient, because by the early 1960s, international prestige had made its way to the top of the regime's agenda. The regime knew that offering an image of modernity and openness, however cosmetic, was the only way to achieve acceptance and economic investment from the rest of the continent and the US at a time when it needed such support. From the 1960s, Spain made economic and cultural efforts to become European and make itself worthy of participation in Europe's democratic institutions. If the regime wanted films that could show some modernity to the world, it needed to meet demands for a liberalisation of censorship. A change of tactics in the early years of the decade meant that some of these young cinephiles and trained film-makers were put to the service of the aims of the dictatorship.

Cinema was part of the strategy to present a modern image and these young men who could deliver 'modern cinema', a New Spanish Cinema (the already mentioned *NCE*), were put under the care of García Escudero. IIEC/EOC graduates such as Camus, Martín Patino, Saura and others were given access to the industry. Producers such as Juan Miguel Lamet, and former classmates like Querejeta gave the movement a decisive economic kick-start by accessing state subsidies (Torreiro, p. 310). Later, Alfredo Matas, the main professional behind the Academia, supported some crucial New Cinemas' projects. The results were a few award-winning films in international film festivals: *La caza/The Hunt* (Saura, 1966) (Golden Bear at the International Berlin Film Festival, 1966), *Nueve cartas a Berta/Nine Letters to Bertha* (Martín Patino, 1966) (Silver Shell for First Work, San Sebastian International Film Festival, 1966) and *Peppermint Frappe* (Saura, 1967) (Silver Bear at Berlin, 1968).[12] EOC alumni in Barcelona also benefited from this relaxation of censorship. But they only really arrived at the end of the 1960s when funds had dwindled, and, unlike their Madrid counterparts, they underplayed engagement with reality in their films. Their destiny was not to join the hegemonic group that created the Academia, but to act as a beacon for those outside the dominant film cultures, an avant-garde at the periphery, as we will see in Chapter 5.

García Escudero listened to these young men's demands for a censorship that would, at the very least, be expressed in terms that were clear enough to know what could be done. The Censorship Code of February 1963 was the result.[13] Unlike the cinephiles, García Escudero was a Francoist civil servant with a military background and strong religious convictions who saw a need for censorship (Monterde, 'Continuismo', pp. 246–7). But the regime's emphasis was on creating conditions in which films could be tolerated rather than endorsed, confident in the belief that their destiny was foreign film festival audiences and their purpose winning prizes for Spanish cinema at the international festivals of Cannes, Berlin and Pesaro (see Hopewell, *Out of the Past*, p. 65).

Meanwhile, the late 1960s and early 70s saw the production of other films, made for the internal market, that were not fit for export and were unlikely to win prizes abroad. These were genre films without any ambitions to be art cinema and compatible with censorship constraints because they were compliant with the regime and preached conformity with the status quo.[14] These mostly modestly, but sometimes generously, budgeted pro-regime comedies and dramas championed the anti-modern, anti-democratic values of Francoism and the moral strictures of the Catholic Church (see Triana-Toribio, *Spanish National Cinema*, pp. 98–104). As Pedro Lazaga, one of the producers of these films declared at the time: 'Perhaps the topics are not transcendental [*temas transcendentales*] but why do we all have to make a transcendental cinema?' (see Montero, 'Una manera', p. 10). Leaving the *temas transcendentales* (code for dealing with issues challenging for the regime) to the *NCE* generation and their auteurist endeavours meant that mainstream producers like Lazaga would not pollute the minds of Spanish audiences with ideas of progress, democracy and modernity, but made films that were popular and profitable.

The legacy of the bulk of film production – the Old Spanish Cinema made by producers and directors, such as Lazaga and Pedro Masó – will be addressed in Chapter 4. For the purposes of recounting how the future creators of the Academia positioned themselves vis-à-vis the Old Spanish Cinema, it is crucial to know that these conformist genre films were despised by García Escudero and both the *NCE* and Escuela de Barcelona cinephile film-makers and critics. Producers and directors of the Old Cinema and their films are marginal to the construction of the Academia, a strategy which had serious and long-term repercussions. García Escudero empowered a generation to depart from the Old Cinema, and without his intervention, there would probably be no examples of individual directors able to cultivate a consistent style across different films that now count as the backbone of Spanish auteurism. And it was precisely these films that provided the template for what the Academia, at least in its inception, wanted to craft: 'good' films modelled on a narrow version of European cinema. This concept of European art cinema – the auteurist model – had by the 1980s in France and elsewhere been rigorously problematised and its definition taken apart to reveal the contradictions and exclusions it produced, but no such questioning took place in the Spain of the 1980s, nor has it occurred subsequently to a significant extent.[15]

THE REGIME'S LONG WATCH OVER CINEMA

As well as working within European models of cinema, what concentrated this generation's minds (whether Madrid- or Barcelona-based) was the fight against censorship, which was to last much longer than the 1960s and survive even the

'Where are you going, Ernesto?', 'I'm off to see *La prima Angélica*', 'One of these days you are going to come to harm'

dictator himself well into the late 70s. Just as much as directors, film magazines and critics had been in the forefront of the fight against censorship and the regime. A few publications took it upon themselves to challenge the state about the existence and function of censorship, even daring to name the censors and alerting readers to which films were cut, and paying a high price for their boldness (see Riambau, 'Fotogramas', p. 373). Audiences also joined in the fight. In the early 1970s, as a more affluent Spain was becoming better educated, better travelled and eager to enjoy the same freedom of expression and consumption as the rest of Europe, the more progressive filmgoers risked life and limb to see *La prima Angélica/Cousin Angelica* (Saura, 1973). The Amaya cinema in Madrid and the Balmes in Barcelona were attacked by the far-right paramilitary group Guerrilleros de Cristo Rey (Warriors of Christ the King) for showing the film (see Diego Galán, *Venturas y desventuras*, pp. 127–31). The plight of audiences was put across pithily and humorously by film-maker and cartoonist Summers for the magazine *Sábado Gráfico*. The cautious male moviegoer dons a crash helmet, since going to the movies has become such a high-risk activity.

In *Cousin Angelica*, Querejeta and Saura had tried to put across the perspective of the losers in the Spanish Civil War, something new in Spanish cinema at the time.

The film was more explicit in its representation of the vanquished and the winners, abandoning to a large extent Saura's allegorical strategies of the 1960s, in earlier work such as *The Hunt*. The backlash against *Angelica*, and its banning by the Francoist state as a consequence, is highly illustrative of the very contradictory and volatile final years of the dictatorship, when there was a degree of opening up and modernisation, but when political dissent was still met with disproportionate censorial harshness. As Saura explained in *Nuevo Fotogramas* at the time of the ban in 1974:

> I believe this is the first time that a film has been made in Spain about the Civil War from the standpoint of those who lost ... And showing this film in Spain without censorship could perhaps bring some hope of an opening, of facing certain themes that have so far been taboo but can be discussed today. But I'm no longer sure ... (Cited in 'Actualidad: un caso alarmante', p. 17)

Understandably, for moments such as these that made Saura despair, this period of late dictatorship is mainly remembered as the time in which the dying powers lashed out against the dissident cinema which he spearheaded. *Canciones para después de una guerra/Songs for after a War* (Martín Patino, 1976), a film made with archive footage from the state-controlled NO-DO (short for Noticiarios y Documentales [Newsreels and Documentaries]) and from feature films from the 1940s and 50s to which a soundtrack of popular songs of the same epoch had been added, became another cause célèbre.[16] This banned film made by a former *NCE* member was still awaiting its premiere in 1975, when the readers of *Nuevo Fotogramas* were alerted to the fact that the release of *Liberxina 90* (1970) – similarly steeped in political criticism, and made by Escuela de Barcelona member Carlos Durán – had also been delayed (Cambra, pp. 8–9). In the same article, Cambra challenged the then General Undersecretary of Cinema, Rogelio Díez, to admit that censorship of films and underfunding by the state were the twin obstacles preventing Spanish cinema from being marketable in Europe (of European quality, in the parlance of the time) and winning European prizes (ibid., p. 9).

As illustrations of the type of intervention the Academia wanted to make on film culture a decade later, these examples of sequestered or banned films have two purposes. Judging by the number of prizes garnered abroad by Saura's films – *Angelica* won awards at Cannes in 1974 as Spain's official entry, and *The Hunt*, as we have seen, was awarded a Golden Bear at Berlin in 1966 – they were among Spain's finest examples of quality cinema. More importantly, as Diego Galán argues, these were the *only* films of European quality, even in the eyes of the Francoists, citing the selection process of *Angelica* for the Official Selection of the Cannes Film Festival in 1974 as evidence:

> Mr Maurice Bessy [the General Envoy of the Festival] watched several Spanish films from which he chose *Cousin Angelica*, a film selected for him in advance by the Ministry of Information and Tourism. There was not among the selected titles presumably any of those running in Madrid's cinemas in May: *Lady Doctor* and *Si fulano fuese mengano/If Joe Bloggs Was Joe Bloggs*, both by Mariano Ozores ... (*Venturas y desventuras*, p. 90)

Galán also mentions that the Critics' Week award at Cannes had gone to Érice's *El espíritu de la colmena/The Spirit of the Beehive* (1972), a film that has since joined the European canon of art cinema. *Spirit* also assumed the perspective of the losers in the Civil War. Selection for European consumption in festivals and success abroad was all the evidence critics belonging to the auteurist generation such as Galán needed to argue that, if more Spanish producers were encouraged to adopt this model of film-making, Spanish cinema would recoup its investment internationally from those new European audiences.

In parallel with Spain's increased levels of wealth and education came a growing demand for more films based on the memories and experiences of the losers and the repression and hardship under Franco. Judging by the letters section in *Nuevo Fotogramas*, it is clear that by the mid-1970s, readers were articulate and knowledgeable about banned films and European cinema trends, and expected Spanish films to be more challenging in form and closer to the films emerging from the rest of Europe. Spanish cinephiles were becoming more *belicosos* (belligerent), to the point that this adjective was used as the title for a subsection of the letters pages. By the end of 1975, correspondents were consistently demanding more: more films and to know more through films (about sexuality, about history, about politics). They also questioned the limits imposed on their freedom to see films, even within the constraints of censorship.[17]

In 1975 in the same magazine, Rosa Montero addressed this change in the nation's taste with the Old Spanish Cinema producer and director Lazaga, who conceded: 'It's true that audiences are changing very rapidly. We used to go to the cinema out of habit but now we go out of curiosity, when a film interests us' (Montero, 'Una manera', p. 10). Lazaga as good as admits that more audiences were becoming cinephiles in their filmgoing practices. Montero and Lazaga cited as evidence of these changes the good box-office returns of films such as *El amor del capitán Brando/The Love of Captain Brando* (Jaime de Armiñán, 1974), produced by Matas, and *The Spirit of the Beehive*, produced by Querejeta. And yet, when Montero suggested that Lazaga himself could be producing films closer to this now-profitable auteurist cinema model, he declared, with honesty, that this was not his calling: 'I'll keep on making films that people want to see, but at the same time, the kind of films I know how to make' (ibid.).

Unlike Lazaga, the film professionals at the helm of the Academia in gestation were convinced – as the critic Montero certainly was – that since the habits of mainstream filmgoers were changing, if more producers could be persuaded, the European auteurist cinema model might become a commercially viable cinema. Also, it was clear in letters to film magazines such as *Nuevo Fotogramas* that a growing sector of the population wanted to learn about the Civil War from the perspective of the losers. The themes, too, seemed to be the right ones for a cinema for democracy. These were convictions held dear by the creators of the hegemonic Spanish cinema in democratic times and by the Academia founders.

Censorship was a long process, but the stage that is most critical for understanding the creation and ethos of the Academia is the last one, from 1976 to 1978. These years straddled dictatorship and democracy, like the founders of the Academia themselves. As Trenzado Romero and others have noted, this phase was characterised by alternating hesitant deregulation and resolute reforms as Francoism was being left behind after the dictator's death at the end of 1975. Key moments were the suppression of the censorship of scripts prior to shooting in 1976 and the definitive abolition of state censorship in November 1977, then justified using the new democratic discourse: 'Cinema, a basic component of cultural activity, must be in accordance with the **democratic pluralism** in which our society is immersed ...'[18] (Trenzado Romero, p. 60; my emphasis).

The twilight years of censorship were a time of contradiction. They produced royal decrees which looked modern, democratic and European on paper, but the early post-dictatorship was marked by uncertainty and backlash from conservative forces. One such backlash was the high court ban of Pilar Miró's *El crimen de Cuenca/ The Cuenca Crime* in 1979, which, unlike *Angelica* and *Songs for after a War* (finally released in November 1976), was not allowed to be screened in cinemas even after the dictatorship was definitively abolished.

Miró's meticulous use of period detail and of uncompromisingly explicit representations of violence in her first feature film, *La petición/The Request* (1976), had already resulted in a fight with the censors and a reputation for headstrong defence of her work against their scissors (see Pérez Millán, pp. 87–112). The explicit represen-tation of torture was also adopted for *The Cuenca Crime*.[19] The film is based on an infamous miscarriage of justice in the 1910s. Two landless workers were falsely accused of being responsible for the disappearance of a third man. The Guardia Civil (Civil Guard) obtained a false confession through torture and the complete degradation of the two men using 'savage methods' (Miró quoted in ibid., p. 136). With the help of the victims' descendants, Miró, scriptwriter Lola Salvador and cinematographer Hans Burmann constructed detailed scenes of torture, using frequent close-ups, some of them involving the victims' genitals.[20] The film exposed in no uncertain terms the brutality of the Guardia Civil and portrayed them as the henchmen of corrupt political masters. Such a tale was incendiary in the nascent democracy, when the rump of the dictatorship was still in control, under the guise of party politics (the first elected president, Adolfo Suárez, was an ex-Francoist minister). *The Cuenca Crime* may have been set in 1910, but with reports circulating about abuses and the torture of political prisoners in Francoist prisons, alongside those about Argentinian and Chilean prisons, the real target was clear (Diego Galán, *Pilar Miró*, p. 131). On paper, censorship had been abolished in 1977, and the Spanish constitution, recently approved through a free democratic referendum, defended freedom of expression. And yet, Miró was threatened with court martial by the Spanish military for having insulted the Civil Guard, which the military considered part of the army, and her producer, Matas, faced punishment as well.[21] As she pithily put it, 'it seems that above the Spanish Constitution, hovers a three-cornered hat of the Guardia Civil' (Miró cited in ibid., p. 133).

On 23 February 1981, a Civil Guard division disrupted the proceedings of parliament in an attempted *coup d'état*; and Miró and Matas's damning portrayal seemed validated. The last real threat to the young democracy came from the army, and the deployment of the Guardia Civil as its visible head. As history records, the new Spanish king, Juan Carlos I, sided with democracy in the end, unlike some in the army of which he was chief commander. Spanish voters aligned with the new system as well, and very publicly turned their backs on the centre-right UCD party (Unión de Centro Democrático [Coalition of Democratic Centre]), made up almost entirely of former

Francoists. In the general elections of October 1982, the winner was the unambiguously left-wing Spanish Socialist Party, voted in by a landslide. The cultural and political conditions changed significantly from then on.

POLICIES AND ORGANISATIONS FOR A EUROPEAN SPAIN

Both Matas and Miró became symbols of the uncompromising fight for democracy, and their closeness to the Spanish Socialist Party and the liberal left was turned now to their advantage. In December 1982, Miró became General Undersecretary of Cinema, ushering in a time of change for Spanish cinema, the seeds of which were planted by that group of cinephiles of the 1950s and 60s. After decades of fighting the forces of Francoism, it is no wonder that a chief priority for Spanish cinema was freedom of expression and doing away with censorship's shackles to tell the repressed memories and present the experiences of the losers in the Civil War. Among the strategies to support these films economically was a new administrative structure brought in during the Socialist Party's first legislature (1982–96). Once in power, the Socialist Party tasked Miró with transforming the Francoist General Division for the Cinema into the democratic Institute for Cinema and Audiovisual Arts (Instituto de la Cinematografía y las Artes Audiovisuales, known as the ICAA – the Spanish Film Institute). The changes also involved new legislation (known popularly as *Ley Miró*/Miró Law) that involved a new form of financing for Spanish cinema designed 'to strengthen the film industry and to achieve a production culturally more valuable and commercially more competitive' (Miró quoted in Ansola González, p. 105). This strengthening of the industry took the form of a new state subsidy paid in advance, following the French system of *avances sur recette*, and the creation of a Film Protection Fund, from where the financing would be drawn (see, among others, Hopewell, *Out of the Past*, p. 86; Riambau, 'La década', pp. 339–447). Directors and producers were meant to join forces to apply for subsidies by submitting their projects to a Subcommittee for Technical Valorisation.[22]

For Thomas Elsaesser, France is the only European country to have something akin to a genuine film industry and culture (p. 36). It is therefore unsurprising that this neighbouring country has always served as a beacon for Spain's cinephiles. When France is invoked as a model for legislation and film culture, it is clear that this is a way of approaching Europe while putting distance between Spanish cinema and Hollywood's commercial practices. This emulation of the French model, of which the creation of the Academia must be considered a part, cannot be fully understood without addressing another auteurist obsession: the liberal left's all-pervading belief that Europe was the solution to Spain's problems. Throughout Franco's dictatorship, but particularly towards its end, progressive and liberal anti-Francoists looked to Europe as an ideal of democracy, modernity, affluence and progress that Spain and Spaniards should aspire to. This is why admission to the European Community in 1986, eleven years after Franco's death, was such an important achievement for the left. As Mary Farrell explains, '[e]ntry to the European club was in fact a high point of the long post-Franco transition period, marking the culmination of the reformist aspirations of the previous decade' (p. 215).

During the late dictatorship and early transition, the process of modernisation was already well advanced among those who controlled and financed cinema in Spain, and who tended to belong to the progressive and liberal opposition (Hopewell, *Out of the Past*, pp. 63–8). The constant fight against censorship from film magazines and professionals can be seen as evidence that this Europeanising process was well under way, whether it was based in Madrid or Barcelona. This process was accelerated when the Socialist Party won the elections in 1982, and became so associated with the Party's actions that it became widely known as the socialist change.

BY INVITATION ONLY

Meanwhile, Matas, the producer of *The Cuenca Crime*, preferred another method for modernising and Europeanising Spain's film culture. Unlike Miró, he did not seek direct power through the control of finances or by joining the administration. As part of the country's administrative apparatus, the ICAA would inevitably change hands as different parties won elections, but a non-governmental film academy could, in theory, keep some distance from elected politicians and, therefore, include all professionals, even those not aligned with political groups. Certainly, that was the image of BAFTA and AMPAS.

On 12 November 1985, Matas invited some of the best-known and most representative figures of Spain's cinema industry to lunch in the Madrid restaurant O'Pazo. Among those invited were his close friend García Berlanga, whose films he produced, and Saura. Directors of production Tedy Villalba and Marisol Carnicero represented fellow producers, and also present were the well-known actors José Sacristán and Charo López. Pablo García del Amo (known for, among other films, *The Spirit of the Beehive*) and José Luis Matesanz represented the editing profession, and Manolo Matji scriptwriters. Film music director and composer José Nieto, DP Carlos Suárez and the art director Ramiro Gómez were also invited. Matas's assembled guests discussed their worries about the industry, about the need to establish a census of all the professionals working in film-making and about whether film awards could improve the quality of films and also entice audiences (Granado, p. 13).

This lunch is usually taken as the foundational act of the Academia, and the *espíritu de O'Pazo* (the spirit of O'Pazo) has become shorthand for the original intentions of the Academia founders. Under discussion at the lunch, and at subsequent meetings, were the main aims of the Academia; their focus was on elevating all the film-making trades as professions in the public eye, and dignifying Spanish films in particular by encouraging their study and research in scholarly contexts and creating annual awards for published research on film (Granado, p. 14). Soon other professionals joined and by the end of that month thirty had signed up, with actors forming the largest professional group, followed next by directors, setting a pattern for the future (García Fernández, 'Los miembros', pp. 51–5).

Matas imagined an association of professionals that would act as a mouthpiece for the entire film industry in dealings with the administration and would have prize-awarding rights. He knew that his own political allegiance would stand in the way of the Academia, which was trying to be an inclusive, pluralistic organisation by recruiting across the entire political spectrum. According to founding member Tedy Villalba, Matas was convinced that many would suspect he had an axe to grind in the creation of the Academia and the prizes, particularly in light of his connection to *The Cuenca Crime* and his position, alongside Querejeta, as one of the frankest critics of censorship.[23] Thus he suggested that, after assembling the film professionals, he would step back and become a regular member without any executive role. This remained the case until his death in 1996.[24]

Matas's eagerness to be offstage, and Villalba's equal eagerness to confirm that this was the case, is crucial for our understanding of the Academia and the film culture models that it and the Goya prizes wanted to inspire. Whatever sympathies or connections the membership might have with the Socialist Party, it was vital to give the appearance of uncoupling party politics from Spanish cinema. At the same time, the rhetoric about the Academia's foundation has always emphasised that it is not, and never has been, a trade union. Gómez Bermúdez de Castro is at some pains to argue this point in an article in which he analyses and contextualises the legal statutes of the Academia:

> The most important question to clarify was the exact configuration of the organization the members wanted to join. The academy was not founded as a forum of political representation, or union representation. ... Everything leads one to believe that the writers of the statutes were scrupulous from its first draft ... this paragraph is part of the first article: 'The Academia excludes the aims of a trade union, and is independent from any political or ideological group.' This text was not deleted or modified in any subsequent versions. (p. 25)

These words come from a comprehensive survey of the Academia carried out by the members of the AEHC, the Spanish Association of Film Historians, in 1998, on the twelfth anniversary of the organisation, and published in one of the Academia's own periodicals, the scholarly *Cuadernos de la Academia* (no. 4). The AEHC has worked closely with the Academia on several academic events and publications, including the compilation of a *Dictionary of Spanish Film* to coincide with the celebrations of the first century of cinema in 1995. The Association was thus directly integrated into the Academia's network, and invested in a particular version of Spanish film history and part of the hegemonic Spanish film culture. For these reasons, their comments cannot be seen as entirely neutral, their rigour as scholars notwithstanding.[25]

In the survey, the separation of the Academia from politics and trade unionism is argued and reiterated so many times, in article after article, that one eventually grows suspicious at so much protestation, necessary though it may seem to writers who are fully aware of the political affiliations of the Academia's founding members. One historian, Esteve Riambau, goes so far as to argue that 'as an institution it came from nothing, it was not trying to take anyone's place' ('Una institución imprescindible', p. 45), and follows this with a series of disclaimers about the Academia as a non-political institution. Distancing itself from political sides is vital for the Academia if it is to be legitimately associated with pragmatic and neutral aims such as 'encourag[ing] the national and international dissemination of Spanish cinema' and 'defend[ing] film professionals', aims it must pursue as an interlocutor with the Spanish Film Institute and other formal bodies of the state which affect cinema, regardless of which party is in government. Politics had to be out of the equation for the organisation to be formally inclusive, and also for it to be the main point of contact for AMPAS, which, as Riambau tells us, it has been since 1986, when it selected the first Spanish film to be considered for the Best Foreign-Language Film Oscar (ibid.).

And yet, despite all the avowals of political neutrality, the Academia will always live with the consequences of the fact that the party in power when it was created, and the political groups and individuals that demanded the mechanisms were put in place for the creation of a modern, European, democratic cinema during the transition, were associated with the liberal left even when not Socialist Party members themselves.

The Socialist Party – and the film-makers and critics associated with it in the 1980s and early 90s – sought social extension in cinema not just by screening the repressed stories of the vanquished in the Civil War, but by granting access to cinema to groups that had been excluded from film-making. In their wish to see the dominant ideology of Francoism challenged in early democracy, they upheld, at least in their writings, the Marxist doctrine that 'the class which has the means of material production at its disposal, has control at the same time over the means of mental production ...' (Marx and Engels, p. 64). As Fernando Lara argued idealistically in 1975 ('El cine español', pp. 221–43), giving the working class access to film-making would challenge the dominant ideas of the dominant class (the bourgeoisie).

In practice, there *was* a redistribution of the means of cinematic production after the O'Pazo lunch. In order to achieve the aims of the Academia, financing had to be provided by the state, at least in part. With the Academia advising and the state providing, producers of the Old Spanish Cinema and other commercial cinema producers were disadvantaged, while those from the auteurist generation who became known as 'independent producers', such as Querejeta and Matas, benefited. The skill at playing the system by some of the independent producers eventually provoked accusations of cronyism, and a range of public criticism.[26] So, one further consequence of the O'Pazo meeting was the sidelining of producers and film-makers who did not belong to the favoured Matas group. We know who were invited inside the tent; now we need to know who were excluded.

NO FREE LUNCH

The following film trades were represented at the O'Pazo lunch: direction, production, acting, editing, scriptwriting, music, film photography and artistic direction. Matas drew on his closest collaborators and friends, whose names are recorded for posterity, but it would be just as instructive to draw up a list of those who were not invited, and would not have been welcome. Such a list would include first the distributors and exhibitors who sought to profit from Hollywood production, and who, as Trenzado Romero argues, fought the new protectionist systems every step of the way (pp. 115–16). So hostile were they to the screen and distribution quotas of the Miró Law that they challenged the new legislation before the Constitutional Tribunal in 1984 (see Lara, 'La hora', p. 43). Also excluded from lunch were the film professionals who produced 'S-rated' films, the many co-productions of horror cinema and pornographic films, which constituted two-thirds of Spain's film output, and did not count as 'good' films, to use Miró's term (p. 44). Producers and directors such as Lazaga, Pedro Masó or Mariano Ozores fell into this category and were not supposed to benefit from the new conditions, and their priorities were not contemplated in the aims of the proposed Academia.

Jesús Franco, who exited the EOC with a fail in direction, was not approached, even though he had gone on to make more films than any of his former classmates, establishing in the process an international cult following. Antonio Lázaro-Reboll argues that Franco's cinema diverged from oppositional film-making, as did the films of another prolific contemporary, Paul Naschy. Both directors were exported, and had transnational and profitable careers (Lázaro-Reboll, *Spanish Horror Films*, pp. 52–93). Naschy and Franco worked in the co-production margins of the industry making exploitation films that kept Spain's film infrastructure alive by providing jobs and training in adverse times, particularly when the crisis in financing at the end of the 1960s and early 70s made auteurist film-making impractical. Spanish cinema was a small industry in terms of the number of professionals involved in the 1960s, and the 'migration of actors between popular and art cinemas [was] a source of major overlap between the two'; the same applies to art directors, cameramen and women editors who worked in both the commercial and the art cinema sectors of the industry (Faulkner, *A Cinema*, p. 12).

Successful commercial producers of the 1970s had profited in a market-driven model, but their films – conservative comedies and melodramas which championed traditional Catholic and authoritarian values – were far from what the Academia cinephiles wanted, particularly if a national cinema was to be built for both a democratic Spain and for Europe. For the auteurist generation, Lazaga, Ozores and Masó were bywords for subproducts and *cine de barrio* (neighbourhood/outskirts cinema). They objected to them on ideological grounds but also for reasons of class and distinction. These films were powerfully associated with the pervasive lack of literacy under Francoism, with rural working-class taste drawn to popular forms of stage comedy and musical, such as *sainete* and *revistas*. Such forms were consumed enthusiastically by rural émigrés dwelling on the outskirts of expanding cities. There was also an element of fear of contamination in the auteurist distaste for these films, since this was the class that some of them had just left behind, with their university education in the 1950s and 60s, and with their cultivated cinephilia. Others, like Gubern, Jordà, Miró, Saura and Portabella, were born into the established bourgeoisie.

So, through reasons that mixed a desire to emulate European quality models with a requirement to consign to oblivion the genres associated with retrograde Francoist values and an underdeveloped lower-class rural experience, the new financing system that was crafted to elevate all national production was predicated on channelling the bulk of funds away from the commercial cinema to satisfy modern and Europeanised filmgoers. The purpose of protective legislation, endorsed by the Academia, was in other words to foster different consuming habits in audiences, encouraging participation in the culture of transition, and so help to create more Spaniards like those who had become better educated, more travelled and keen on their urban identities in the 1970s. But in terms of strengthening the industry, the protective legislation simply did not deliver. Instead, 'Spanish cinema gradually became a sum of political, creative and personal projects to the detriment of its organized and structured business side,' as Álvarez Monzoncillo and Menor Sendra put it (p. 25).

Significantly, the lunch invitation did not include anyone from television. The defenders of the pervading model of cinema at the time, based on the hegemonic European auteurist model, could not envisage an association which, like BAFTA today, includes television. And yet, many of the EOC alumni who went on to become the *NCE* directors had worked in television when state money was scarce. A particularly striking case was Miró herself, who developed a sustained television career and made many prestigious films for the small screen. Her award-winning work for television – effectively classified as 'training' by her biographer José Antonio Pérez Millán – in fact became an obstacle to her career in film-making, or, as Pérez Millán calls it, 'actual cinema' (p. 82).

Other recently graduated EOC members moved to television during the financing crisis of the 1960s and early 70s. But they did not see this medium as their natural home and, once they had formed the Academia, translated this prejudice against television to their nascent organisation, despite the fact that all of them had been involved in it. In the words of Javier Maqua (film-maker and critic of the 1970s):

> The sixties are the television years: many *EOC* alumni spent a stint working in television, while developing a complex of 'slumming it'. There is a clear hierarchy of work among the Academia members: serious people work on cinema and the little people who do not have the courage to tough it out in the industrial cinema, seek refuge in television. But they all worked in television, every single one of them. (Cited in Minguet *et al.*, p. 418)

Television suffered from a lack of prestige, and quality cinema sought to distance itself from it. According to Antonio Carballo Dávila, who was editor in chief of *Cineinforme*, a prestigious industry magazine, this short-sightedness is one serious obstacle impeding the Academia's officially stated desire to be inclusive. He argues that without addressing this problem, the Academia will never achieve that foundational aim of the organisation. Carballo maintains that, true to the 'O'Pazo spirit', the Academia only represents those invited to lunch (p. 7).

In the same editorial, Carballo complains bitterly about the lasting legacy of the exclusion of so many potential stakeholders, 'of all of us who were not directly associated with film production' (ibid.). Even twenty-five years after O'Pazo, he warns that the Academia is failing and will continue to do so until it accepts onto its steering group key industry players such as distributors, exhibitors, laboratories and television channels:

> Did I say television channels? Yes, indeed, television channels. One of the topics I insisted upon the most with Matas was that the Academia would benefit enormously if it included television alongside cinema, following the model of the British BAFTA. (ibid., p. 8)

The relationship between television and the Academia is fractured, as Carballo observes, but far more complex than one of simple exclusion from the foundational moment. In fact, the Academia relies on television for its existence not only because it broadcasts the revenue-generating annual film award ceremonies (Ortega, p. 144), but also because television channels (both private and state-owned) were obliged from the late 1990s to contribute to film financing, following the French model. Some of the consequences of the intervention of television in film financing after 1999 will be addressed in Chapter 4.[27]

Another absence from the O'Pazo lunch that has had a detrimental effect for the Academia and for the appeal of Spanish cinema to a wide audience is that of commercial cinema. It has to be pointed out that the decisive canonisation of the auteurist model of cinema espoused by the *NCE* generation and its professionals did not mean that all elements of the popular Old Cinema could be permanently erased from the picture.

The Academia rewarded and encouraged a particular type of Spanish film and made the careers of film professionals, who in their turn ensured that by 2010, as Belén Vidal puts it, 'Spanish cinema can hardly be called a minor or peripheral cinema' ('Memories of Underdevelopment', p. 211). However, there were clear casualties of this campaign, and by ostracising the commercial cinema at the start of its existence, the Academia also ostracised a large number of Spanish filmgoers. As we will see in subsequent chapters, the Academia has difficulty conciliating the degree of migration and overlap between the commercial and the auteurist cinema of the past, and working out how to recognise the contribution of certain film professionals while negotiating the potentially subversive meanings of awarding prizes to those too closely identified with ideas of cinema contrary to their funding principles. For these reasons, Pedro Masó and Jess Franco did not receive Goyas de Honor until 2005 and 2009 respectively. This problem with commercial values remains unresolved. In 2007, the election of the popular auteur Álex de la Iglesia as president of the Academia was supposed to bring the institution closer to the people, in the process acknowledging the problem of distance. The main instrument through which both a distance and an attraction between hegemonic film culture and 'the people' was created is the subject of the next chapter: Spain's cinema awards, the Goyas.

2

And the Winner Is …

Given this fundamental orientation towards the task of judgment – the upholding of cultural standards by means of reward and rebuke – the academies were naturally disposed toward prizes and awards.

(English, p. 39)

The Academia is true to its natural disposition, and it shares this natural inclination to judge with all academies. Awarding prizes is the Academia's most distinct and public function. Awarded every year since 1987, the *premios Goya* – Goya awards or prizes – are a central feature of Spanish film culture. Spanish and foreign critics use the adjective 'Goya-winning' to endorse films and performances for prospective national and international audiences; Goyas are in turn routinely mentioned as part of the publicity; and re-released DVD cases of the winning films proudly display stickers announcing their accolades. A new term was even coined in 1987: a film or professional honoured with a Goya has been *engoyado/a*.

The Goyas are not just a set of prizes, but crucially also a key event in the Spanish cinema calendar. Between 1987 and 2011, the annual award ceremony (*la Gala de los Goya*, henceforth Gala) was the most important showcase for hegemonic Spanish cinema, and continues to be so to this day. The Gala is a theatrical and also a televisual event, with all the attendant build-up in the press and other media, the corporate sponsors, and the red carpet moments with couture frocks and celebrity gossip. Each Gala is staged in front of a live audience of members of the Academia, including Spain's transnational film professionals: Amenábar, Banderas, Bardem, Juan A. Bayona, Isabel Coixet, Cruz, Maura, Eduardo Noriega, Maribel Verdú and, occasionally, Pedro and Agustín Almodóvar. The considerable audience shares for this event range from double-figure percentages – for example, 33.5 per cent in 1999 and 20.5 per cent in 2007 – to single figures (9.8 per cent) in the lean years of 1992 and 1993, when it was shown by the private channel Antena 3, instead of the state-owned TVE1 or La 2 (Granado, p. 309).

From the Galas' inception, Spain's highest state representatives have patronised this celebration of Spanish cinema. Former monarchs, Juan Carlos and Sofía, attended the first award ceremony on 16 March 1987, and their son, Felipe, was also present in 1999. José Luis Rodríguez Zapatero was the first and only Spanish prime minister to attend in 2005 (Granado, p. 274). The Galas welcomed government members, especially the minister of culture, although some have been made to feel like gatecrashers at the party of Spain's film professionals. There are also those who dread rather than look forward to the Gala and whose concerns will be taken up towards the end of this chapter.

This chapter is divided into two parts: other prizes, and Goyas and Galas. Before exploring how the Galas and Goyas act as instruments of hegemonic film, I will first consider how they are only the most prominent part of a wider award-giving culture. The Academia also bestows less public awards that cultivate the idea of film as cultural good rather than industrial product. These include the *Medallas de Oro* (Gold Medals), and other prizes such as the González-Sinde award given to those using cinema to benefit society as a whole, the Muñoz Suay award for the academic study of cinema and the Alfonso Sánchez award for film criticism. There are also yearly homages to those who have given extended service to Spanish film. All these prizes are decided upon by small committees and ratified by the Board of Governors. Although it is never overtly stated, these lower-profile prizes exist as a way of settling accounts with the past and have priorities that the Goyas, more oriented towards the box office, cannot accommodate.

These low-profile internal awards form a critical background against which the publicly staged Galas negotiate Spain's geopolitical position as a national cinema aiming at international markets by giving its films and film professionals 'award capital' that may enable them to travel transnationally. At the same time, in Goya season, the Academia struggles with its own and Spain's political present and past. The Goyas have defined the best of Spanish cinema for the last thirty years, but in many ways they remain caught up in the principles and practices established in the earliest years. Close scrutiny of those early years is therefore vital to understand the wider agenda of the Goya system. As for the Galas, they became most interesting whenever the PP was in power, when they turned into a site of struggle for the competing interests of the hegemonic film culture. From 2001 to 2003 in particular, a left-leaning sector of the hegemonic film culture, wedded to an idea of cinema as a medium that engages with reality and conceiving of film professionals as politically and socially committed, treated the Gala as a political platform. In the years when the political fight receded, the role of the annual Gala as a pageant of cinematic taste became easier to discern.

THE ACADEMIA'S LESS PUBLIC AWARDS

Just as the Academia needs to be understood in relation to the institutions it replaced (see Chapter 1), so the film prizes of democracy should be seen in the context of their genealogy. To appreciate how awards function as instruments of reward for 'good' film-making habits (and punishment for 'bad') and foster a particular kind of understanding of cinema, it is crucial to explain why they exist in the first place. During the Franco era, many prizes fulfilled the reward-and-punishment function at a national level: these included the National Awards for the Cinema and the various National Interest (created in 1944), Military Interest (1946) and Special Interest awards (from 1962). As Bernard Bentley has shown, the extensive array of prizes from the Dirección Nacional de Cinematografía served to 'reward productions that appeared to endorse the values of the regime' (p. 85). There were also National Film Awards (*Premios Nacionales de Cinematografía*) for the best scripts. However, as Bentley explains, 'these prizes did not necessarily coincide ... since too many separate government offices had a say in the production and distribution of each individual film' (ibid.).

During the Franco era, prizes came from various sources, and they aimed to please different groups, such as the military, whose stake in the national cinema was high in a dictatorship that installed captains, generals and admirals in all government positions – including overseeing cinema – to the end of its days.[1] In addition to the awards mentioned above, there were those issued by the Circle of Writers for the Cinema (Círculo de Escritores Cinematográficos), a professional body which judged scriptwriting.[2] The Church also had a considerable role in policing films. Besides its presence on censorship boards, it created prizes of its own. These included awards presented to Spanish and foreign films at the Festival de Cine Religioso y de Valores Morales (Festival of Religious and Moral Cinema), which was founded in 1956, and was the antecedent of the Semana Internacional de Cine de Valladolid (International Film Week of Valladolid) (see Combarros Peláez, p. 24).

Rather than opting for consolidation, the Academia created a battery of prizes and a frenzy of awards that echoes the practices of the Franco era. This proliferation started with the formation of the institution in 1986 and continued well into the last years of the following decade. The abundance of awards is partly the logical translation into the Spanish context of 'the rise of the prize' that is pervasive, particularly in the cinema world (English, p. 323). But it also has a strong element of Spain and Latin America's inherited habits of cultural (particularly literary) prizes of the sort satirised by Roberto Bolaño in 'Sensini', a tale of impoverished writers who make a living by regularly entering literary contests. And then, perhaps, there is the not-so-residual mindset that requires constant paternalistic validation from higher authorities. The perceived need to validate arts and culture through prize-giving is long-standing: José Cadalso made the case for them in his *Cartas marruecas* in 1775 (pp. 96–7).

In democracy, as under Francoism, there were many stakeholders beyond those directly involved in film production, distribution and exhibition. Between 1986 and 2011, film-making depended heavily on government funding and was implicitly asked to justify its usefulness for society. To satisfy these demands and prove Spanish cinema's value as a cultural good, some of the Academia's awards encouraged the amelioration of society, rewarding, for example, the dissemination of human rights or health education. With this remit of recognising cinema's usefulness, the González-Sinde award was created in 1998. The name honoured the Academia's first president, the director and producer José María González-Sinde (1986–8), father of the writer and director Ángeles González-Sinde, herself Academia president (2006–9), and minister of culture between 2009 and 2011.[3] This award was given to institutions or individuals.[4] Among the winners was the Fundación de Ayuda contra la Drogadicción (Foundation for Help against Drug Addiction), which was awarded the prize in 1999 for its screenings of anti-drug films for children, while in 2000, the Fundación La Casa del Actor (Actors' House Foundation) was decorated for establishing a residence for retired actors.

Other prizes were less concerned with social impact and more with parcelling out different areas of film culture, which were not film-making in the strict sense, but nevertheless justified cinema's existence and enhanced the place of films in Spain's culture. With the Muñoz Suay award, created in 1997 to commemorate the death of the influential critic and key participant in the Salamanca conference of 1955, the Academia celebrated the best historical academic research on Spanish cinema.[5] As we saw in the previous chapter, the critic Muñoz Suay championed film-making in defiance of Franco, and defended the Catalan movement Escuela de Barcelona at the end of the 1960s. As an undercover member of the Communist Party, he was instrumental in bringing Luis Buñuel to Spain to shoot *Viridiana* (1961).[6] Naming a film research award after him therefore gave an unambiguous political inflection to the long-cherished aspiration of the auteurist generation to legitimate cinema culturally. In the 1950s and 60s, as Pujol Ozonas explains, and as we saw in the previous chapter, the auteurist generation advanced cinema's legitimation by contributing to periodicals and magazines that displayed 'a new form of seeing and thinking about cinema' – that is, in *writing* about cinema (p. 127). With the mechanisms of the Academia behind them, these cinephiles could now elevate cinema to an object of study, and give it the attention that it had only fitfully received in the periodicals of the 1950s through to the 70s. Here, then, is an example of a prize that belatedly recognised figures who were uncomfortable to the Franco era.

Through prizes for scholarship, such as the Muñoz Suay, the Academia was trying to encourage rigour and significance in reflections on and memorialisations of Spanish cinema, be it through academic study or journalistic film criticism. Rigour and significance, for these purposes, has mainly meant archival work and data-gathering, rather than, for example, the philosophical or conceptual adventures valued in some other film cultures. It inevitably follows that the awards have been most closely linked with the AEHC, a network of scholars with whom the Academia partnered most successfully in the journal series *Cuadernos del Cine Español* from 1997 to 2005.[7] Since film cultures encourage a set of protocols and a particular process of selection in determining what needs to be conserved, it is important to acknowledge the decisive role of the sixth Academia president, José Luis Borau (1994–8), in the creation of one of the key strategies of canonisation: the compilation of a dictionary of Spanish film. The *Diccionario del cine español*, coordinated by Julio Pérez Perucha, Esteve Riambau and Carlos F. Heredero, under the guidance of Borau, aligns its values and priorities closely with the hegemonic auterist programme.[8] During the period covered by this study, the bulk of the recipients of the Muñoz Suay award were members of the AEHC. In parallel with Muñoz Suay is the Alfonso Sánchez award, which judges the value of critics and journalists who use their work to promote Spanish cinema in the media and celebrates non-academic film research. Finally, there is the Segundo de Chomón award, which honours the memory of the early cinema pioneer who worked with the Pathé brothers in France, and recognises technical innovation.[9]

There is only one Goya dedicated to lifetime achievement – the *Goya de Honor* – but many more potential candidates for lifetime recognition, so to this battery of internal Academia prizes we can add the yearly homages to distinguished film professionals whose contributions fall short of deserving a more public garland. Perhaps the most prestigious of these are the Gold Medals, forty-six of which were given out at once in 1996, as part of cinema's centenary celebrations. This bumper harvest of Gold Medals was integral to making up for lost time, a function that Spain's democratic prizes have taken on to ensure that no previously neglected film professional passes away before their contribution is recognised.

In the establishment of these many new awards, the practices of the Academia resemble those of earlier professional and regulatory bodies, but at the same time, new urgencies quite unambiguously replaced old priorities. We need to ask what values replaced those of the patriotic military or the pious Church, when they no longer had a say about which films were celebrated under democracy, particularly during the Socialist Party administrations of 1982–96 and 2004–11. At the head of the Academia's list of key values have always been the rights gained with democracy: freedom of speech and the inclusion of all voices. As I indicated in the previous chapter, the defence of *democracy*, *pluralism* and *participation* are still stressed on its website. Therefore, it is social responsibility and activism through cinema that the organisation values and commends with awards.

The Academia and all its elements are products of Spain's journey from dictatorship to democracy, a journey that involved the transformation of the old regime's institutional apparatus for the cinema and the cooperation, or co-optation, of the auteurist group that cut its teeth in the fight against the dictatorship.
The numerous 'other prizes' awarded by the Academia carry the burden of history by participating in the cleansing function that cultural prizes and events undertook during the transition, and particularly during the first decade of the Socialist Party's period of office (1982–92).

This cleansing function consisted of two processes: awarding prizes to those who had been denied them because of their opposition to the regime, and allowing some institutions and individuals, tainted by their previous Francoist incarnations, to receive awards, present them and organise events under democracy as if 'their hands were clean'. Both processes were part of the pact of silence: 'the tacit agreement among all the political forces to avoid a public debate on the Second Republic, the Civil War, and Franco's dictatorship' (Balfour and Quiroga, p. 158).

The first process – awards to those who had been overlooked for political reasons – was intended to give recognition to those for whom it was long overdue.
Cultural prizes (such as the Miguel de Cervantes literature award) recognised figures who had only been spoken about in hushed tones during Francoism because of their associations with the Second Republic, or their ideological incompatibility with the authoritarian and Catholic status quo. In a study of the Cervantes award, Sarah Bowskill argues that cultural prizes helped restore Spain's positive image abroad. As she explains, authors who accepted the prize

> could confer political legitimacy on the emerging regime at an international level. Thus Spain could try to rejoin the literary present from which it had been largely excluded under Franco by (belatedly) consecrating those authors most associated with literary modernity. (p. 296)

The second process at work in the prizes was the significant 'suspension' or 'bracketing off' of the past involved in the mechanics of award-giving under early democracy.
The pact of silence forged during the transition manifested itself in film culture through absence and omission, in those moments when Spaniards conveniently forgot to remember, or had to repress their memories of the recent past in public award

ceremonies. A principal beneficiary of this repression was Spain's monarchy, as Bowskill argues in the case of the Cervantes prize. By being associated with this literary award and handing it to high-profile, left-wing writers – even returnees from exile such as the poet Jorge Guillén – the Spanish monarchs acquired both cultural capital and democratic credentials (pp. 296–7). The most prestigious cultural prize worldwide, the Nobel Prize, is closely related to a democratic monarchy, where King Carl Gustaf of Sweden hands the medals to the laureates (English, p. 55). By imitating this gesture, the Spanish monarchy could hope to project the same aura of legitimacy, rather than being a constant reminder of Franco. It was, after all, the dictator who imposed monarchy as a form of government and Prince Juan Carlos de Borbón y Borbón as his successor, thus continuing to exert his will on Spain after his death (Preston, pp. 27–38).

In the pursuit of consensus and without endangering 'the possibility of living together' (Echevarría, pp. 28–9), such connections with the dictatorial past were made opaque. For figures too closely associated with the regime who could not be easily recuperated for democracy, but who needed to be validated for political reasons, the less public awards of the Academia served an important purpose. This was the case with the Gold Medal awarded to Vicente Casanova, the owner of Cifesa, the powerful production company of the 1930s–50s, and 'the regime's ideological standard bearer' (Peter Evans, 'Cifesa', p. 215). Casanova's conformist views and 'his friendships with high-ranking [Francoist] politicians like Carrero Blanco' (ibid.) were put aside to award him the Academia's first Gold Medal. But, for several reasons, which included Casanova's advanced age, this recognition was not made in public, nor was it widely publicised. Instead, the vice-presidents of the Academia travelled to Casanova's home in Biarritz in 1986 to hand him the institution's first award (Sánchez Salas and Sánchez Salas, pp. 81–3).

Other associations with the regime were not 'put aside', however. This was the case with Ana Mariscal, who died in 1995 without any significant recognition from the Academia, public or otherwise. A pioneer woman in film direction and production, she taught at the EOC (Martin-Márquez, pp. 85–140), and had acted in many key films of the 1940s and the 50s, such as *De mujer a mujer/From Woman to Woman* (Luis Lucia, 1950), in which she performed opposite the first female recipient of a Best Actress Goya, Amparo Rivelles (see Triana-Toribio, 'Ana Mariscal', p. 193; Faulkner, *A History*, pp. 60–4). One of her most iconic roles was as the hero's girlfriend, Marisol, in *Raza* (José Luis Sáenz de Heredia, 1942), a film based on a story by Franco, scripted and directed by a cousin of the founder of Spain's Fascist party. The same process of forgetting to remember which rescued institutions directly connected to the dictator, such as the monarchy and production companies like Cifesa and its owner, Casanova, could not do the same for her. The hegemonic film culture of democracy has shown other inconsistencies, besides the latent sexism which condemned Mariscal.

ENGOYADOS

If the cultural and social priorities of the Academia are catered for through internal awards, the Goyas provide guidance to the national and international audiences of

Spanish films. In general, they have succeeded in supplying indices of quality, for award-winning films always have a second life at the box office after the ceremony. Translating award capital into economic gain is a principal aim of film prizes, as James English argues in his study of the growth and function of cultural awards.

English explains that all the prizes created by 'official societies, academies, and professional organizations in the less legitimate arts, the fields of "entertainment"' (p. 69) are modelled on the Oscars, particularly the way prizes translate into box-office success. Even so, the Goyas have to be viewed as more than simply the result of Oscar envy, since establishing a direct line to the Academy Awards is problematic.[10] In the previous chapter, I showed how democratic organisations such as the Spanish Film Institute are in effect revamped Francoist bodies, geared in early democracy to provide favourable conditions for auteurist cinema and the hegemonic film culture.

While the Francoist prizes were replicated in the not so public awards such as the González-Sinde, the newly minted Goyas were also steeped in connections to earlier prizes. Historical accounts of the Goyas make two things clear: first, they were created to replace the Francoist awards of the SNC and the CEC, and second, this link makes historians uncomfortable. For example, Luis Fernández Colorado acknowledges that '[a]fter the disappearance of the old National Entertainment Union awards, instituted in the Franco era and viewed with suspicion due to their official prejudice, a disorienting landscape remained which did not benefit Spanish cinema' (p. 114).

Historians of the Academia are at pains to distance the Goyas from previous prizes for obvious reasons. The SNC may have been tasked officially with rewarding achievement in film-making during the dictatorship, but they equally policed cinema for left-wing content. As Fernández Colorado puts it, awards were tainted by the recipient's political ideology 'or with considerations for the propagandist mileage that the regime expected to obtain' (p. 119). After decades of condemning these awards for their official prejudice and suspicion, little would have been achieved by historians in democratic times by invoking them as models. Yet, Fernández Colorado's words reveal that the disappearance of the *Premios del Sindicato* provoked the need for the Goyas.

Muñoz Suay, of the future Muñoz Suay award, spearheaded the denunciation of the old prizes. In 1975, as censorship was waning, practices of cultural coercion by the regime were openly contested in the media, and one such contestation resulted in a bitter exchange of accusations between Muñoz Suay and Ángel Falquina.

Falquina represented the CEC, and Muñoz Suay published a weekly column about Spanish cinema in *Nuevo Fotogramas*. The subject of this argument was the CEC awards of 1975. In his column of 14 February, the critic complained that Saura's name was absent from the winners. For this reason, members of the audience disrupted the proceedings as the awards were presented to the other recipients. Muñoz Suay explained that, years before, similar events had taken place when Bardem and Berlanga were passed over ('Lágrimas de cocodrilo', p. 6). He employs one of the key conventions of award-bashing: questioning the very purpose of the prize. If prizes won abroad do not translate into national success, he asks, what exactly are national juries celebrating?

> What has been or will be the purpose of this award? If the official and less official awards are given to others, is it not the case that the organizations are there to do just that, to deny

awards to those who deserve them? ... The issue or issues are deeper and it is not ... [the jury members] who have the last word but, in the end, it is *forces beyond cinema* [*motivaciones extracinematográficas*]. (ibid.; my emphasis)

Falquina responded two weeks later in a letter to *Nuevo Fotogramas* (p. 36). With some condescension, he remarks that Muñoz Suay inevitably shows bias for Saura's work, since they belong to the same generation, and he confirms that, exactly as Muñoz Suay surmises, international prizes do not count at all. Finally, he explains that a democratic vote cast by the members of the CEC decides the winners (ibid.).

In return, Muñoz Suay dismissed the authority of the judges, arguing that some CEC members were closely connected with the regime, and he finished by stating that a future critics' association 'fit for the European market' should be made up of those who judge cinema from purely intellectual perspectives ('Réplica', p. 7). The CEC was not the only body found wanting. By the end of the 1970s, the SNC prizes had also lost their credibility, as the collective of film critics 'Marta Hernández' explains. Its jury membership may have been opened to film professionals as well as regime bureaucrats, but old-guard civil servants, such as the censor Pascual Cebollada, were still involved, and this compromised their decisions in the eyes of younger critics. With the sarcastic and sceptical tone that characterises their writings, the collective delivered a damning denunciation of both prizes and juries, and concurred with Muñoz Suay on the need for change (Hernández, p. 158).

But regardless of the disrepute into which these awards had fallen, by the end of the 1970s, when their demise coincided with the dismantling of the apparatus of the Franco era, the context was such that film culture was too dependent on prizes to give them up. Using them as orientation and recommendation for audiences had become too engrained and naturalised in film criticism, both in popular and cinephile magazines, as even a cursory look at the letters section of best-selling magazines at the end of the dictatorship shows.

According to Fernández Colorado, prizes were needed under democracy in order to offer guidance to persuade audiences to back Spanish cinema. Members of the Academia whom I interviewed in 2013 and 2014 universally held this belief. A world without film prizes seemed unthinkable – indeed, bad – for audiences, and it is even suggested that the main reason behind creating the Academia itself was 'the desire to create a series of awards to promote Spanish films' (Fernández Colorado, p. 113). So, there was no question of doing without prizes, but two changes needed to be made. First, as was the case with other awards, the civil servants and censors who made up the juries in the old regime were replaced by juries suitable for democratic times. Second, the prizes needed a new name.

The 'new name' debate illustrates the contradictions and negotiations that the politics of consensus in the new democracy provoked. One obvious choice would have been *Premios Luis Buñuel*. Picking this name would have instantly linked the films celebrated in democracy with the last period of democratic government in Spain – a time when Spanish cinema was last connected with modernity and Europe: the Second Republic of 1931. As Ginette Vincendeau observes, the concept of influence rules film history (pp. 56–7). Following Vincendeau's logic, choosing Buñuel would be coherent with a film culture seeking legitimation by 'relat[ing] subsequent films to an earlier, golden movement' (ibid., p. 60). Not only did Spanish cinema experience a Golden Age in production and creativity between 1931 and 1936 (Gubern, 'El cine sonoro', p. 129), but the early 1930s were also a time when an avant-garde cinema movement developed through cine clubs, such as the one Buñuel directed, and in thriving publications like *La Gaceta Literaria*, where some of Spain's most prestigious writers discussed the new art (Escobar López, pp. 32–5). *Premios Luis Buñuel* would have especially commemorated *Nuestro Cinema* and its key editor, the critic Juan Piqueras, a pivotal figure of the film culture of the Republic who was captured and killed by Francoist soldiers in 1936. The auteurist generation established their credentials as cinephiles by writing for *Nuestro Cine*, a magazine's whose title was a direct homage to *Nuestro Cinema*, and they considered Piqueras a crucial precursor. However, they had to put aside this attachment when it came to making choices in democracy that would endow cinema cultures with prestige and credibility, when these choices put consensus at risk.

They did not (or could not) choose the name Buñuel – so as not to, as Fernández Colorado puts it, 'personalize the prize excessively and so that the comparison would not offend anyone' (p. 119). This seems a curious explanation, since the name chosen was equally personalised (Goya) and since it beggars belief that any Spanish director contemporary to Luis Buñuel would have had the audacity to rank himself above the veteran director or be thus classified by historians. More likely explanations are Buñuel's anti-Francoist credentials, and the awkwardness that his close association with the Communist and Socialist parties of the Second Republic created for the founders of the Academia, always in search of consensus. Add to this the fact that he famously refused the king of all film prizes, the Oscar, and the name of the Aragonese director was too loaded to be used.[11] Like the name Miguel de Cervantes, retained for the major literary prize, Goya was a much safer choice, located further back in the past and, crucially, safely embraced by the liberal left without being too much of an assault on the right's sensitivities in the 1980s.[12] In short, Goya was more fitting for the needs of a country still tentative about how much 'memory' of the losers of the Civil War could be unearthed and celebrated without incurring the wrath of the right.[13]

The composition of juries also had to be changed and now only film professionals were fit for membership. What the Goyas involved more than anything else was a change of guard. When founding Academia member Tedy Villalba said, 'we were anxious to create the prizes as soon as possible' (quoted in Sánchez Salas and Sánchez Salas, p. 67), the 'we' refers to this new guard. As a consequence of the new composition of the Academia juries, a director like Saura moved from being overlooked in national prizes to becoming an undisputed arbiter of value. He occupied a position of prestige not just as a founding member of the Academia, but also because his films, ignored by Francoist prizes, had collected more valuable critical capital through success at foreign film festivals during the 1960s and 70s. As Marvin D'Lugo argues, 'European festivals have regularly rewarded or castigated certain political positions', and Saura benefited from festival prizes he won not simply for the cinematic values of his films but for his political positions too ('Carlos Saura', p. 129). The record of success at European festivals has to be factored into the evolution that saw the auteurist directors of the 1970s and 80s move from the margins to the centre of this new hegemonic Spanish cinema for Europe.

VOYAGE TO SOMEWHERE

As I pointed out in the previous chapter about the creation of the Academia, accounts of the foundational meetings consistently choose to forget that film professionals had belonged to a professional body only a few years before: the SNE. So, when Riambau argues 'as an institution, [the Academia] came from nothing, it was not trying to replace anybody – it has always separated itself explicitly from the administration and from any political adscription – and it had Hollywood as a referent' ('Una institución', p. 45), he is being aspirational rather than expressing the actual truth. As we have seen, the rhetoric about Academia prizes is comparable, with everyone behind the institution emphasising that the awards and the Academia should not have 'any political, trade union, or corporate slant' (Fernández Colorado, p. 119), when quite clearly the less public awards were designed to redress past oversights and advance a specific sociopolitical agenda.

In the same way, the more public Goyas served to settle past accounts under democracy. Early Goyas helped restore Spain's positive image abroad and internally by belatedly celebrating unsung heroes, those film professionals long associated with the fight against the dictatorship. For example, in awarding the first Best Actor award in 1987 to the actor, director, scriptwriter and novelist Fernando Fernán Gómez for his work on *Mambrú se fue a la guerra*/*Mambrú Went to War* (Fernán Gómez, 1986), the Academia made clear its preferences.[14] More importantly, in also awarding him the first Best Film award for *El viaje a ninguna parte*/*Voyage to Nowhere* (1986) as well as the first Best Director and Best Screenplay awards, the Goyas were presenting a model of exemplary cinema for the producers and film-makers to follow, and at the same time celebrating a group that had been distrusted during the Franco era: the acting profession.

Voyage to Nowhere is the story of a travelling theatre company and the hardships its members endure while touring Spain's devastated countryside after the Civil War. The film is exemplary of the 'good' films (Miró, p. 44) encouraged by the Miró Law: it is a heritage project (a literary adaptation of Fernán Gómez's acclaimed memoirs set in the 1940s and 50s); it meticulously reconstructs the experiences of the losers under Franco from an unquestionably left-wing perspective; and it represents the stories of a group that had been silenced. In short, it was a film that would have been censored a decade earlier. Its 'goodness' was also evident in the quality of the production: its large budget went towards carefully reproduced period detail and costume design.[15]

The film encapsulates what critic Carlos Losilla called 'the pretty film, tasteful, agreeable to eyes and ears even if the topic seems unseemly' ('Legislación', p. 41), which evokes Bourdieu's definition of middlebrow art and condenses exactly what the Goyas needed to celebrate to make up for lost time.[16] By awarding the film multiple Goyas in 1987, the Academia also neatly closed a circle within post-dictatorship film cultures, explicitly endorsing the aesthetic and thematic selection criteria of the Committee for Cinema Classification and the Subcommittee for Technical Valuation. By using the recently passed Miró Law, the Committee had awarded *Voyage to Nowhere* a large amount of state funding. Faulkner (*A History*, p. 186) argues that this film was a rather indulgent project: nostalgic, derivative and overlong. This may well be the case, but the Goya agenda does not often match with the assessment of more detached critics, seeming to reward not so much the work at hand but its symbolic weight.[17]

With these first Goyas, the Academia addressed past neglects, giving recognition to Fernán Gómez, whose prolific, politically engaged, anti-establishment career had made him emblematic of the opposition to Franco (Perriam and Triana-Toribio, pp. 332–3). Although his own directorial efforts did not fit within the neorealist programme of the 1960s (Pérez Merinero and Pérez Merinero, p. 21), Fernán Gómez's acting featured prominently in prestigious work by companions of the auteurist group and in films that have become standard examples of oppositional films: in *The Spirit of the Beehive*, he played Fernando, an archetypal exiled-within, defeated, republican intellectual; and he was again Fernando, in *The Love of Captain Brando*, playing once more the republican intellectual, but this time a returning exile.

Significantly, part of Fernán Gómez's activism had been as a spokesperson for the acting profession, as the actor who represented his peers at the historic Salamanca conference in 1955. There he delivered an impassioned vindication of the acting profession, and denounced the marginalisation and vilification suffered by actors before, but particularly under, Francoism, when they were viewed with moral and political suspicion.[18] But Fernán Gómez was not just a paragon of the left-wing activist actor, and by 1987 could function as a good consensus choice. He was also well liked – or well enough liked – by more conservative audiences, who knew him as a comic actor in the popular cinema of the 1940s and 50s (D'Lugo, *Guide*, p. 224). And he was also admired for his roles in popular theatre – for instance, in one of Spain's most acclaimed works, the farce *La venganza de Don Mendo/Don Mendo's Revenge* (Pedro Muñoz Seca, 1918), a play he adapted and directed for the cinema, and in which he played the main role in 1962.[19]

Fernán Gómez wrote both the script for *Voyage to Nowhere* and the homonymous novel on which it is based, a novel which includes much autobiographical detail. The correspondence between the author and a particular ideal Spanish actor deserving belated recognition could not be clearer. What sort of actor is this? Also importantly, what sort of actor is this not? Fernán Gómez is synonymous with the *engagé* actor, exemplary of the heteronormative male actor as a professional, sober and dignified figure. As D'Lugo puts it, he achieves 'the difficult balance between light, comic roles and a number of strikingly serious, brooding characters' (*Guide*, p. 225). His acting is diametrically opposed to that of a *galán* (leading man), 'the term habitually associated in Spanish with Clark Gable' (Perriam, p. 2) and also translatable as 'matinee idol'. Fernán Gómez, although from an acting family, had worked his way up from the ranks as a *secundario* (supporting actor), thus earning his status through acting ability, and not through conventional good looks, which he did not possess.

There were also clues in those first Goyas of 1987 about the kind of acting that was *not* to be celebrated in women. The Best Actress award was given to Amparo Rivelles for her role in *Hay que deshacer la casa/The House Must Be Unmade* (José Luis García Sánchez, 1986). Rivelles, born in 1925 and so of the same generation as Fernán Gómez, had returned to Spain in 1977 after thirty years of absence 'as something of an icon of conservative drama' (Mira Nouselles, p. 263). She had enjoyed a long career that included major roles in films considered iconic in the filmography of the regime (certainly complicit with its values), but, within their complicity, showing unquestionable prestige, including literary adaptations of the 1940s such as *El clavo/The Nail* (Rafael Gil, 1944) (Faulkner, *A History*, pp. 47–54).[20] Rivelles's prestige derives from her respected acting family (her parents were María Fernanda Ladrón de Guevara and Rafael Rivelles) and from her 'elegant, sophisticated, haughty' acting style (Mira Nouselles, p. 263).

Crucially, Rivelles was another *sober* actor, untainted by connotations that marred the careers of many female actors of the Franco era: their association with either 'folkloric' musicals, with eroticism or with the horror genre. As Perriam tells us, 'a significant feature of Spanish media and leisure culture through the Franco years had always been the fixation on the female stars of stage and screen musical with "folkloric" emphases' (p. 3). In early democracy, members of the Academia were wary of red carpet glitz, frivolity and 'star gossip' conjured up by the female actors who appeared in glossy magazines such as *¡Hola!* or *Diez Minutos*, or who were too connected to popular music and television – for instance, Marujita Díaz, Carmen Sevilla or Carmen Maura (Perriam and Triana-Toribio, pp. 333–5). Nude appearances on the cover of magazines such as *Interviú* or *Nuevo Fotogramas*, or a close association with the S-film phenomenon (Kowalsky, p. 189), may not have been enough to dilute a reputation for serious acting for those who shared the liberal and non-religious values of the auteurist group, among them Rivelles's fellow nominees in 1987, Ángela Molina and Victoria Abril. However, Molina (who had worked with Buñuel) and Abril had appeared in sexualised roles and on magazine covers, and so were unlikely choices of consensus. Rivelles had been away from Spain during the boom years of the S-rated films, and with her star persona untainted, she was a very safe choice.[21] The bestowing of the Goya on Rivelles was a perfect counterpart to the many awards given to Fernán Gómez, because it rewarded the same idea of sober heteronormative acting.

As for the man of the moment in 1987, Fernán Gómez did not attend the award ceremony, and, while not entirely dismissive of it, declared himself sceptical of awards, fanfare and prestige, thus reinforcing this idea of a heteronormative sobriety that the hegemonic film culture aspired to, a matter to which I will return in the next chapter on Almodóvar. Finally, we should remember that the plot of *Voyage* fleshes out the past lives of the professional group that made up most of the membership of the Academia. In the process of singling out a 'good' film and celebrating an overlooked profession, the Academia therefore served itself, while also serving cinema.

THE BIG FILM PRIZES TELL A STORY

I have already suggested in *Spanish National Cinema* that the Goya prize is a key instrument for Spanish film cultures (p. 116). Here, I want to show how the hegemonic Academia uses the Goya prizes as an instrument to shape Spanish cinema – to 'reward and rebuke', in the words of James English (p. 39). It does so with a dual purpose. On the one hand, just as we saw above with acting, the Goyas value a specific type of professional and performance style that once elevated can be used as a model. But as well as these cinematic values, the Goyas have historically praised specific subject matters and specific genres, subject matters and genres that have changed over time.

In the prizes' early years, when relieved of market pressures by the Miró Law, Spanish independent producers and directors could make the films they thought Spain needed, ignoring audience preferences and aiming to please the commissions which decided what money was awarded to which project (see Ansola González, pp. 102–21; Hopewell, '"Art"', p. 119). Much can be learned from the type of films that received the Academia's stamp of approval in these early years in the main three categories: Best Film, Best Director and Best Screenplay. The table below outlines the main winners between 1987 and 1991.

It is impossible to separate the stylistic and political elements of the successful films. The 'pretty film, film pleasing to eyes and ears' (Losilla, 'Legislación', p. 41) invariably followed the conventions of realism and told the stories of 'the little people' in Spain's past. However, the academicians sought a consensus in their choice of stories, particularly at the start of the awards' life. The early winners represented a cross-section of society, but their main protagonists were never the victors of the Civil War or those who might have benefited from the dictatorship.

Three out of the first five Best Film winners were set in the past and offered a mix of rural working- and middle-class characters: *El bosque animado/The Animated Forest* (José Luis Cuerda, 1987), *¡Ay, Carmela!* (Saura, 1990) and *Voyage to Nowhere*. The two exceptions were *Mujeres al borde de un ataque de nervios/Women on the Verge of a Nervous Breakdown* (Pedro Almodóvar, 1988), set in a resolutely post-Francoist Madrid, and *El sueño del mono loco/Twisted Obsession* (Fernando Trueba, 1990), set in Paris. Two exceptions out of five may not sound like exceptions at all, but when *Voyage* was awarded Best Film, the choice was reinforced when, besides the big three, the film received several other Goyas. This happened again in 1988, when the Best Film for *The Animated Forest* was underlined by three other Goyas in different categories, as well as by Rafael Azcona's award for Best Adapted Screenplay. When *¡Ay, Carmela!* was chosen

	Best Film	Best Director	Best Original* Screenplay	Best Adapted Screenplay
1987	*El viaje a ninguna parte* (dir. Fernando Fernán Gómez)	Fernando Fernán Gómez for *El viaje a ninguna parte*	Fernando Fernán Gómez for *El viaje a ninguna parte*	
1988	*El bosque animado* (dir. José Luis Cuerda)	José Luis Garci for *Asignatura aprobada*	Rafael Azcona for *El bosque animado*`	
1989	*Mujeres al borde de un ataque de nervios* (dir. Pedro Almodóvar)	Gonzalo Suárez for *Remando al viento*	Pedro Almodóvar for *Mujeres al borde de un ataque de nervios*	Antonio Giménez Rico and Manuel Gutiérrez Aragón for *Jarrapellejos*
1990	*El sueño del mono loco* (dir. Fernando Trueba)	Fernando Trueba for *El sueño del mono loco*	Agustí Villaronga for *El niño de la luna*	Fernando Trueba, Manuel Matji and Menno Meyjes for *El sueño del mono loco*
1991	*¡Ay, Carmela!* (dir. Carlos Saura)	Carlos Saura for *¡Ay, Carmela!*	Montxo Armendáriz for *Cartas de Alou*	Carlos Saura and Rafael Azcona for *¡Ay, Carmela!*

* Neither *El viaje a ninguna parte* nor *El bosque animado* are original screenplays. The category of adapted screenplay was not introduced until 1989.

in 1991, the endorsement of the Academia by multiple awards went into overdrive: the film received a total of twelve Goyas, in addition to Best Film.[22]

If, during Francoism, the administration had one cinema for export and another for national consumption, new democratic Spain could not afford such luxury: the same films had to play out inclusion and democratic values internally and signify Spanish cinema's achievements externally. Francoism could accommodate external prizes going to one type of cinema destined for international festivals, while box-office success and internal prizes validated another type of cinema. In contrast, the cinema generated by the Socialist-created Spanish Film Institute and Academia had to multitask if it was to represent a democratic nation.

Ideally, a multi-Goya winner navigated more than one imperative and ticked heterogeneous boxes – that is, demonstrated appeal overseas, but also satisfied the agenda for consensus of a Socialist administration holding the purse strings. In some cases, in this desire of the Academia to win matches both at home and away, a greater emphasis was placed on reaching the external audience, with the outcome films such as *Twisted Obsession* (based on a novel by Christopher Frank and starring Jeff Goldblum and Miranda Richardson) and *Remando al viento/Rowing against the Wind* (1988) (about the life of Mary Shelley and featuring Hugh Grant and Liz Hurley). Here, the casting and non-Spanish subject matter were clear attempts to reach international audiences and so demonstrate Spain's capacity to compete with other democratic nations. Neither of the films met their internal financial targets, and must be considered halfway houses of Goya success.

The model for how to realise both agendas was a film that just predated the Goyas: Mario Camus's *Los santos inocentes/The Holy Innocents* (1984). This adaptation of a Miguel Delibes novel set in rural Spain in the 1960s plays out the class dimensions of the aftermath of the Civil War in a deeply sober and didactic fashion. *The Holy Innocents* won awards at Cannes and was also successful with critics and audiences internally. Its presence can be strongly felt in both *The Animated Forest* and *¡Ay, Carmela!*, the two early winners that come closest to the Platonic ideal of the Goya-winning film.

The Animated Forest is a quality project that imitated a trend for heritage films current in the French cinema industry, which, like Spain's, was seeking to strengthen itself by making fewer films but with larger budgets (see Hayward, p. 54). Most notable among these in the mid-1980s were Claude Berri's *Manon des sources* (1985) and *Jean de Florette* (1986), both successful adaptations of Marcel Pagnol novels inspired by his Provençal family history, which evoked a rustic rural past and met with the approval of national and international audiences (ibid., p. 285). *The Animated Forest* is based on a series of short stories by Wenceslao Fernández Flórez (1885–1964), a politically conservative writer and journalist, but also an intellectual whose conservative ideas were tempered by more enlightened views: he was critical of the army, the Church and of populist entertainment such as football and bullfights, which he thought retrograde (Obelleiro, n.p.).

The film's interconnected stories unfold in the early 1930s in the peripheral northwest region of Galicia, predominantly rural at the turn of the twentieth century and cut off from the social and political movements that were raging through Europe and Spain, including, crucially, the tensions leading up to the Civil War. The first story

The Animated Forest (1987): atemporal, timeless forest of the Spanish northwest

tells how Malvís (Alfredo Landa) decides to become the bandit Fendetestas to make a living. Unfortunately, his scheme to make money without working fails, as he cannot strike fear in his fellow villagers, who all recognise him under his useless disguises. Later stories develop the lives of other inhabitants, including those of the milkmaids and a local lad in love with a woman who leaves the village.

At the level of film style, *The Animated Forest* is very much what Losilla called a 'pretty film' in the middlebrow vein, with cinematography by Javier Aguirresarobe (who did not get a Goya on this occasion) stressing the beautiful Galician landscape and often employing fog effects in order to recreate the atmospheric conditions of the Spanish northwest, rendering the landscape atemporal and dreamlike, and shrouding the stories and characters in a fairy-tale timelessness. This is particularly evident in the night scenes, when the forest reveals its ghosts, and when the *Santa Compaña* (The Saintly Company) appears on two separate occasions as a string of lights floating in a heavy ribbon of haze among the trees.[23] The production design and costumes by Félix Murcia and Javier Artiñano carefully colour-coded the peasants (mostly dressed in earthy tones and blues, in the case of the milkmaids), and the kindly landowner Mr D'Abondo (Fernando Rey) and his family, who wear blinding white costumes throughout. Artiñano won a Goya, as did José Nieto, whose soundtrack, inspired by Galician Celtic music, added to the authenticity of the heritage style.

The aesthetic of the blurred past was already evident in *The Holy Innocents* (see Triana-Toribio, *Spanish National Cinema*, p. 124). In that canonical film, careful reproduction of period detail contributed a strong texture of pastness, while the most pressing aspect of the past – the Civil War – remained unnamed, ever present and yet inchoate. The same effect is at work in *The Animated Forest*, with the influence of *The Holy Innocents* especially evident in the casting. The Goya winner in the Best Actor category was Landa for his portrayal of the bandit Fendetestas. Landa remained a popular national star first and foremost, even after the success of *The Holy Innocents*, so his casting does not seem to signal a desire to reach an international audience. The actor in *The Animated Forest* best known outside Spain was Fernando Rey, who had appeared in Buñuel's *Viridiana, Tristana* (1970), *Belle de jour* (1967) and *The Discreet Charm of the Bourgeoisie* (1972), as well as *The French Connection* (William Friedkin, 1971). However, Rey plays a very secondary character in Mr D'Abondo.

The Animated Forest's transnational credentials are most evident in its imitation of the foreign trend for big-budget literary adaptations steeped in countryside nostalgia and period detail. Overall, this heritage strategy worked with internal audiences, achieving very respectable ticket sales of €694,019 and grossing €1,325,309. In this instance, the Goyas proved their worth by directing internal audiences to the right kind of films, whereas the next case achieved this aim and worked transnationally as well. With the Civil War theme of *¡Ay Carmela!*, international audiences got 'what is expected from Spain', to borrow D'Lugo's phrase ('Lo que se espera', p. 39), and with it a star that Almodóvar had already made international: Carmen Maura.

WHERE THE TASTES OF AUDIENCES AND ACADEMICIANS MEET

¡Ay Carmela! is without a doubt the tent-pole film of the Academia in its early years and the film that reveals best how the institution's preferences had swiftly become formulaic. It is an adaptation of a play with a highly successful run in Madrid theatres. Set towards the end of the Civil War, it features 'the little people': powerless bystanders caught in the conflict. Paulino (Andrés Pajares) and Carmela (Maura) are members of a travelling variety theatre troupe entertaining the Republican side, who, lost in the fog, end up in Francoist territory. The troupe includes Gustavete (Gabino Diego), who has a disability and is, if not a child, much younger than the main characters (a reminder, therefore, of the disabled characters in *The Holy Innocents*, and also of the proclivity of this generation to show Civil War plots through the eyes of children traumatised by the conflict). Captured by the Francoist side, they are obliged to perform for their captors in a makeshift prisoner-of-war camp, a performance which ends with Carmela's death.

The film also features idealistic members of the International Brigades, who are depicted here as heroic young men who fought for Spanish democracy even if they could not pronounce the name of the country they were fighting for. Awarding *¡Ay Carmela!* a multitude of Goyas, the Academia singles out a film that establishes a seamless link to the past work of its founding members, particularly Saura, who, as we have seen in a previous chapter, suffered at the hands of censorship for telling stories about the Civil War at a time when the point of view of those defeated could not be put across. As D'Lugo puts it, in *¡Ay Carmela!*, 'Saura underscores the need to rebel against the imposition of political conformity by reaffirming individual creativity within the performance of social life'. Saura's message, combined with

Maura's 'intensively political' performance ('Carlos Saura', p. 130), connected strongly with international audiences.

A recent enthusiastic reappraisal summarises the film's didactic achievements:

> The simplicity of the narrative style and the dialectic elements represent the past from the point of view of a re-evaluation of historical memory to speak of personal dignity, violence and, above all, a sense of solidarity with the members of the International Brigade who came from abroad to fight for the ideals of the Spanish Republic. The film allows the spectator to visualize literally the horrors of war against a background of destroyed buildings, repression and famine. (Barrenetxea Marañón and Garrido Caballero, p. 128)

As the writers further state, these elements 'were a winning recipe that made the film a Spanish blockbuster': ¡Ay Carmela! sold over 900,000 tickets, and received thirteen Goyas (ibid.). Box-office success meant that the subsidy from the ICAA and the Italian backers had been well spent by independent producer Andrés Vicente Gómez and director Saura. International awards rubber-stamped the endorsement of the Academia and ensured further critical capital for Saura and the film. For instance, Maura received the European Film Award for Best Actress in 1990. The judgment of the Academia was also confirmed externally when Andrés Pajares won the Best Actor award at the Montreal Film Festival.

The purpose of the Academia, as I indicated at the start of this chapter, is to uphold cultural standards, and at the beginning of its life as an institution, the perception was that much work needed to be done to elevate Spanish cinema to European quality. We may fault them for other later choices, but with *The Animated Forest* and *¡Ay, Carmela!*, their idea of 'good' films coincided with audiences' tastes. The Goyas supported the hegemonic model of cinema in the late 1980s and early 90s, and as audiences trusted the Academia's judgment, the Goyas achieved their aim of guiding filmgoers. Critics of protectionist legislation have argued that one of the main problems for the hegemonic film culture was that it continued, until the end of the 1990s, to pour public money into films against evidence from the box office (Ansola González, pp. 102–21). But by the end of the first decade of the Academia's existence, the Goyas were undisputedly Spain's versions of the Oscars, granting a second life in theatrical exhibition to films that had been *engoyado*.

GALAS

In spite of abundant evidence to the contrary, the rhetoric surrounding the Goyas presents them as an entirely new institution. In contrast, the Galas are truly new, since Spanish cinema had never before had an open award ceremony that was broadcast publicly. Here too, the Academia succeeded in inventing a tradition. Yet the past still weighs heavily in this protocol of the hegemonic film culture. This is partly because the Gala sought from the outset validation from another invented tradition, the Spanish monarchy imposed by the dictatorship.

The first Gala was presided over by King Juan Carlos I and Queen Sofía. Juan Carlos received the 'number 0' Goya trophy, a statuette by the Spanish sculptor

Berrocal (Granado, p. 33).[24] Berrocal was chosen over other Spanish sculptors due to his connection with the royal family, who collected his work (see Sánchez Salas and Sánchez Salas, p. 70). Such an arrangement might have been expected to generate some disquiet in a PSOE-dominated Academia, and indeed its curiosity was noted by some. As Tedy Villalba confesses: 'It was not that there were monarchists in the Academia. I don't think any of us was. I think most of us were republicans' (ibid.). But the need for validation and consensus in those early years overrode all other concerns.

A number of ghosts from the past haunted the Galas during the period of this study, particularly in its last decade (2001–11), making this ceremony a peculiarity among film award ceremonies in the amount of attention it received within Spain. Looking back over that decade in 2012, Borja Hermoso from *El País* observed,

> In all honesty, … considering what is going on in the world, even in the cultural field and its weakened industries, the largest amount of space we should be using for reporting on the Gala is half a page of the newspaper; one full page, being generous. That is what they do in Europe. All it should take is accounting for what is after all a recurring event. But inextricable psychological/journalistic mechanisms will force us (and the rest) to craft elaborate feasts of pages, broadcasts, images and bytes. ('El Goya nuestro', n.p.)

Why are the Galas such an anomaly in the context of award ceremonies in Europe? Why does this event 'force' journalists to diverge from what is the norm in other film cultures? Some of the reasons have already been outlined in the previous chapter, where I detailed the origins of the Academia and the ways that Spain's hegemonic film culture since the 1980s put cinema to the service of the political process of democratisation. This has earned the Academia critics and enemies in the right-wing PP and fierce opponents from less moderate right-wing media.

The key moment when the Gala became an affront to the PP occurred in 2003, when film professionals openly opposed the PP government's decision to take Spain into the second war in Iraq, and used that year's Gala as an anti-war platform. Prize-winners and presenters came on stage wearing stickers proclaiming 'No a la guerra', and the ceremony's hosts, Guillermo Toledo and Alberto San Juan of the activist theatre group Animalario, gave a running anti-war commentary throughout the event. This was followed by the Gala in 2004 when controversy over Julio Medem's *La pelota vasca/The Basque Ball* (2003) eclipsed the award-winning films. Nominated, but unsuccessful, in the documentary category, Medem's film gave voice to both sides in the Basque conflict, including interviews with victims and perpetrators. The film was violently criticised by both sides, and the Asociación de Víctimas de Terrorismo (Association of Victims of Terrorism) staged a protest outside the Gala site, while inside there were passionate onstage statements in favour of freedom of speech (see Stone, pp. 178–9). Then, in 2005, by which time the Socialist Party was in power, it was Alejandro Amenábar's euthanasia-themed *The Sea Inside* which stirred up anger in the Catholic Church in the lead-up to the award presentations.

In response, the right-wing press gave up entirely on reporting who won which award and focused instead on which political campaign was aired at the Gala. One eloquent example is Juanjo Alonso, writing for the extreme right-wing online newspaper *Libertad Digital*. In his survey of the Galas from 2003 to 2012, Alonso titled his columns as follows: in 2003, 'No to War'; in 2004, 'The Association of Victims of Terrorism against *La pelota vasca* by Medem'; in 2005, 'Zapatero Attends the Gala to Support Spanish Cinema'; and so on. From the right-wing perspective, the Galas were primarily a left-wing political event, and not a celebration of the best films, and the year zero was 2003 (see Alonso, n.p.).

If the reaction of the right to the Galas is an anomaly in Europe, it is not anomalous that film professionals, particularly actors, should be active in championing political, humanitarian and environmental causes. This is a transnational phenomenon, evident in Hollywood, Bollywood and other star systems, and something which stems from long-standing and '[s]trongly naturalized connections between performance and politics in theatre' (see Perriam and Triana-Toribio, pp. 336–8). It must be remembered that actors are the largest professional group of the Academia and therefore the Galas have been seen as a natural platform for campaigns that unite the acting community and other film-making professionals.

SHAPING THE TELEVISUAL SPECTACLE FROM 2005 TO 2011

In the years 2005–11, with Spain once more under a Socialist administration – led by prime minister Rodríguez Zapatero – the Galas turned to film professional concerns, and reporting about the event focused again on the merits of award winners and, more frequently, on the Galas as televisual spectacle. As a result, the Galas' work as instruments for the formation of film culture came once again to the fore in newspaper and television debates.

As James English observes, award-bashing is a common genre in reporting on such ceremonies, with the genre serving to indicate the status of the reporting journalists as insiders to an economy of prestige (see English, p. 211). Between 2005 and 2011, there was indeed a strong element of Gala-bashing in the reports of key commentators such as Diego Galán, Maruja Torres, Elsa Fernández-Santos, Inés Muñoz Martínez-Mora (from *El País*), and Hermoso (from *El Mundo* and then, from 2007, in *El País*). Among the instances of Gala-bashing, two themes predominate, themes which emerge naturally from two key principles of the hegemonic film culture that were established at the foundation of the Academia and remained current twenty-five years later.

The first principle that guides the Galas and the reporting on them is the ambivalent relationship with Hollywood. In 2009, Hermoso argued that the Galas reflect the Spanish film industry's collective delusion about the existence of an industry and star system. Since other European cinema industries are similarly structured, with small independent production companies working in tandem with large television channels, and have star systems that boast mostly internal celebrity, they can only appear deficient in comparison with Hollywood. When the Galas were described as 'more Hollywood-like' and 'No longer looking like an event held in a shopping mall', these amounted to backhanded compliments (Muñoz Martínez-Mora, n.p.). Against this background, different presidents mentioned in their address at the start of the Gala the need to defend Spanish cinema against Hollywood domination. In the 'exultant' Gala of 2010, President Álex de la Iglesia even argued bullishly that

Spanish cinema had the potential to compete with Hollywood (Elsa Fernández-Santos, 'Los Goya', n.p.). Whether the atmosphere was euphoric or mournful, Hollywood was ever present on Gala nights.

The second principle is class- and taste-based: if a Gala is geared towards popular taste and away from the core middle-class art cinema audience cultivated by the Academia, critics' knives come out finely sharpened. Perhaps the clearest illustration of this was Hermoso's article in *El País* after the 2009 Gala, entitled 'Ceremonia jurásica', in which he argued that public money should never again go towards a Gala of this type broadcast on a state-owned television network. The 'Jurassic Ceremony' had caused him to cringe with embarrassment, largely due to its *prescindible* (disposable) qualities. Hermoso considered *prescindible* Carmen Machi, a highly recognisable television actor who appeared as the Gala's MC that year. The Academia and TVE had no doubt turned to Machi after the Galas of 2007 and 2008, which had audience shares of 20.5 per cent and 18.1 per cent, losing many viewers to the Telecinco sitcom *Aída* (2005–12), which had a higher share on both nights (up to 29.5 per cent). *Aída* starred Machi, who was already a household name through the sitcom *7 vidas/7 Lives* (Telecinco, 1999–2006). For Hermoso, Machi's presence meant that the Academia had stooped too low: it had pandered to popular taste, to the televisual taste of the private channel Telecinco, no less, and thus delivered an uncouth ceremony. For him, Machi compared badly with Catalan actor Rosa María Sardá, who presented the ceremony in 1994, 1999 and 2002. Sardá, famous for a distinguished career in cinema, theatre and television and for playing Rosa in Almodóvar's *All About My Mother*, also directed the Galas of 1999 and 2002.

Among the many tensions that these ceremonies revealed were the contradictions created in Spanish film culture by the tug-of-war between an Academia intent on demonstrating its academicism and rigour through a formal ceremony, and the interests of television channels such as Telecinco, TV3 and TVE, which had been heavily financing Spanish cinema since 1999 and so demanded their needs be met through audience and television-friendly Galas featuring television stars. When Hermoso declared the ceremony obsolete and distanced himself from the popular taste that it was seeking to satisfy, what he failed to acknowledge was that the most popular and populist television channels had a large stake in the making of Spanish cinema. Perhaps it is in fact Jurassic to insist on imagining a film culture divorced from other audiovisual media, particularly television, in the manner Hermoso does. In the next chapter, we will see how understanding popular taste and satisfying it, among other qualities, put Pedro Almodóvar at the centre of a large part of Spanish film culture, even if not at the centre of the hegemonic one.

3

Being Different: Almodóvar and the Academia

It is cool to do things on your own, it is fun to be ignored and insulted by those around you. It is life affirming to 'get' and embrace matters that most others don't.

(Kugelberg, p. 46)

That Kugelberg's words appear at the start of this chapter may surprise those who think of Almodóvar as the undisputed star of Spanish cinema; the film-maker whose films must be credited with having attracted the world's eyes to the cinema of Spain and keeping them firmly there. His influence on Spain's film industry and future generations is undeniable, and yet, this influence emanates from someone who, like the punks, Kugelberg tells us, has been at odds with his peer group. I want to start this chapter with the events of one Valentine's night years ago.

14 February 2010 was a night to remember. The new president of the Academia, Álex de la Iglesia, responsible for box-office and critical successes such as *El día de la bestia/The Day of the Beast* (1995), pulled out all the stops to make sure it was. The preparations started in late 2009 to ensure that his first Gala at the helm was seen as a complete success and a clean break from the past. Previously, we saw how Borja Hermoso panned the Gala of 2009 in Spain's most prestigious newspaper, *El País*, calling it 'Jurassic' ('Ceremonia jurásica', n.p.). He complained that it had been populist, humourless, tacky, and far too dependent on the target audience's familiarity with and affection for the presenter Carmen Machi. As I mentioned in Chapter 2, Machi rose to fame playing Aída in Telecinco's high-rating and 'ground-breaking' sitcom *7 Lives* (see Smith, 'Family Plots', pp. 29–50),which, just before the end of its last season, generated the spin-off *Aída* (2005–14) set in a tower block neighbourhood on Madrid's outskirts. Aída is a working-class housewife whose malapropisms and ignorance derive from a quaint *españolada* and keep the laugh track busy. Telecinco is Spain's most popular and populist private TV channel, 'devoted to profitability and controlled by foreign interests' (Smith, 'Quality TV?', p. 17), including Berlusconi's media conglomerate Mediaset. Targeting a Telecinco audience, as the Gala of 2009 clearly did, was in Hermoso's view an error, since the Academia should be associated with prestige and quality, and attract an educated middle class. His review hinged on the fact that, for him, the Academia in 2009 had been courting viewers from the wrong age, social class and education ('Ceremonia jurásica', n.p.).

Whether or not de la Iglesia read Hermoso's broadside, every effort was made to leave behind that 'failed' Gala. But not precisely to build up a 'quality' event of the kind that Hermoso sought. De la Iglesia is committed to an idea of cinema that is not wedded to the quaint, 'low class', Spanish humour associated with *Aída* and other television series, but that is free nevertheless to draw on popular genres such as horror, sci-fi, and contemporary Spanish and Hollywood comedy. Crucially, he is a film-maker who does not see cinema as divorced from other audiovisual media.

As part of the build-up to the event, details about the new presenter for 2010 were revealed with much fanfare, both online and in a press conference held on 16 November 2009 at the Academia site in central Madrid. The revelation's style was consistent with the genres of comedy, horror and the thriller in which de la Iglesia's films are rooted. With a nod to his own *The Day of the Beast*, de la Iglesia staged the kidnap of the popular Catalan TV comic Andreu Buenafuente, the Letterman-style late-night talk show presenter of *BNF* (2007–11), at the time the tent-pole programme of LaSexta (the sixth channel). Buenafuente was hauled onto the stage to face the cameras tied to an office chair on castors. Photos of de la Iglesia grinning, and with his hands firmly on the back of the chair while a bound-and-gagged Buenafuente gesticulated mock resignation, made the front covers of many newspapers the next morning (see Povedano, n.p.). De la Iglesia's choice of presenter was seen as confirmation of the new president's confessed intentions: to renew the image of the Academia and consequently of Spanish cinema; to unite an Academia whose members were divided on many issues (to the point that some had left); and to bring the Academia, and Spanish cinema, closer to national audiences (who were staying away), particularly to the younger demographic of twenty-five to forty-four-year-olds, where de la Iglesia's core fanbase is situated (see Rocío García, 'De la Iglesia', n.p.).

Some commentators saw the choice of Catalan Buenafuente as a way of appealing to trendier, liberal and non-Castilian audiences, and as part of a wider PR campaign to renew the image of Spanish cinema that de la Iglesia had been engaged in before running for president (Payán, n.p.). As Jordan explains, de la Iglesia was already known for championing the cause of Spanish cinema in publications such as *El País*, defending the industry through letters to this newspaper against accusations of endogamy and the misuse of public funds (*subvenciones*) to provide a soap box for left-wing film-makers ('Audiences', pp. 25–9). De la Iglesia insisted that blank accusations against Spanish cinema – that it does not interest anyone – were unfair and unproductive. He fought to dispel the myth that public funding was generating too much *cine social*, or films about the Civil War (de la Iglesia, 'Carta a *El País*', n.p.).

For the Gala of 2010, one other cherished Catalan, the much acclaimed actor, presenter and director of earlier ceremonies, Rosa María Sardá, was recruited. Just as crucially, Spain's transnational stars, Penélope Cruz and Javier Bardem, were also among the theatre audience at the Palacio de Congresos (Conference Palace) where the event was staged. But a much bigger surprise was waiting in the wings. At the 2010 Gala, Pedro Almodóvar returned. He and his brother Agustín had suspended their membership of the institution in February 2005 over disagreements about the voting system and after what they considered unfair treatment of his work by the Academia (Rocío García, 'Los hermanos', n.p.). The director had been absent from the award ceremony since 2004.

For the Almodóvar brothers, the treatment of *La mala educación/Bad Education* (2004) – left out of the shortlists of finalists in most categories in 2005, and awarded no Goyas – was the last piece of evidence of a bias against his work, the signs of which can be found very early on in the life of the institution (see Agustín Alonso, n.p.). So, for example, although *Matador* (1988) was released in time to have been a candidate for the first Gala, it received only one nomination (for Antonio Banderas as Best Supporting Actor). Then began a series of apparently symptomatic slights and oversights. The academicians nominated *¡Átame!/Tie Me Up, Tie Me Down!* (1989) for fourteen categories in 1991, but, uniquely in the period of study, awarded it no Goyas. Perhaps most notoriously, in 2003, the Academia selected *Los lunes al sol/Mondays in the Sun* (Fernando León de Aranoa, 2002) as Spain's candidate for nomination in the foreign-language film category at the Oscars over Almodóvar's *Talk to Her*. With the benefit of hindsight, this was a gross miscalculation on the Academia's part, since Almodóvar was not only nominated for the Oscar for Best Director for this film in the major categories but, more importantly, won the Oscar for the Best Original Screenplay in 2004.

Almodóvar may have downplayed the importance of this award, as D'Lugo explains in his study of the director (*Pedro Almodóvar*, p. 114), but in terms of international recognition for Spanish cinema, both nomination and award were great achievements, and ones that awkwardly called attention to the Academia's conflicting priorities. *Mondays in the Sun* was a realist film addressing pressing national social concerns such as high unemployment – what critics call within Spain 'a necessary film' – that for this very reason risked performing badly when seen outside Spain's specific sociopolitical context (see Fecé and Pujol, pp. 147–65). We will address how the Academia navigates its Oscars' dilemmas in Chapter 6. In any case, Almodóvar's triumph (no thanks to the Academia) was recorded in the institution's official magazine (see Academia, 'Premiados en festivales internacionales', p. 6).

The picture is not clear-cut though, since not all Almodóvar's films have been overlooked at the Galas. The national and international critical and audience successes, *Women on the Verge of a Nervous Breakdown* (nominated in eight categories, winner in seven), *All About My Mother* (with fifteen nominations and seven wins) and *Volver* (2006) (nominated in fourteen and successful in five) were clear winners with the Academia in the third (1989), fourteenth (2000) and twenty-first (2007) Galas. Even here though, the recognition is relatively begrudging. When Almodóvar wins, he does not win big: none of the three most garlanded films – *Mar adentro* (fourteen), *¡Ay, Carmela!* (thirteen) and *Blancanieves/Snow White* (2012) (ten) – are by the director who is most acclaimed internationally and who represents Spanish cinema worldwide. Therefore, after this 'blowing hot and cold' of the Academia, his appearance at the award ceremony in 2010 could be read as a gracious gesture, particularly since it was followed by an official return to the Academia and Pedro and Agustín's renewal of their memberships in April 2011 (Rocío García, 'Los hermanos', n.p.)

Almodóvar's return, the return of Spain's most successful transnational auteur, was such momentous news that the next day's front cover of *El País* showed him, dressed in black suit and shirt, walking onto the stage to present the Best Film award. His words were also reported. He declared he was moved by the standing ovation from Academia members that greeted his arrival, and that his return had everything to do with de la Iglesia's insistence. 'You have a very, very stubborn president,' he joked. This welcome positioned him as a prodigal son of sorts. Like the biblical character, he may be a prodigal son, but he was, however, far from humbled by the reception, and his language revealed that he still saw himself as liminal to the organisation. Within his speech to the members, he let it be known that even if he was embraced by the institution, he was not back in it yet, pointedly speaking of de la Iglesia as 'your' president. He also mentioned casually that in three weeks' time he was travelling to Hollywood to present the Oscar for the Best Foreign-Language Film at the AMPAS ceremony. At this juncture, he could be forgiven for thinking that presenting the Best Film Goya (to *Celda 211/Cell 211* [Daniel Monzón, 2009]) was small beer among his transnational engagements.[1]

THE MAKING OF AN OUTSIDER

In a recent comprehensive companion to the director and his work, Josetxo Cerdán and Miguel Fernández Labayen deal excellently with the difficult topic of the reception of Almodóvar within Spain. They speak of '[t]he persistent characterization of the director as upstart and interloper on the part of both critics and relevant cultural institutions' (p. 129). The Academia, although not directly mentioned, is clearly among those institutions, and those in the know would place it first in line for this accusation. In fact, most studies of Almodóvar and his films feel the need to include sections which address, particularly for the benefit of baffled foreign readers, why Spain's most famous and exportable director is so reluctantly acclaimed by his own. Paul Julian Smith has highlighted how foreign critics take Almodóvar more seriously than his compatriots (see *Desire Unlimited*, p. 61), and Smith became proof of that with his own scholarly work. Smith's work often clarifies such issues as why Almodóvar has created a cocoon in his tightly knit production arrangements to protect himself (ibid., p. 4). My first ever talk as a PhD candidate in the UK in 1989 was entitled 'Why Do Spanish Critics Hate Pedro Almodóvar?' in response to being constantly asked this question by fellow students, and in many ways the question has not gone away.

Cerdán and Fernández Labayen address in their study the paradox that sees Spanish critics dismiss the director and his films, while at the same time being forced to 'acknowledge his talent in the face of growing recognition beyond Spain's borders' (p. 129). This contradictory response to Almodóvar has posed a challenge to the scholarly study of his films, which without fail run up against the issue of their contested cultural value (see, particularly, Smith, *Desire Unlimited*). Over a period of almost thirty years, the views of the Academia and Almodóvar sometimes overlapped. In general, though, the director and Spain's cultural institutions have held each other at arm's length, a situation that is and was inevitable, since they inhabited from the start discrete – when not antagonist – positions within Spain's film cultures, separated by understandings of what Spanish cinema should be.

As I have shown in previous chapters, the Academia pinned its colours to the conventions of realism and *cine social*, and to the genres and modes of representation that would be compatible with the cultural recuperation of the history repressed under Francoism, continuing thereby two cherished strategies of the auteurist generation in the transition. Their belief in the superiority of realism was generated partly by training together as a group in institutions like the IIEC/EOC, which also had the effect of forming a particular taste through shared habitus, a habitus that dictated privileging in their work European art cinema traditions such as neorealism. At the start of this study, we highlighted how this predilection for a cinema that communicated the idea of high art – for arthouse realism and literary adaptation – was already antiquated at the time the auteurist generation made it hegemonic. Holding on to these values by awarding state funding only to certain films and encouraging only those film-makers and producers who followed suit through awards such as the Goyas was one of the strategies for constructing the Spanish cinematic field.

For Bourdieu, the cultural field is a construction that

> takes into consideration not only works of art themselves, seen relationally within the space of available possibilities and within the historical developments of such possibilities, but also producers of works in terms of their strategies and trajectories, based on individual class or habitus, as well as their objective position within the field. (Johnson, p. 9)

The Academia, as an organisation of these 'producers of works', as well as other cultural agents, deployed the Goyas and Galas as mechanisms through which those who had made their names in the profession (the auteurist generation) in the late Francoist cinema could assert their power over the field. This is what I called in the Introduction 'academicism' – that is, an authority over film cultures. The Goyas and other modes of recognition had the desired effect of 'freezing the movement of time, fixing the present state of the field for ever', as Bourdieu describes the workings of French cultural production in the 1960s (Bourdieu, 'The Production of Belief', p. 106). Making a particular model of Spanish cinema present for ever froze in time realism and the cinema of social values and high art values, accomplishing the *espíritu O'Pazo* to the letter. As Smith explains, Almodóvar's work of the early 1980s, with its 'embrace of artificiality and caricature', 'ugly aesthetics', 'ungainly camerawork' – which thrilled and frustrated critics such as Diego Galán and Alberto Fernández Torres (cited in Smith, *Desire Unlimited*, p. 14) – could not be used for the purposes that the Academia at its inception wanted Spanish cinema to embrace. According to Smith, the rigid hegemonic models continued well into the early 2000s: 'the Spanish cinematic field remains highly distinctive, with texts, producers and institutions combining and continuing to valorize high aesthetic qualities in a way that is not characteristic of other European territories, such as the UK' ('Resurrecting the Art Movie', p. 147).

Such valorisation of quality and realism was, of course, not shared by Spanish audiences. Films that were popular with funding bodies and cultural administrators, such as the Academia and the Spanish Film Institute, were by the 1990s not at all popular with audiences (see Ansola González, pp. 102–21). The exceptional *¡Ay, Carmela!*, which we studied in Chapter 2, was successful with both international and national audiences and critics, as well as with the Academia and other institutions such as the European Film Academy. However, as well as being an exception, it marked the end of an era.

In production contexts, the game changed in the early 1990s, particularly after legislation known as the *Ley Alborch* of 1994 was brought in to produce a legal framework that responded to wider European concerns (these are the years of the modifications of the General Agreement on Tariffs and Trade) to 'diminish the importance of advance subsidies' (Yáñez, pp. 27–8), thus making film professionals more market aware (see, for example, Jara Fernández Meneses, pp. forthcoming). Between 1990 and 1997, the Goyas appeared to recognise a need to adjust and respond more to the box office. The turn to the now transnational auteur Alejandro Amenábar in the late 1990s seemed a clear sign of a change at work, demonstrating a greater will to compromise between the cherished literary-political high aesthetic qualities and the genre conventions that worked with audiences. Market-aware films such as Amenábar's *Tesis/Thesis* (1996) and the Civil War drama by an Academia veteran, Trueba, *La niña de tus ojos/The Girl of Your Dreams* (1999) saw their success translated into Goyas (Best Film in the eleventh and thirteenth Galas respectively).

Almodóvar's films packed film theatres in the 1990s: the maternal melodrama and thriller *Tacones lejanos/High Heels* (1991), a co-production with France's Ciby 2000, reached well over 2 million spectators (2,072,921). The subsequent co-productions with Ciby 2000, *Kika* (1993), *La flor de mi secreto/The Flower of My Secret* (1995) and *Carne trémula/Live Flesh* (1997), were seen by 1,037,808, by 981,750 and 1,433,397 spectators respectively in a decade when exceeding the target of a million spectators was an outstanding box office (see Ministerio de Educacíon, Cultura y Deporte, n.p.). Still, these are the years in which Almodóvar's films were in the wilderness, if not with audiences, at least with the Academia. The institution's misgivings about Almodóvar survived right through the mid-1990s, when his films adopted more orthodox forms of representation, displayed technical virtuosity and engaged successfully with realism, during what Smith has termed his 'blue' period of classical austerity ('Preface', p. x).

In 1992, *High Heels* received four nominations but no Goyas, and in 1996, the melodrama *The Flower of My Secret*, five nominations and no Goyas. Next, the thriller *Live Flesh* was acclaimed abroad for its 'direct engagement with the characters, coherent integration of the plot, and a sense of psychological, social and historical depth' (Smith, 'Absolute Precision', p. 9). This was a film in which, as Smith argues, Almodóvar 'managed to integrate the concerns of an earlier, more sober Spanish cinema characteristic of directors such as Carlos Saura' (ibid.). Smith remarked that the film was 'once more passed over by Almodóvar's peers in nominations' for the Goyas (ibid.), winning just one Goya for Best Supporting Actor for José Sancho.

The 2000s opened with a moment of confluence for Almodóvar and his peers at the Academia, with seven Goyas going to *All About My Mother* and five to *Volver* in 2007. But as we will see in Chapter 5, the Academia and Spain's hegemonic film culture were preoccupied in the period of study about not departing too much, or for too long, from high aesthetic qualities and the values of realism designed for 'transforming audiences rather than satisfying them' (Álvarez Monzoncillo and Menor Sendra, p. 26). The unexpected and uncharacteristic success of the avant-garde film *La soledad/Solitary Fragments* in 2008, which will be examined in more detail in Chapter 5, can only possibly be understood as a correction to the praise and prizes (including Best Director and Best Film) heaped on *Volver*, a popular melodrama, the year before. The director who splintered from the hegemonic idea of realism and high art values but who, in *Volver*, made a clear homage to neorealist cinema seemed to be reconciling himself with the traditions of realism. Many critics must have hoped for a second *¿Qué he hecho yo para merecer esto?/What Have I Done to Deserve This!!?* (1984), his only film to be lauded by Spain's hegemonic critics. Almodóvar declared that he cast Cruz as a modern-day Anna Magnani, citing Magnani's performance in Luchino Visconti's melodrama *Bellissima* (1951) as inspiration (see Smith 'Women, Windmills', p. 16). The aspects he borrowed from neorealism, however, take Spanish cinema far from the ideal of sober realism of its *cine social* auteurs to the acting styles and costumes of Giuseppe de Santis's dramatic *Riso amaro/Bitter Rice* (1949) and Visconti's *Bellissima*, tales of working-class women torn between duty and desire. The gaudy *mise en scène* in *Volver* also contributes disparity. The very sober and experimental *Solitary Fragments* is the obverse of melodramatic, and thus seems to restore the balance.

WHAT KIND OF OUTSIDER IS ALMODÓVAR?

In order to understand what kind of outsider – how different Almodóvar is from the men and women who populated the Academia in the period of this study – we have to return to the beginning of his career. Almodóvar had been the voice of dissent against the chorus in favour of European realism and against genre in the 1980s, and continued his success nationally and abroad during the following decades. What once had been a dissenting positioning that marked him as divergent from the Academia founders became, during the 1990s and early 2000s, the strategy that many film-makers had to imitate to survive: make concessions to genre, make films for the box office, often displeasing state-founding commissions and the Academia heterodox. Let us look into the strategy Almodóvar developed over the years, because it is a combination of factors.

a) An outsider who makes virtue out of necessity and finds his own way

> I've always worried that I don't have sufficient knowledge to do these things I'm doing. That's why everything I've done is highly imaginative, although a little amateurish, because I didn't have the means and the know-how. I was always clear about the fact that a boy such as myself, from a humble family, etc. etc. etc., was not going to wait for a wonderful and marvellous opportunity where everything was going to be handed to him; I was going to have to steal that chance and make it mine. (Almodóvar to Montero, 'Pedro Almodóvar', p. 24)

In early interviews with Rosa Montero for *El País Semanal* and for *Fotogramas* critics Maruja Torres (1982) and Nuria Vidal (1988), much was made of the fact that Almodóvar's way into film-making did not follow the traditional pattern from training to apprenticeship to direction that was the norm for film-makers such as Camus, Érice, Martín Patino, Miró, Molina and Saura who trained at the IIEC/EOC. In the first study on Almodóvar by María Antonia García de León and Teresa Maldonado (a sociologist and a journalist respectively, *not* film critics or film scholars, and women), the director's origins and access to the industry are central to the contextualisation and interpretation of both his work and his authorial persona. If this fact was remarked upon so often (by detractors and by fans), it was principally because film-making in Spain in the 1980s was a closed environment, almost exclusively male, and resolutely middle and upper class.

Budding directors had gained direct entry to careers in film-making after training in the same craft (often via television, as was the case with women directors such as Molina and Miró, or, for other EOC women like Cecilia Bartolomé, never managing to secure a foothold in the industry), or after a stint as critics, as in Érice's case. As García de León and Maldonado state, in 1987, in a country without general access to university education, future film-makers and film critics attended university, and even 9 per cent had studied film-making abroad, particularly in the IDHEC (Institut des Hautes Études Cinématographiques) in Paris (*Pedro Almodóvar*, p. 64).

Among Almodóvar's contemporaries, Fernando Colomo was an EOC alumnus (Losilla, 'Fernando Colomo', p. 242), and Fernando Trueba went from a degree in film studies at the Facultad de Ciencias de la Información (School of Journalism) in the Universidad Complutense de Madrid in 1972, to film criticism in *El País* (1974–9) and the magazine *Casablanca*, to film-making (Ortiz Villeta, p. 868). Iván Zulueta, whose father was director of the San Sebastian International Film Festival, attended the EOC (Joaquim Romaguera i Ramió, p. 925).

In 1986, those who had, in Almodóvar's words, 'the knowledge to do these things', who had the training and opportunity to access film-making networks that he lacked, were in the process of creating the Academia; and Montero stresses in her interview that what defines the director from La Mancha is precisely his detachment from those networks: 'Almodóvar wasn't part of that coterie' ('Pedro Almodóvar', p. 24).

Hand in hand with not belonging to the auteurist generation by class and education came a rejection of its values. This rejection was first voiced when Almodóvar was a self-taught underground director in the 1980s, with a day job as a civil servant at the then state-owned Spanish telephone company Telefónica. He argued that a production that sidelined genre cinema, privileged realism as a mode of representation and held a heteronormative worldview had had its day. As García de León and Maldonado state, Almodóvar adopted the role of the attacker and the polemicist as an early authorial persona (p. 59).

In a second early interview I want to draw attention to, it is significant that Almodóvar emphasises how a lack of training was not simply important in that it set him apart, but also because it freed him from the obligation to use the Spanish canon as guidance and to adhere by a school of film-making rules. In this interview for the respected specialist film journal *Contracampo*, the interviewers Juan Ignacio Francia and Julio Pérez Perucha could not be more different from Almodóvar. Francia, perhaps closer, was starting his career as journalist, and was part of one key youth culture phenomenon in the 1980s, the influential radio station Radio 3. Pérez Perucha was destined to assume – and at the antipodes of Almodóvar – one of the most hegemonic roles in Spanish cinema as film historian and critic and president of the Spanish Association of Film Historians (already discussed in the previous chapter). He was also the editor of the canonical tome *Antología crítica del cine español 1906–1995*.

In 1981, as young-ish critics for *Contracampo*, they captured Almodóvar in this polemical controversialist mode that García de León and Maldonado indicated. The budding director stated that the only valuable recent films in the 1980s had been the soft-porn movies made during the period of relaxation of censorship at the end of the 70s:

I think that the most important movies in the last five years of Spanish cinema are those of Agatha Lys, María José Cantudo and Barbara Rey [stars of S-rated films] ... All of that is more interesting than what the serious boys are doing ...: [Emilio] Martínez Lázaro, [Fernando] Trueba etc. (Francia and Pérez Perucha, 'First Film', p. 4)

The interviewers put some distance between themselves and Almodóvar when they argue that, unlike those up-and-coming directors of the 1980s, he does not create 'characters with whom it is easy to identify, such as educated professionals' (ibid., p. 7).[2] Their subsequent questions are about 'carelessness', about lack of knowledge. In response, Almodóvar declared himself not willing to be discouraged by difficulties. *Pepi, Luci, Bom y otras chicas del montón/Pepi, Luci, Bom and Other Girls on the Heap* (1979–80) may be poorly shot, but it is not a film where cinematography matters, he said. Not having a formal training, he reasoned, meant not having to follow the priorities of those who were EOC-trained and part of the hegemonic Spanish cinema (ibid.).

In 1982, Almodóvar declared in a very candid interview to the short-lived Barcelona *Magazine Moda 1* that those 'serious boys' who knew what they were doing – making films alongside him, and who were thirty and forty years old in the early 1980s, such as Trueba and Fernando Colomo – made a *cine costumbrista* (films of local colour). 'It's an antiquated cinema, not interesting in the least' (Rivas, p. 61).[3] He illustrated his opinion by arguing that *Ópera prima/First Work* (1980) by Trueba, for instance, focuses on a main character who is an archetype of Madrid men of the age of the directors. They are *progres* (short for progressives) – that is, men with a past history of (timid) activism against Franco, with lukewarm left-wing ideals, who are now university-educated professionals. These middle-aged *progres* are unable to fit in the democratic world inhabited by a younger, more modern generation that was not attached to former political ideals because they had only experienced the dictatorship as children. This age division is in fact palpable in *First Work*, where the female cousin of the title is the representative of this generation. A younger woman (played by Paula Molina), she is a distant relative for whom the protagonist (Óscar Ladoire) yearns.

Almodóvar emphasised the difference of his own first work, which precluded the identifications that these realist comedies were overtly dependent on. In *Pepi, Luci, Bom* and *Laberinto de pasiones/Labyrinth of Passions* (1982), Almodóvar explains that he constructed characters who were the obverse of those of his contemporaries, and with whom identification was not the point. Figures such as Pepi (Carmen Maura) – an heiress whose intention to sell her virginity to the highest bidder is thwarted by a rapist policeman (Félix Rotaeta) – were deliberately outrageous and non-naturalistic (Rivas, p. 62). He also explains that his own stylistic loyalties were not to European New Cinemas but to American mainstream and New York experimentation. Almodóvar linked his recitals of phonetic poetry with Herminio Molero in venues in Madrid with his interest in the underground cinema of Andy Warhol and the avant-garde work of Jonas Mekas (ibid., p. 61). 'To tell you the truth,' he confessed to Rivas, 'the generation of ten years ago is more interesting than my contemporaries' (ibid., p. 62). Smith argues 'that the much remarked "freshness" of *Pepi, Luci, Bom* resulted not only from its chronicling of a new sociological model "beyond the camera" but also from its articulation, however unwitting, of new forms of representation' (*Desire Unlimited*, p. 14). With declarations and work such as these, it is perhaps no surprise that Almodóvar was not invited to lunch by Matas four years later at O'Pazo. While Martínez Lázaro, Trueba and Colomo were recognised as the new generation and soon were incorporated into the workings of the Academia (Trueba became president in 1988, albeit for a brief period, after the first incumbent, José María González-Sinde), the Almodóvars never contributed to the organisation's inner workings, even though their membership started in 1987.

As well as dwelling on Almodóvar's lack of higher education, cinematic or otherwise, these interviews and studies focus on his rural working-class origins in La Mancha (see, for instance, the start of Francia and Pérez Perucha's cited interview of 1981; García de León and Maldonado, pp. 29–35; Nuria Vidal, pp. 87–92). Being born in the poor countryside, rather than in an urban environment, will be turned into an asset, much in the same way as lack of training. But since these are not the normal environments for a film-maker, I want to turn to the strategy Almodóvar employed to find access into film-making, and to the capacity of permanence in the face of hostility.

b) An outsider with his own look and way into the industry

Much has been made of the influence of the punk movement in Almodóvar's early career (see, for example, Triana-Toribio, 'A Punk Called Pedro', pp. 274–82). If it can be argued that, from 1977, lack of training was no longer the stumbling block it once had been in pursuing a career in the arts and Almodóvar took advantage of this, the truth is that he was also in the right place at the right time. Emerging out of the dictatorship, Madrid in the late 1970s was a hub of creativity and had the world's attention (see Vernon and Morris, 'Introduction', pp. 5–8). Both factors explain his access to and success in film-making. Johan Kugelberg defines the legacy of punk as 'the immediate implementation of DIY grassroots culture among the young' (p. 46). In the late 1970s and early 80s, Spanish would-be creators, inspired by punk philosophy, dispensed with musical training and formed punk and pop bands such as La Banda Trapera del Río, Ramoncín, Kaka de Luxe, Paraíso, Parálisis Permanente and Derribos Arias. Almodóvar did the same in film-making and often collaborated with these freshly minted musicians. Countercultural publications such as the Barcelona magazine *Star*, fascinated by the punk movement, commissioned Almodóvar to write 'a lewd and somewhat parodic story of the punk movement, sometime around 1977' (Francia and Pérez Perucha, p. 4). This story, which became the script for *Pepi, Luci, Bom*, further cemented Almodóvar's association with punk. Soon the charges of incompetence that reviewers meant as an insult, intended to make him desist, were embraced by Almodóvar as a badge of honour much in the way punk musicians did.

It has often been noted that Almodóvar's position as an outsider obliged him not only to adopt DIY methods, but to find indirect ways into film-making (see, for instance, Smith, *Desire Unlimited*, pp. 18–20; Vernon and Morris, 'Introduction', pp. 1–18). It should be pointed out here that outsiders also included those women who graduated from the EOC such as Miró and Molina (the latter the first woman to graduate in the field of direction), who were likewise forced to find indirect routes, regardless of their pedigree or training. Even if Miró eventually became central to the hegemonic cinema and created the Spanish Film Institute, formulating the key financing strategies of her fellow classmates and teaching at the EOC, she carved out a career in film-making, 'making them forgive me for being a woman', as she once declared (García de León, p. 168).

Almodovar's indirect ways led him into a 'celebrity author' version of auteurship, as Marvin D'Lugo argues, in which he was seen as 'a multitalented entrepreneur of a new cultural paradigm: writer, performer, film-maker, actor, and authenticator of a counter-cultural style' (*Pedro Almodóvar*, p. 7). He became a 'celebrity author' through exposure in several media. Visibility also involved his ubiquitous presence at the *terrazas* and parties of the *Movida*, which started as an underground cultural movement but was soon commodified by the media, as Vernon and Morris have pointed out ('Introduction', pp. 8–11). Rivas declared in 1982:

> Now he is a celebrity [*un personaje de moda*]; [his presence] obligatory in any party or gathering worth its salt, courted by producers, chased by hacks, accosted by aspiring actresses, idol of the punk, New Wave, or Romantic (new or old, or whatever) youth ... (p. 60)

He performed in the music venue Rock-Ola in Madrid, alongside drag queen Fabio McNamara (Fabio de Miguel), with whom he formed a glam rock duo, and released an EP and the album *¡Cómo está el servicio ... de señoras!/Goodness Me, the State of the Ladies Toilets!* (1982). The title, revealingly a pun on a popular comedy of pre-democracy, *¡Cómo está el servicio!* (Mariano Ozores, 1968), makes the most of the fact that *servicio* in Spanish means both 'toilets' and 'domestic help'. With this title, the director clearly signalled his thematic and generic allegiances, but he also indicated that there were cinematic references at the core of all his extra-cinematic activities.

García de León alluded to the notorious and multitudinous spectacle-premieres of his early work such as that of *Labyrinth* and *Entre tinieblas/Dark Habits* (1983), which provoked the kind of extreme reactions that Spanish cinema had not seen since the late Francoist first screenings of Saura's *Cousin Angelica. Dark Habits* was premiered with a bomb threat hanging over the theatre, and two Madrid cinemas refused to show *Labyrinth*, fearing a riot (García de León and Maldonado, p. 61). By 1983, the gains of Almodóvar's celebrity strategy were already evident; he was invited by music and talk show presenter Paloma Chamorro to make a trailer (*Trailer para amantes de lo prohibido/Trailer for Lovers of the Forbidden*) for the cult programme *La edad de oro/The Golden Age* (TVE, 1983–5).[4] Within the trailer, he promoted his next film, *What Have I Done to Deserve This!!?*

The image of Almodóvar as the 'king of parties' gave way, over the years, to that of a very recognisable persona central to the publicity campaigns for his films. The celebrity label has stuck, but Smith argues that it is important to see beyond that cliché ('Women, Windmills', p. 18). With the success of these 'celebrity author' tactics, Almodóvar demonstrated that one of the weakest points of the hegemonic Spanish cinema was its approach to promotion and marketing. But while high visibility and identification with his or her films during the launch campaign is something to be expected of film-makers aware of the commercial value of auteurism (see Corrigan, pp. 101–36), actively seeking this visibility also distanced him further from the auteur image cultivated by the auteurist generation and the Academia. The type of media-friendly images of himself, and of his films, that were circulating – particularly in the late 1980s and early 90s – were not the 'correct' ones, because Almodóvar's early visibility was predicated on frivolous, flamboyant and female-identified images. Think of him singing onstage in a housecoat and heavy make-up, or wearing a bright yellow jacket for his appearance on *La edad de oro* in the 1980s.

Images such as these clash with the heteronormative image of the sober and *engagé* Spanish cinema auteur. Consider, for instance, Carlos Saura with his characteristic dark-rimmed glasses in the 1960s, which became gold-rimmed as he grew older, and his image of bohemian scruffiness composed of well-worn tweed jackets, sloppy jumpers and earth-tone scarves. As Pujol Ozonas argues, the cinephile imaginary is male and heterosexual (p. 40), and this includes what they exude through their attire. García de León comments that, in 1989, critics were agitated over whether Almodóvar was gaining weight, observing that this 'does not feature in the data that is aired about other directors' (p. 70). Far from being incidental, the way auteurs look in Spanish film culture is a rich semiotic and political field. De la Iglesia used to be strongly associated with his *gafas de pasta* (thick-rimmed glasses), his penchant for T-shirts and other forms of scruffiness (see his defence of the T-shirt in 'Vindicación de la camiseta', p. 45). The changes that occurred in his wardrobe when he became director of the Academia in December 2009 were remarked upon, alongside his weight loss. He took part in, among others, a photo reportage for *Vanity Fair [España]* in February 2011 wearing designer black jackets and white tuxedo shirts (see Virginia Galán, p. 106). De la Iglesia's departure from the obligatory shabbiness that film directors are associated with in Spanish film culture is so unsettling for some that their reaction was to disavow it. Actor and fellow director Santiago Segura wrote a short comic piece in *El País Semanal* entitled 'Álex de la Iglesia: A Genius Wearing Underpants', which commented mostly on the new image as a pose. Symptomatically, Segura claimed to still be able to glimpse, through these sartorial changes, the real de la Iglesia:

> [N]ow he is the president of the Academy of the Cinema Arts and Sciences (or something along those lines), he makes public appearances in tuxedos and makes judicious and conciliatory speeches. ... But he doesn't fool me. I've known him for twenty years. ... For a while he lived in Carabanchel and I saw him in his underwear. Álex de la Iglesia is a genius in underpants. ('Un genio', p. 45)

The image that defined Almodóvar in the late 1980s and early 90s was not simply frivolous but coded queer. In reference to the image used in the reportage in *El País Semanal* for the release of *Kika*, in which Almodóvar is 'peeking out from between scarlet curtains, a green spotted bow in his black curly hair' (Smith, *Vision Machines*, p. 37), Smith argues that the director and his work are put to different uses by different cultures. So, 'the adoption by a man of this flamboyant femininity serves as an index of homosexuality, defined here not as desire for the same sex, but as identification with the other', enabling a recognition by queer audiences everywhere (ibid.). This image, which serves as a way of indicating his modernity and exportability to some, of signalling a director in tune with a diverse society, who 'places himself on the feminine side of the gender difference' (Smith, 'Preface', p. x), is precisely what provokes questions about his value as a director in Spain, as well as in certain conservative sectors of the foreign press. This is because, as Smith has observed, for critics such as Carlos Boyero (*El Mundo* and *El País*) and Alexander Walker (*Evening Standard*), those who place themselves on that feminine side are inherently inferior (ibid.)

c) An entertainer before an educator who, when he 'educates', gives a 'bad education'

Almodóvar's persona, different class and education were not the sole elements that militated against him in the eyes of the hegemonic film culture. The generation that created the Academia favoured not simply a particular kind of cinema but, as I repeated at the start of this chapter, one that could be used directly for political purposes: as an instrument for democratic education. Any film-maker not singing from that hymn sheet risked being an outsider (see García de León and Maldonado, pp. 64–9; Smith, *Desire Unlimited*, p. 2). Spanish cinema at the end of Francoism was tasked with this educational role not exclusively by internal commentators, as we have seen previously, but also by art cinema publications abroad. Roger Mortimore, writing for *Sight & Sound* in 1974, argued that 'Spanish cinema can do nothing more worthwhile than help the Spanish people to face the past honestly, to conquer their fear of shibboleths' (p. 202). He goes on to defend this didactic and healing mission envisaged for Spanish films, arguing that all efforts should be put towards achieving 'the eradication of the lies that sustained the dictatorship [that] would take decades to dispel' (ibid.).

In the midst of opinions such as these, and a clear favouring of the role of didacticism in Spanish cinema, Almodóvar was declaring the superiority of hedonism and frivolity and of making films as if Franco had never existed, thus inviting charges of apoliticism, irresponsibility and cultural amnesia (see Smith, *Desire Unlimited*, p. 2; Vernon and Morris, 'Introduction', pp. 2–8). Critics may have been misreading his intent, but these were serious charges in a country which had endured a *pacto de silencio* (pact of silence) as the price to pay for democracy.

Almodóvar's refusal to follow suit, to eschew the sobriety of realism for the saturated colours of Classic Hollywood Technicolor comedies and melodramas, with their crowded frames and fast-talking dialogues, when what the hegemonic film culture expected Spanish film-makers to do was to communicate political messages, meant that he could not fit in. The Spanish Film Institute with its funding and the Academia with its prizes were pursuing the creation of a recognisable, identifiable national style within European patterns, and that is another reason why Almodóvar, who was not abiding by their rules, was denied both state funding and prizes. He told Nuria Vidal that *Matador*, his fifth feature film, was the first to receive money from the Spanish Film Institute (p. 30). He was aware that 'although they didn't like my films very much' (ibid., p. 148), once they realised with the success of *What Have I Done*, particularly in the US, that his cinema was exportable, they had to fund him. He tells Vidal, however, that *La ley del deseo/Law of Desire* (1987) was denied state money by the evaluation committees of the Spanish Film Institute and that producers would not touch it: 'A story about a homosexual film-maker, who cares about that?' It was only the intervention of Fernando Méndez-Leite (head of the Spanish Film Institute in 1984) that helped it to be made (ibid., pp. 193–4).

Here is another difficulty that the cultural agents and critics have with his work. It is not simply that Almodóvar chooses queer images for his self-publicity and visibility as an auteur. He has also adopted a 'mainstreaming of the queer', which, as Smith observed in 2003, with regards to *All About My Mother*, is a step too far for critics such as Boyero (see Smith, 'Resurrecting the Art Movie', p. 158). If we read symptomatically into the verdicts of the Academia about his work, we could not be blamed for thinking that the organisation is homophobic. In fact, if we consider that *Law of Desire* is the film that the Academia neglected the most by not shortlisting it in any categories in 1988, thus excluding the director from the Gala, and that *Bad Education* missed the shortlist in most categories and was denied any Goya prizes in 2005, we would be more than justified in thinking that the regulative powers of the Academia discourage any serious engagement with homosexual culture.

And yet, even if he did not adopt their stylistic strategies at the start of his career, and they rejected him outright, it is undeniable that Almodóvar learned much from the auteurist generation, particularly from their incarnation as *NCE*. He learned from film-makers such as Saura and Érice that a director who manages to make a name for himself abroad, at least with selected audiences, and to capture the attention of certain festivals and foreign awards (in his case, Cannes above all) had to be tolerated by the nation. He could endure both censorship and censure if he kept in mind the fate of *Cousin Angelica* at the hands of the Francoist regime and about how the national film awards spurned Saura, and yet he emerged triumphant in democracy.

However, a distinctive feature of Almodóvar's strategy is that he also took lessons at the beginning of his career from the Old Spanish Cinema we addressed in Chapter 1 – from Lazaga, Ozores and Masó – to the point that he was (both correctly and incorrectly) suspected of being their inheritor (see García de León and Maldonado, pp. 242, 248), decades before Santiago Segura established an undeniable link with them (as we will see in the next chapter). From them, he learned that without an engagement with comedy, melodrama, repetition, lowbrow culture and popular culture icons, and importantly with televisual culture, films would not enjoy mainstream success within Spain. From the start of his career, this place that Almodóvar was creating outside the hegemonic film culture was intended to be a space for film-makers who have 'breached the barrier between art and commerce' (Smith, 'Pedro Almodóvar', p. 131), learning lessons from both camps.

Almodóvar's durability in such a hostile environment can be attributed to two factors. The first is the Almodóvar brothers' production company El Deseo S.A., which has protected him against the ostracism of the funding bodies and censorious critics (see Smith, *Desire Unlimited*, pp. 4–5). Lack of support led to independence in funding. 'Almodóvar was the only one who established himself independently from state funding and the only director who understands the commercial priorities of cinema', affirmed Emilio C. García Fernández (*El cine español*, p. 114) when El Deseo was starting out. At the time of writing, it continues to be a very viable, if medium-sized, production company, for his own films and for those of other directors (see Díaz López, pp. 107–28; Triana-Toribio, 'Telecinco Cinema', pp. 424–6). Secondly, he has had more than a little help from academics and critics outside Spain in producing the favourable critical support that the Academia has not provided and that has ensured the critical success of his films in art cinema circuits in the US and Europe. Much to the annoyance of Academia-approved Spanish film scholars, who want to be the gatekeepers of canonicity, Almodóvar made himself indispensable to the Anglo-Saxon academic environment, as Paul Julian Smith explains:

> For academics in the US (and to a lesser extent in the UK) Almodóvar was a dream director, equally exploitable in courses of gender, ethnic, or lesbian and gay studies. Hispanists found a topic which, finally, was attractive for scholars and students in other areas; generalists could flatter themselves that they were taking an interest in a 'minority' area, which proved to be more pleasurable than most. Most importantly ... in his love of fantasy and cross-gender identification, Almodóvar coincides with recent psychoanalytically inspired feminist film theorists. (*Desire Unlimited*, p. 2)

The canonisation that Brad Epps and Despina Kakoudaki define as 'the work of a number of assiduous scholars (and it bears mentioning, fans)' (p. 2) has kept him relatively safe from the brickbats. During the period of this study, his films had received four Césars from the Académie des Arts et Techniques du Cinéma (including an honorary one), two awards at Cannes (script and director) and an award to the full cast of female actors in *Volver*, one David de Donatello, four Baftas from the British Academy of Film and Television Arts, two Golden Globes and two Oscars.

In what might seem an unlikely comparison, but which is in fact a very comparable case, it cannot have been a coincidence that Jess Franco was awarded a lifetime achievement Goya in 2009, only after external recognition: the French Cinémathèque canonised him with a *Hommage-Restrospective* on the director's work in June/July 2008.[5] In the case of Almodóvar, the outside's perception of Spanish cinema has forced the inside to redefine its priorities. Even before Paul Julian Smith, D'Lugo, Epps, Peter W. Evans, Kathleen M. Vernon and others with their work on Almodóvar brought him external validation, MoMA delivered a painful blow to the hegemonic film cultures in 1984. Two years before the Academia was created, the famous museum selected *What Have I Done* over *The Holy Innocents* for its Spanish Film Week. This unambiguous indication that Almodóvar's film was the better choice to show the outside world the changes that had occurred in a modern Spain could not be missed by the hegemonic film cultures (see D'Lugo, *Pedro Almodóvar*, p. 44). In fact, this event is what Almodóvar was alluding to when he confessed to Vidal that although they (the Spanish Film Institute and the Academia) did not like his films very much, they had to continue supporting him, since his cinema was exportable when that of the members of the Academia had fallen flat.

The Spanish media has made much of the real and imaginary quarrels between Almodóvar (representing Spanish cinema to the outside) and the Academia (as the representative of Spanish cinema internally). Part of the insistence of journalists on dwelling on his disagreements with the institution has to do with the fact that both Almodóvar and the Academia are highly media friendly, and their disputes all the more so. A telling interview was published in 1995, when Almodóvar was chosen by *La Revista de El Mundo* to represent Spanish cinema in a special issue dedicated to the Centenary of Cinema. Journalist Elena Pita commented, 'it may seem paradoxical to you that we have selected you to represent Spanish cinema, since you have always played at being the "[enfant] terrible", the outsider' [in English in the original] (p. 36).

Almodóvar responded that it did not surprise him and that he did not set out to be an outsider. Later on in the same interview, Pita suggests that, since the Academia selected *The Flower of My Secret* to be submitted to AMPAS for the foreign-film Oscar, this perhaps meant an end of the hostilities between the Academy and the director: 'So, that little battle you had with the Academia and with the Spanish directors, those envious men, is over now, right?' (ibid.). Almodóvar replied that it was not the case. His relationship with the Academia was still tense and 'among my circle of friends I don't count a single film director' (ibid.) In short, the entire interview insists on setting up a scenario in which Almodóvar is on one side, with the Academia and the rest of Spanish cinema on the other. It is the journalist who establishes the scenario, but the director is also willing to play along with it.

The scenario set up by journalists, and played along with by Almodóvar, conceals as much as it reveals, even if it contains a kernel of truth. Almodóvar was indeed different, and the Academia has employed the means at its disposal to discourage him, or, at the very least, to contain him. But they have failed, and this failure is exemplary to others. Almodóvar is not unique in having had a troubled relationship with the Academia. Future president, Álex de la Iglesia, whose career was kick-started by El Deseo, also had his share of difficulties, as we will see in the Chapter 4. Meanwhile, de la Iglesia's early collaborator, Santiago Segura (also examined in the next chapter), inhabits a place outside the Academia, and was led to it following in Almodóvar and de la Iglesia's footsteps. Almodóvar's shadow looms large over Segura and de la Iglesia's generation, because he is not simply a film-maker outside the tent established by the Academia, he is *the* film-maker who created the space outside the tent. He demonstrated with his independent approach the benefits of being an outcast. Almodóvar shares much with Segura, whose work shows clear signs of Almodóvar's influence, not least the use of commercial popular culture and a penchant for scatological and bad taste comedy in the *Torrente* saga. Guided by the pioneering punk Pedro, others have also chosen liminality from the institutions that rule Spanish cinema, and a new generation of auteurs has learned to inhabit the outside successfully.

4

Rogue Males, 'Bad' Films and 'Bad' Loyalties: Santiago Segura and Álex de la Iglesia

There are similarities between Almodóvar's relationship with the Academia, discussed in the previous chapter, and that of the younger directors I concentrate on in this one, as well as that of those even younger, who will be addressed in Chapter 5. Just as with Almodóvar, the Academia has in turn demonstrated approval and disapproval by the giving or withholding of Goya awards. Equally, the presence of Santiago Segura (b. 1965) and Álex de la Iglesia (b. 1965) at the Galas makes trade papers and even national press headlines, because, like Almodóvar, Segura and de la Iglesia are recognised for more than their work: they are household names in Spain, often part of public debate.

The reputations of Segura and de la Iglesia have not been built transnationally to the same extent as Almodóvar's. Although they have enjoyed box-office success in Spanish-speaking territories such as Argentina and Mexico, their popularity relies firmly on national audiences. And yet, even if they are best known for making box-office hits, they are not strictly speaking domestic film-makers. Their transnational financing strategies often rely on co-production, in the case of de la Iglesia, and follow Hollywood models, in the case of Segura. Predictably, they were treated during the period of study in a similar way to Almodóvar: the Academia kept these directors and their films at bay for not conforming, but, equally, kept them close due to their media friendliness and credibility with mainstream audiences. The difference is that both Segura and de la Iglesia were very visible rogue academicians, but academicians nonetheless. They have not left the institution in protest – although, as we will see in the second case study, de la Iglesia did resign from his post as president.

In the Introduction, I argued that those film cultures in competition with the hegemonic Spanish cinema have articulated their identity in disagreements with the Academia. Here I will show what this looks like in practice. The aim of this chapter is to examine the effectiveness of these popular film-makers, their beliefs and their films in challenging the particular film culture that the Academia built through three factors: its academicism, its 'academy effect' and the Goyas. This challenge reveals the existence of emerging film cultures from which another type of cinema feeds: the genres of horror, melodrama, the musical and the comedy, including romantic and teen comedies – films that are shown mostly in multiplexes to young audiences. These popular genres, some of which are drawn on heavily by Segura and de la Iglesia, are more closely connected with platforms such as television and the internet, about which the Academia has misgivings. To explore some of these connections, I will in this chapter focus closely on one film, Segura's *Torrente 4: Lethal Crisis* (2011), and on de la Iglesia's role as president of the Academia from 2009 to 2011.

THE TURN TO GENRE

The hegemonic film culture and the Academia's pursuit of the middlebrow realist European model only reigned uncontested for a few years after the institution's foundation, from 1986 to 1993. During this time, with the awarding of the Goyas, the Academia worked hard to give visibility to 'good' auteur films, promoting them not simply as part of the national cinema, but *the* national cinema. It was hoped that expurgating embarrassing genre films of the past (the 'bad' Old Spanish Cinema of the late 1970s particularly, discussed in Chapter 1) and offering national audiences the auteur quality of *¡Ay, Carmela!* or *The Animated Forest* would change national mainstream filmgoing habits. Perhaps predictably, it did not. The success of the Academia's ideal film, in which socially relevant or political topics like the Civil War were leavened with mainstream formulae, such as comedy and the musical (as in *¡Ay, Carmela!*), proved elusive. By the end of the 1980s, the modest box-office returns of 'good' national films, upon which funding and often Goyas had been heaped, made it clear that these had not found an audience inside Spain, however many plaudits they received outside the country (Ansola González, p. 121).

Yet those at the helm of the Spanish Film Institute in the late 1980s (such as Fernando Méndez-Leite) stubbornly insisted that what mattered was the higher quality of the Spanish films being made (Losilla, 'Legislación', p. 33), and the hegemonic view remained in favour of these policies, even in the face of audiences' rejection of these 'better films', and the evidence of film theatres closing down. Then, in 1988, during the Socialist Party's second term in office, Jorge Semprún, as the new minister of culture, brought in legislation to force Spanish producers and directors to listen more to the markets. Within the Academia, the response to Semprún's more market-led policies, with their intention of attracting more private financing, was to demand the return of the levels of protection that cinema had enjoyed in the past. Academia president Antonio Giménez-Rico, while admitting that the previous favourable fiscal context had not genuinely bolstered the industry, argued that 'at least films were made' (see Granado, p. 57).

But change was on the way that would make it difficult to maintain the view held by Giménez-Rico and other producers that what mattered was to keep making quality films financed by the state. The 1990s brought transnational trends that effected deep changes in Spanish cinema production. As Tim Bergfelder observes, many European film-makers 'moved increasingly towards popular genres and narratives previously considered the domain of Hollywood' (p. 318). He cites examples from French and German cinema, but without a doubt, Spanish cinema, by then seriously starved of state funds, was part of this phenomenon as well. This decade ushered in 'a central epochal shift in Spanish cinema' (Beck and Rodríguez Ortega, p. 3) with market-aware strategies and the return of what had been expurgated from Spanish cinema: genre. '[P]opular audiences favoured such changes and new directors set forth to reinvigorate genres such as comedy, horror, melodrama and the musical for both national and international markets' (p. 4). This turn to genre owes much to the national and international success of Almodóvar, whose own embrace of comedy and melodrama, alongside lowbrow popular culture, subculture and European and Hollywood influences, showed the way to other directors. Spanish critics such as Manuel Hidalgo in the weekend film section of the daily *El Mundo*, 'Cinelandia', celebrated these changes, as well as the challenge the new economic conditions issued to the hegemonic film culture and how they were impelling and energising a younger generation. In his article of 15 May 1993, he lauded a new group of 'directors, actors, technicians, designers, scriptwriters, musicians, producers, critics, all of them film-makers, that seem to be springing up everywhere' and who revelled in working in these new more market-aware contexts (p. 1). Beatrice Sartori provided a detailed alphabetical list of new names (pp. 3–5), among them the producer Santiago Tabernero (1961–). Tabernero declared himself ready to challenge the realist, political model subsidised by the Spanish Film Institute and cherished by the Academia, and to listen instead to the box office, regretting that 'Spanish cinema recently has been far more interested in pleasing the ministerial commissions [for state funding] than audiences' (cited in Sartori, p. 4).

Not surprisingly, the two directors I focus on in this chapter were at the top of this list of new talent. These children of the 1960s, both born in 1965, launched their careers in the early to mid-1990s. So too did the actors, scriptwriters, artistic directors and music directors who became their regular collaborators: José Luis Arrizabalaga (1963–), Karra Elejalde (1960–), Jorge Guerricaechevarría (1965–), Mariano Lozano (1961–). The centrality of de la Iglesia and Segura to this new breed is clear from the main heading of Hidalgo's article, which is in fact a manifesto of the 1990s generation, and alludes directly to de la Iglesia's first feature, *Mutant Action* (a film produced by Almodóvar and where Segura made his debut as an actor). The article is titled 'Mutant Action in Spanish Cinema: The New Spanish Film-makers Are Here'.

The Academia adjusted somewhat to these changed national and international contexts by acknowledging the work of the 1990s generation as promising talent. In 1990, the Goya's fifth year, the category of Best New Director was introduced. It was an opportunity for the Academia not only to welcome a new generation, but also to acknowledge the rise to prominence of women in the film industry. Three of the six shortlisted newcomers were women: Ana Díez (1957–) – the winner with *Ander eta Yul/Ander and Yul* (1988) – Cristina Andreu (1958–) and Isabel Coixet (1960–).

Segura received his first Goya in 1994 – Best Fictional Short Film for *Perturbado* (1993) – thus designating him as a 'new kid on the block' from whom much could be expected. In 1995, he was back at the Gala to present the award for Best Animation Short. He won an acting award for *The Day of the Beast*, and in 1999, he won Best New Director for *Torrente, el brazo tonto de la ley/Torrente, the Stupid Arm of the Law* (1998). That was his last prize until 2011. De la Iglesia, Chus Gutiérrez (1962–) and Julio Medem (1958–) were shortlisted in 1993, but de la Iglesia missed out on the Best New Director prize with *Mutant Action*. The award went to another promising newcomer whose cinema was more clearly aligned with middlebrow auteur cinema models that the Academia favours. Julio Medem's direction of *Vacas/Cows* (1992) gave clear indication that he was well equipped to produce accessible yet auteurist films, something he did with later successes such as *La ardilla roja/The Red Squirrel* (1993) and *Los amantes del círculo polar/The Lovers of the Arctic Circle* (1998). As I have observed elsewhere, critics such as Carlos F. Heredero pinned their hopes on Medem at the time, and declared him the only film-maker of his generation who could lay claim to the title of auteur (see Triana-Toribio, *Spanish National Cinema*, p. 149).

De la Iglesia's best year at the Goyas was 1996, when he won Best Director for *The Day of the Beast*. Since then, his films made the shortlists for prizes throughout the late 1990s and early 2000s, and frequently were awarded for special effects, art design and sound, while missing out on the big prizes (Best Film, Best Director, Best Screenplay), an all too familiar scenario for Almodóvar, as we saw in the previous chapter (see Buse, Triana-Toribio and Willis, pp. 120–2, 137).

Segura was invited back to present prizes throughout the early 2000s, when his own films were not even in the running. And, as Carlos Boyero suggests in his review of the 2014 Gala (n.p.), for the Academia, the ceremony remained an opportunity to keep de la Iglesia in his place. Unlike Icíar Bollaín (1967–), Coixet, Fernando León de Aranoa (1968–), Medem and other directors of the same generation more assimilated into the hegemonic film culture and, thus, winners of the big three prizes, de la Iglesia and Segura have stayed more or less resolutely within the genres of comedy and comedy/horror, which are associated with lowbrow taste rather than middlebrow respectability, and have proven beyond the pale for the hegemonic culture.

WHEN THE WINNER DOES NOT TAKE IT ALL

In previous chapters, I traced the steps that the Academia, bolstered by the Goyas, took to encourage the model of cinema that I have been discussing as hegemonic. In short, reward the 'good' with Goyas and punish the 'bad' with no awards. I want to address what these rogue directors, their films and interventions in the Academia may reveal about the relationship between the auteurist models of European cinema, espoused by the Academia from 1993 to 2011, and the emergent genre film culture of the mid-1990s represented by de la Iglesia and Segura that has inspired more box-office-attuned strategies. Ventures such as the transnational productions of Spain's Filmax (see Lázaro-Reboll, *Spanish Horror Films*, pp. 222–5) owe much to these trailblazers.

The auteurist and hegemonic models that I have broadly outlined so far are built, as it were, on the 'four articles of faith' that are presented below in summary form as context for the two case studies that follow:

1. Form: There is a superior class of cinema that provides the 'good' films, and this is 'European art cinema'. European art cinema means realist cinema (however reductive this view may be). There is an inferior class of cinema: genre cinema, particularly those genre films that seem to imitate Hollywood cinema too closely, be they comedies, horror films, melodramas or thrillers. More expensive films that translate investment into high production values are an aspiration. Following these European patterns, Spanish films should be able to cross borders and be successful internationally, at least in festivals if not in wider distribution channels.
2. Content: There are superior contents – themes and subject matter that film-makers should be dealing with, and these change over time only slightly: screening

the past so that Spain can learn to live together again; representing the repressed realities of the past (1980s and early 90s); addressing the social problems of the present (2000s).

3. Finances: There is also a superior type of financing, and that is the state subsidy. Since cinema is a cultural good that should be protected from the demands of the market, the state should pay for 'good' films and act as the leader in film production (this was the case during the mid-1980s and 90s). As the state becomes less willing or able to pay for film production – partly because the hegemonic films do not work at the box office, and partly because the content of films is not appealing to the party in government (when the party is not the Socialist Party) – the private sector, from 1999, has to be embraced in the form of the television channels, at the producers' behest. Gradually, it is accepted that this shift in financing will bring necessary sacrifices regarding the first two articles of faith, but the Academia could ensure, via its awards, that the divergence from them is not too great.

4. Theatrical and DVD releases are the key platforms, and there is a distrust of other media platforms, particularly the internet. This is due to the very real threat that piracy poses, although this threat affects Hollywood films much more than Spanish cinema: 'In the global context, by 2008, 20 per cent of all digital downloads for the top-grossing films worldwide originated from Spain' (Brannon Donoghue, p. 23). Domestic films are expected to recoup their investment during theatrical runs, and this mindset had not changed much by 2011. A key concern of the Academia's founders was the difference between the 'televisual' and the properly cinematic. This is a prejudice that has a long history, and, as we saw in Chapter 1, is one of the reasons why television companies were not invited to join the group that set up the Academia. If film-makers are interested in true cinema, in 'cine/cine', as Meritxell Esquirol and Josep Lluís Fecé put it (p. 31), they should stay well clear of the televisual.

CASE ONE – NOT FIT FOR EXPORT AND NOT FIT FOR GOYAS: SEGURA'S *LETHAL CRISIS* (2011)

Lethal Crisis is the fourth in the *Torrente* saga. This profitable franchise of films has been addressed by Spanish film studies as something new: films that assume a position among a series of entertainments on offer and follow as closely as possible Hollywood blockbuster strategies (see Esquirol and Fecé, pp. 27–39). Each film stars Segura as José Luis Torrente, a corrupt and bungling ex-policeman turned private detective from Madrid, whose principal attributes are extreme right-wing views, racism, sexism and homophobia. He is also characterised by his attire ('tacky Sonny Crockett clothing', as Lázaro-Reboll ['*Torrente*', p. 219] puts it), his corpulence, his vulgarity and poor hygiene (see Triana-Toribio, 'Santiago Segura', p. 153). Finally, he is famous for his working-class/popular allegiances to football team Atlético de Madrid and *copla* (popular Andalusian song) singer El Fary. In short, he is the comedic obverse of iconic, refined, high-society and sexually potent detectives or secret agents such as Ian Fleming's James Bond, as played by Daniel Craig.

Lethal Crisis finds an impoverished Torrente doing odd security jobs as the economic crisis grips Spain. Desperate for work, he accepts an offer as a hired assassin. His accomplice in this is Julito Rinrín (played by the celebrity son of a bullfighter and a *copla* singer, Kiko Rivera). He befriends Julito in a brothel, surrounded by voluptuous sex workers in lingerie. When Torrente attempts to kill his target, he discovers that the victim is already dead. Framed for this murder, Torrente ends up in prison. There, inspired by the Hollywood film *Escape to Victory* aka *Victory* (John Huston, 1981), he organises a football match between inmates and guards, hoping that it will provide a distraction to enable his escape through a tunnel that fellow prisoner Antoñito (TV singer/comedian Cañita Brava) has spent years carving out with a spoon. Torrente's girth collapses the tunnel, suffocating Antoñito, Peralta (played by Yon González of the successful TV series *El internado/Boarding School* [Antena 3, 2007–10]) and Torrente's long-lost uncle Gregorio (veteran 1960s and 70s actor Tony Leblanc). Once out of prison, Torrente blackmails those who framed him, but in the process of getting his revenge is captured and put back behind bars. The derivative plot serves as a loose frame on which to hang humorous sketches in which Torrente displays his incompetence and his bigotry when faced with a multicultural, pluralistic, democratic contemporary Spain.

Torrente 4: Lethal Crisis (title in English in original) is without doubt a 'bad' film that had no chance of Goya success, and yet, its release was Spain's main cinema event of 2011. The purpose of *Lethal Crisis* was clearly not to win Goyas, and it was not shortlisted in any categories, as Segura reminded the Gala audience. Equally, it did not circulate abroad via festivals, and is not amenable to political readings that speak across cultural and national boundaries, and therefore by certain measures is not a transnational product. And yet by a different set of indicators, it was Spain's most transnational film of its year: one of Warner Bros. most successful local-language productions (LLPs) in Spain (Brannon Donoghue, p. 8). According to Brannon Donoghue, LLPs represent 'an industry-wide experiment in systematic localization across the global film market', part of the transformations that Hollywood studios are undergoing due to the '[l]arger processes of globalization, conglomeration and convergence which are increasingly reshaping studios' operations outside the Anglophone market in different ways' (ibid., p. 4).

Lethal Crisis was Spain's first feature film shot entirely in HD 3D. It had a €10 million budget ('Technicolor', p. 18), and on its first day, 11 March 2011, opened with €2.5 million, breaking the previous record in Spain set by the second instalment of the Twilight Saga, *New Moon* (Chris Weitz, 2009), which had made €2.2 million on opening. On its first weekend, *Lethal Crisis* broke records as well: it was seen by over 1 million spectators and made €8.3 million (Marín Bellón, n.p.). It went on to make almost €20 million on theatrical distribution in Spain.[1]

Lethal Crisis's huge success is far from the norm for a Spanish release in its home territory. Spanish films in the decade 2000–10 had rarely been successful with national audiences. In fact, *Lethal Crisis* set new box-office records only weeks after the national press reported disappointing box-office data for Spanish films released in 2010.[2] In February 2011, several articles lamented that Spanish filmgoers continued to spurn the national cinema in favour of Hollywood films, and that Spanish films had an ever-diminishing market share at a time when other European national cinemas were connecting better with their 'natural' audiences (see Marín Bellón, n.p.).

In addition to being shot in HD 3D, the film was also, at great expense, premiered on multiple screens on a fixed release date, simulating as much as possible Hollywood's film release strategy. These costly conditions would be normal for US 'tent-pole' films, which aim to recoup their large investment through revenue in various territories, but *Lethal Crisis*, although a Warner Bros. LLP, could not aspire to several sources of income. As Segura declared: 'I don't have a world market, either I make the €10 million back in Spain or I'm dead' (Crespo, p. 87). The film had no pan-European distribution and, according to IMDb, it has been shown only in Hungary and in Paris, as part of the Absurde Séance film festival.[3] Warner Bros. assumed from the outset that it was not going to be bankable in many territories. As Brannon Donoghue explains, since LLPs are not expected to do well transnationally, 'there is even more pressure to recoup costs during domestic theatrical runs' (p. 8).

Lethal Crisis can tell us much about the gatekeeping strategies of the hegemonic film culture that the Academia put in place with its academicism and its prizes. My contention is that within its diegesis and by its success, *Lethal Crisis* confirms how the particular kind of state intervention in the national cinema that was encouraged with state subsidies and Goya prizes, and that intended to create a Spanish cinema fit both for transnational consumption (particularly European) and national audiences, had not succeeded with the national mainstream. Having traced the history of intervention in Chapters 1 and 2, I will return to some of its key details here in order to explain how the Academia's loss is Segura's gain.

In Chapter 2, by providing concrete examples, I gave substance to the claim that the Academia uses its instruments to set examples of 'good' cinema. This drive to create 'good' films depends, of course, on an understanding of what constitutes a 'bad' film. Therefore, we need to locate the badness that made the auteurist group despair about the Spanish cinema that came before the establishment of the Spanish Film Institute and the Academia. In Chapter 1, I referred to two men, Lazaga and Masó, who did not attend the lunch that marked the creation of the Academia. This producer/director team made comedies and melodramas that, for the leftist and auteurist cinephile critics and film professionals of the 1960s and 70s, were the quintessence of all that was embarrassing and reprehensible about Spanish cinema.

In order to read the success of *Torrente*, we need to see beyond the doxa that Lazaga and Masó (and others) crafted 'objectionable' films. They were particularly successful in creating a popular formula at the time known as *sex-comedies celtibéricas* (Guarner, p. 24). *No desearás al vecino del quinto/Thou Shall Not Covet the Fifth Floor Neighbour* (Ramón Fernández, 1970) is perhaps the most illustrative of these popular films. Co-produced with Italy, as was often the case, *Thou Shall Not Covet* capitalised on the desires for sexualised images of a deeply repressed nation with an inferiority complex about lagging behind its more liberated European partners. As I have argued elsewhere, in films such as these, sex was implied, but censorship rules were adhered to from the outset, ensuring that the sexual act was never actually represented. These films did not fight against censorship; they embraced it[4] (Triana-Toribio, *Spanish National Cinema*, p. 98).

For those who believed that cinema was a cultural good and a vehicle for change in Spain, these films were anathema. Lazaga and Maso's comedies and melodramas were vehicles for the status quo and demanded no change, and no modernisation – rather, quite the opposite. The same critical voices that chastised Lazaga/Masó praised Saura,

Martín Patino, Miró and Duran for their films. Rosa Montero, a cinephile film critic and contemporary of the auteurist generation, declares in an interview with Lazaga in 1975 (mentioned in Chapter 1) that his films are truly awful, and criticises him (albeit gently) for the way that *sex-comedies celtibéricas* are full of 'all the Hispanic topics of the repressed male and the stereotypical woman with big thighs and exciting cleavage' ('Una manera', p. 9). They may have been retrograde, but these films were hugely popular with a large sector of Spanish cinemagoers during late Francoism. In fact, they were made at a time when Spain had one of the most prolific and successful film industries: between 120 and 150 films were made each year, and the share of the national market by local films was around 20 per cent, a very high percentage (see Álvarez Monzoncillo and Menor Sendra, pp. 24–5).

The winning formula of local comedies rested on that happy acceptance of the status quo, but they were also popular because they drew on a home-grown star system familiar through television and variety theatre, and because they addressed everyday issues that were crucial to their audiences, as well as the male/female relationships that gave them the 'sexy' label. These everyday concerns included: the housing shortages; the transition from an agrarian to an urban economy, and the need to migrate from the countryside to the cities or even abroad (principally to Germany); the more open-minded morality of tourists in the face of a Catholic environment; the inadequacy felt by the recently-rural-now-urban dwellers among the established city-wise middle classes; and the generational gap. All these themes were addressed in the diegesis of *sex-comedies celtibéricas* in a light-hearted manner, ensuring that tradition was upheld and that the dictatorship was not criticised for producing these conditions.

Their plots addressed a society that was becoming more affluent and educated, but where there were pockets of resistance to change, and deep insecurities. For instance, they often use the fact that Spain was increasingly in contact with the rest of Europe as a motivation for conflict and comedy: for example, in *El turismo es un gran invento/What a Great Invention Is Tourism* (Pedro Lazaga, 1968) and in the contemporary *Celos, amor, y Mercado Común/Jealousy, Love and the Common Market* (Alfonso Paso, 1973). Comedies such as these negotiated changes through characters who were experiencing difficulties adapting to modernisation and Europeanisation. In *Jealousy, Love*, for example, modernity and embracing European customs means adultery for protagonist Felipe (played by Leblanc). Films such as *Los económicamente débiles/The Economically Weak* (Lazaga, 1960), also starring Leblanc, *El cálido verano del señor Rodríguez/Mr Rodríguez's Hot Summer* (Lazaga, 1963), with López Vázquez (who a few years later played the main character in Saura's *Cousin Angelica*, the film that provoked the ire of the right-wing paramilitary Warriors of Christ the King, as we saw in Chapter 1) and *Jealousy, Love* drew much of their inspiration from Italian comedies of the 1960s and 70s.[5] These films are not the only ones that confirm how this popular comic tradition was far from divorced from European influence. The sources, however, were not principally in art cinema or the New Cinemas movement, but in European genre cinema – French and Italian particularly.

There was another genre that made the auteurist generation, destined to become hegemonic, even more uncomfortable. In the early 1970s, a brief loophole in censorship allowed for the proliferation of soft-core pornography in the *películas S* (S-rated films), which were widely available although not recommended family viewing. Auteurists bemoaned that much of film production in the late Franco regime had degenerated into such embarrassing films. As we saw in Chapter 1, soon the Socialist Party policies produced milestone triumphs in external recognition and started to erase that image of frivolousness and over-sexualisation: the AMPAS award for Best Foreign-Language Film in 1983 went to the very sober *Volver a empezar/ Starting Over* (José Luis Garci, 1982), and *The Holy Innocents* received awards at Cannes. As Teresa Vilarós explains, each success abroad (of the right kind of film)

> was greeted in Spain [...], not simply with satisfaction but also with a feeling of having cancelled a pending debt, of an account with *an embarrassing past* being settled, something which placed us, at last, in the right position to have access and the opportunity to compete in an international arena. (p. 241; my emphasis)

Segura's *Torrente, the Stupid Arm of the Law*, the first instalment in the *Torrente* franchise, is key to the epochal shift to genre that critics speak of. Segura's strategy from the start was to distance his franchise from the earlier Goya-winning 'good' films, which is ironic given that the film won Segura the Best New Director Goya. *The Stupid Arm* was released with the publicity tagline 'just when you thought that Spanish cinema was getting better'. This was a direct taunt to the hegemonic cinema model, and the *Torrente* franchise has subsequently continued to position itself as the antithesis of the Goya-winning films. *Lethal Crisis* declared itself 'the crowning work of bad-taste cinema' in its publicity campaign in early 2011. The same phrase appeared on the DVD cover in the place where other Home Entertainment releases would have displayed Goya wins.

Why do these films so blatantly reject the Goya-receiving, state-sponsored cinema? The main reason is that the *Torrente* franchise has been very careful to signal from the outset that in genre, themes and casting, it aims to bring back memories of those embarrassing earlier comedies. So the sexy Spanish comedies and the *películas S* appear in the form of male chauvinistic representation of women, who appear either scantily clad or matron-like and asexual. Another important reminder of these racy comedies of the 1970s is the casting of plenty of TV celebrities and actors. The principal actor linking the two periods is Leblanc, who starred in many of those 1960s and 70s films as well as in numerous popular programmes of Francoist television. Segura himself started out in Spanish television, and the use of and allusion to this medium in his films is key to understanding the success of the *Torrente* franchise.[6]

As seen on TV

The presence in *Lethal Crisis* of actors known for their work on the different Spanish TV channels is constant, but at its most intense in the scenes set inside the prison. In these episodes and throughout the film, the celebrities and/or television actors, if they are not already known for comic turns, are constructed as figures of fun, deflating their public personas and rendering them ridiculous through *mise en scène* and characterisation. For instance, Yon González, teenage idol of *Boarding School*, who appears as prison inmate Peralta, is dressed in a fishnet vest and lurid blue elasticated tracksuit bottoms, and has a stutter. The colour of the tracksuit bottoms alludes humorously to the actor's most famous role as Iván Noiret, whose boarding school uniform includes a blue jumper. We could argue that this reference to a teen series indicates the film's target audience, but the casting of other actors such as Leblanc or the stand-up comic Cañita Brava, who are likely to elicit recognition from older if not all age groups, complicates this first reading. Leblanc's presence in *Lethal Crisis* is key. As Quintana puts it, in Leblanc, Segura finds a putative father for his cinema ('El cine como realidad', p. 19). The casting of Leblanc is crucial in suturing the *Torrente* franchise to the pre-democracy cinema, but this actor was also inextricably linked to iconic televisual moments in Spain. In his obituary of Leblanc in November 2012, *El País* film critic Gregorio Belinchón reminded readers that justice could not be done to his career and star persona without including his television appearances ('Muere el actor', n.p.).[7]

The scene of the football match between inmates and guards is particularly rich in examples of the thick-and-fast assault of celebrities in incongruous cameo roles. Football, which is a very important part of Spain's televisual experience, has always been central to the construction of the Torrente character and audiences are already familiar with his support of Atlético. It therefore comes as no surprise that the team of inmates he puts together for the match against the prison guards wears a makeshift kit in which the characteristic Atlético red stripes seem to be painted on. The opposing team – managed by the prison governor (TV actor David Muro) and introduced by him as 'his cousins' – is introduced in a low-angle shot that emphasises their height and shows off their pristine authentic uniforms. The supposed 'cousins', smirking menacingly, are the internationally renowned Real Madrid players Sergio Ramos, Gonzalo Higuaín and Álvaro Arbeloa, as well as the FC Barcelona player Cesc Fábregas. Enjoyment comes principally from two sources. On the one hand, the intertextuality, which is reinforced by the soundtrack as the background music evokes the music from *Escape to Victory* and, as in Huston's film, real footballers play some of the characters. On the other, the exaggerated inequality of the teams and the incongruous positions of the celebrities produce the comedic moments.

The principal jokes in the football scenes rely for their effect on bad taste and challenges to political correctness. The inmates' goalkeeper is El Langui, aka Juan Manuel Montilla, a well-known DJ and rapper, and member of the hip-hop group La Excepción/The Exception. El Langui is affected by cerebral palsy. His disability means that his movements are limited and his posture prevents him from being an effective keeper. The national audience would be familiar with El Langui's public persona as a performer, composer and actor who engages with his disability (in a similar manner to the British stand-up comic and actor Francesca Martinez), and whose songs and acting roles address what it means to live with the condition and confront people's prejudices about CP. The casting of El Langui as the butt of a comic scene could arguably distance the audience, and may go a long way to explaining why this film is not fit for export, as the lack of European distribution seems to confirm. However, his presence has to be viewed in the context of the film's dialogue with the Spanish cinematic past and can in fact be interpreted as direct allusion to the celebrated comedy *Los tramposos/The Cheaters* (Pedro Lazaga, 1959), in which Leblanc pretends to be disabled in order to con people out of their money. This interpretation is substantiated by the fact that *Lethal*

Crisis is not the first film in the franchise to play on Leblanc's performance of disability for economic gain and the cinematic past in which it originated: *Torrente, the Stupid Arm of the Law* introduces Leblanc as Torrente's father and a wheelchair user.

Arguably, El Langui's casting leads us to something else that re-emerges with *Lethal Crisis* and the *Torrente* franchise in general. The return of repressed 'bad' films and the pre-European past goes beyond casting choices and strays into the territory of the politically incorrect and even the politically dangerous. Torrente proudly displays right-wing attitudes that hark back to pre-transition Spain and challenge multiculturalism. The butts of his jokes are traditionally disempowered groups such as people with disabilities, women, migrant workers and homosexuals, who are mocked in the franchise in a manner very reminiscent of their portrayal in the *sex-comedies celtibéricas* in pre-modern Spain. For instance, the homophobic *Thou Shall Not Covet* titillates its audience with hints of homosexuality, but ultimately negates its existence in Spain. The modern and fully integrated European Spain of the 2000s formally and officially rejected such views, and their unapologetic return in *Torrente* confounded many critics. Is this irony? Or is this film displaying blatant nostalgia for Francoism? In their moral panic, critics forgot to look at how Torrente himself is represented as a comic figure for these backward views, but, more importantly, they forgot that the *Torrente* franchise provided something that the films of the 1960s and 70s brought forward: retrograde though they were, these films engaged with the realities and preoccupations of the time. *Jealousy, Love and the Common Market* did indeed address the fact that a Spain opening up to Europe would be faced with moral and economic challenges; by the same token, the underlying worry in *Thou Shall Not Covet* is that Spain is both modern and traditional, and this affects individual lifestyles but also familial structures and communities.

Nostalgia for the past or engagement with the present?

Amidst this resurgence of genre cinema and the huge success of the *Torrente* franchise, auteurist critics persistently declared the superiority of the European art cinema model, particularly because of its potential for an engagement with reality. In Spain, the belief is widespread that European cinema is synonymous with a cinema that addresses social reality, while Hollywood and genre films provide escapism and entertainment. This assumption does not stop with Hollywood. All genre cinema, to an extent, is suspect.

The presumption holds strong that to engage with social themes is what matters most in Spanish cinema. In the early 2000s, those presiding over the ICAA and the Academia still showed a marked preference for films whose subject matter, style and intention emulated the neorealist and art cinema legacy – in other words, models of art cinema emanating from Europe. In 2001, Best Film *El Bola* and Best Director José Luis Borau for *Leo* (2000) had as backdrops child abuse and homelessness respectively (see Triana-Toribio, *Spanish National Cinema*, pp. 155–8). The winners of the principal Goyas (both Best Film and Best Director) in 2003, 2004 and 2005 confirmed the trend: *Mondays in the Sun* deals with unemployment in post-industrial northern Spain; *Take My Eyes* with the subject of gendered violence; and *The Sea Inside* with the much debated right to die.

	Best Film	Best Director	Best New Director	Best Original Screenplay	Best Adapted Screenplay
2001	El Bola (dir. Achero Mañas)	José Luis Borau for Leo	Achero Mañas for El Bola	Achero Mañas and Verónica Sánchez for El Bola	Fernando Fernán Gómez for Lazarillo de Tormes
2002	Los otros/The Others (dir. Alejandro Amenábar)	Alejandro Amenábar for Los otros	Juan Carlos Fresnadillo for Intacto	Alejandro Amenábar for Los otros	Jorge Juan Martinez et al. for Salvajes
2003	Los lunes al sol (dir. Fernando León de Aranoa)	Fernando León de Aranoa for Los lunes al sol	Julio Wallovits and Roger Gual for Smoking Room	Enrique Brasó and Antonio Hernández for En la ciudad sin límites	Adolfo Aristarain and Kathy Saavedra for Lugares comunes
2004	Te doy mis ojos (dir. Icíar Bollaín)	Icíar Bollaín for Te doy mis ojos	Ángeles González-Sinde for La suerte dormida	Icíar Bollaín and Alicia Luna for Te doy mis ojos	Isabel Coixet for Mi vida sin mi
2005	Mar adentro/ The Sea Inside (dir. Alejandro Amenábar)	Alejandro Amenábar for Mar adentro/ The Sea Inside	Pablo Malo for Frío sol de invierno	Alejandro Amenábar and Mateo Gil for Mar adentro/ The Sea Inside	José Rivera for Diarios de motocicleta

Goya winners from 2001 to 2005 (chart compiled from the AACC)

Spanish genre cinema, particularly the thriller, has been mindful of engaging with particular issues that make headlines worldwide and which translate well abroad: the purpose of the prison service, fundamentalist groups, terrorism. And certain genre films made with high production values and destined for the mainstream national market have indeed been distinguished with awards. Two outstanding examples are recent films that address a social ill or a contemporary political/social issue: the prison movie *Cell 211*, with its underlying questioning of the prison system, and the thriller *No habrá paz para los malvados/No Rest for the Wicked* (Enrique Urbizu, 2011), which is based on the 11M bombings in Madrid in 2004.[8] These two films won the Goya award for Best Film in 2010 and 2012 respectively.

The *Torrente* franchise, in contrast, makes no claims to belong to the traditions so valued by the Academia and the Goyas. However, to accuse the franchise of not engaging with reality simply would not hold. The entire franchise, and more precisely *Lethal Crisis*, far from neglecting Spain's present, addresses it explicitly. The title of the film is the first clue to this direct acknowledgment of current reality. The film may eschew a sober engagement with the reasons and consequences of the economic crisis, much in the same way as the comedies of the 1960s and 70s did not delve into the fraught and uneasy relationship between Spain's Catholic morality and the challenges that the opening up to modernity and Europe were creating for the characters in the films mentioned above. But like the plots in those films, *Lethal Crisis* negotiates through humour the effects of the economic difficulties and touches, albeit in a vague manner, on the very foundation of the collective financial difficulties by representing a Spain in which corrupt elites wield power and possess wealth.

Lethal Crisis's opening scene represents a world of corrupt politicians and privileged tycoons, who attend a luxurious wedding party behind high walls, isolated in the wealthy Madrid suburbs. At the start of the film, Torrente's job is to lead the security team protecting the rich guests. Significantly, the elite milieu that serves as an introduction to Torrente's world includes a cameo by dictator Francisco Franco's granddaughter, Carmen Martínez-Bordiú y Franco, a wedding guest with whom Torrente flirts. This cameo is an eloquent reminder of the persistence of the dictatorship in democracy. In the subsequent scenes, Torrente looks for food in the rubbish bins and is sleeping rough in the centre of Madrid, along with other homeless people. The *mise en scène* in those early street scenes shows walls covered in tattered posters and dirty streets. The film may offer, according to popular film magazine critics, escapism through 'mindless humour', a space for 'being vulgar' and 'the chance to forget about political correctness' (Izquierdo, n.p.), but the bulk of the diegesis is taken up by scenes that take place among those economically excluded from the safe world inhabited by the elites, elites that include those very close to the dictatorship whose privilege and wealth remain intact.

As I have shown, the main thrust of state intervention in cinema from the 1980s was the expurgation from Spanish cinema of a type of genre cinema: the old pre-democratic films, particularly comedies, which were hugely popular, relied on cultural specificity and retrograde humour, had a symbiotic relationship with television, and whose setting and characterisation emphasised an engagement with various issues that affected Spain in its transition from the dictatorship to democracy. Since *Lethal Crisis*, and the *Torrente* franchise in general, relies largely on local references and actors – in dialogue with Spanish cinema's past and in closeness with television – its success can be read as a kind of rejection of a particular European model of cinema in favour of a return to the expurgated cinema. This is all the more critical, because issues that affected Spain in its transition from dictatorship to democracy – such as the nation's inferiority complex with regards to its European neighbours, and the weight of its tradition and history – were not tackled in any significant form by the well-meaning and worthy realist and/or historical films of the European model. Yet, we must not forget that *Lethal Crisis* is a film for a media savvy audience whose models of cinema as entertainment come from Hollywood rather than Europe. It is this combination of local and global strategies that have made the franchise an unprecedented success and a key exemplary text in understanding how Spanish cinema has negotiated its relationship with film cultures of the present and the past. This negotiation means that Segura's films can continue to perform the function that the Old Cinema once had – being the embarrassing box-office successes that the Academia and the Goyas will, at best, acknowledge at one remove, by, for example, inviting Segura to present awards at the Galas.

Meanwhile, other films followed in the wake of the *Torrente* franchise, notably *Fuga de cerebros/Brain Drain* (Fernando González Molina, 2009) and *Fuga de cerebros 2: Ahora en Harvard* (Carlos Therón, 2011). Combining bad taste, political incorrectness, and televisual comedy with television stars and the mainstream Hollywood model of *American Pie* (Paul and Chris Weitz, 1999), *Brain Drain* and its sequel were not planned for foreign distribution even though its distributor is 20th Century Fox Spain. These films rely on very culturally specific verbal and slapstick humour, disregarding the *mise en scène* model of the 1980s 'good' films, a *mise en scène* which was carefully crafted with great attention to detail, but which relied on a very substantial budget. *Brain Drain 1* played on 254 screens and made a total of €1,218,545 on its weekend release, 24–26 April 2009 (see Chris Evans, 'Giving Audiences', n.p.; 'Box Office: Data, Spain', p. 26).[9] Like the *Torrente* films, these products are calculated to generate revenue in only one territory.

For Segura it is a win-win situation: being perceived as inhabiting the margins, countercultural, outside the tent partly explains the success of the *Torrente* franchise and his popularity. Segura is complicit in this exclusion – which is why he is a guest at the Goyas, even if only to confer prizes on others – and derives much symbolic capital from being left out of the awards, which adds to his credibility as a pillar of the popular. For all this, Segura is still a full member of the Academia, and, in fact, is not at all marginal. Nevertheless, he knows his place in the national cinema – to make commercial films on the Hollywood model, and financed by Hollywood, that the Academia despises but needs, because they generate large box-office returns and positive headlines for Spanish cinema. It is in this context that we have to understand his humorous address at the Goyas in 2012, when he told his fellow academicians: 'Thank you, for this kind ovation that I really need. I'm sad. I'm depressed. I'm devastated. Here's the thing: there are 29 categories in the Goyas and you haven't voted for me in any of them' (Segura, 'Monólogo', n.p.).

Segura was not sad. He was laughing all the way to the bank.

CASE TWO – ACADEMIA VS. DE LA IGLESIA AND THE INTERNET

Álex de la Iglesia, the popular auteur behind some of the most important films of the post-Franco era, is definitely not one of the arthouse auteurs whose careers the Academia was trying to hothouse with its academicism and its Goyas. As I have argued elsewhere, his films may be far more nuanced and highly crafted than those of Segura, but they have been too candid in acknowledging influences from Hollywood and from Spanish and European popular genres to be to the taste of the cultural gatekeepers (*Spanish National Cinema*, pp. 158–9). Back in the mid-1990s, de la Iglesia and Amenábar were, as Lázaro-Reboll points out, 'the bright hopes of contemporary Spanish cinema' (*Spanish Horror Films*, p. 205). As Lázaro-Reboll explains, both commanded higher than average budgets and were backed by producers well established in the industry and the Academia. El Deseo (the Almodóvar brothers' company) and Lolafilms (headed by Andrés Vicente Gómez) supported de la Iglesia's early scripts. Amenábar's first work was financed by the early Goya-winning director and producer José Luis Cuerda. In a country where film promotion is often the weakest link in a film's production strategy, two of the film-makers' early projects – *The Day of the Beast* and *Thesis* – bucked the marketing trend with large budgets and multi-platform strategies (ibid.). Both Amenábar and de la Iglesia embraced horror and acknowledged Hollywood's influence, while at the same time distancing themselves from the lowbrow Spanish horror genre film traditions of the 1970s and backing 'the bid for prestige' (ibid.), which paid off handsomely. Their films were box-office successes, popular with critics and, crucially, with the Academia: *The Day of the Beast* received six Goyas, and *Thesis* seven, and both directors went on to pursue transnational careers. Amenábar, whose 'sobriety and calculated social conscience' (Buse, Triana-Toribio and Willis, p. 5) made him the poster boy for consensus film-making in 2005, turned to English-language co-productions such as *Los otros/The Others* (2001) and more assertively later with *Ágora/Agora* (2009) and *Regression* (2015), as we will see in Chapter 6.

De la Iglesia, from his early years, was one of Spain's clearest successes with audiences of the turn to genre in the 1990s. His genres of choice are horror and comedy, and his debut film was a sci-fi Western/horror/comedy produced by Almodóvar. Later, still centred on Spanish-speaking markets, he acquired a cult following in Spain and Latin America. Attempts to move to transnational English-language co-productions either never took off (*The Mask of Fu Manchu*, a long-cherished project) or were unsuccessful: *Perdita Durango* (1997), a co-production with Mexico, shot in Spanish and English in Mexico and the US, and featuring Rosie Perez; *The Oxford Murders* (2008), shot in English and on location in Oxford, with John Hurt, Leonor Watling and Elijah Wood heading the cast (see Buse, Triana-Toribio and Willis, pp. 78–96).[10]

By the time he became the Academia's thirteenth president in 2009, de la Iglesia had cultivated a very media-friendly persona, and was closely aligned with the Hispanic subcultures of horror cinema. He was a frequent guest at the most renowned horror and fantasy festival in Spain, Sitges, and had directed a relatively successful TV sci-fi series and one video game. De la Iglesia was an early adopter of Web 2.0 and is known for his proximity to fans through his website, forum, blog and Twitter feed (see Triana-Toribio, 'Auteurism and Commerce', pp. 269–70). He also created through his work and words an image of someone who, even from a left-wing position, could be very critical of the PSOE. However, the stakes remained low as long as he was not perceived as a political director (see Buse, Triana-Toribio and Willis, pp. 23–32).

Early hopes that the critics had for de la Iglesia – that he would mature and his work would become 'more serious' – were in fact unsubtle hints for him to be interpellated by the priorities of hegemonic film culture, which entails supporting openly the campaigns of one party (Socialist) and the condemnation of the other (PP). His films, although never too explicitly, did offer a critical perspective on the early 1990s and the Socialist Party. *The Day of the Beast*, a horror comedy about a Basque priest who thwarts the birth of the anti-Christ, represents Madrid as a dystopian city, rife with right-wing violence, which the film condemns, but as Spanish film critics pointed out at the time, it is also a clear attack on the sleaze and corruption of the left (Buse, Triana-Toribio and Willis, pp. 6, 58–60). Just as the films he directed and co-scripted 'do not accept the fairy-tale of fully achieved modernity' (ibid., p. 25), his actions in the Academia consistently show that he did not equate criticising the Socialist Party in government with supporting the right.

It is perhaps surprising that someone who did not embrace the sober, didactic and political European realist model defended by the Academia was elected by his peers to preside over it. All the more so, since the academicians kept his films at bay with prizes which damned with faint praise by recognising his merits as a *metteur en scène* rather than auteur, with technical awards such as special effects, make-up and art design (see Buse, Triana-Toribio and Willis, p. 4). How de la Iglesia arrived at the presidency, what he did during his tenure and why he resigned reveal much about the inner forces of the Academia, the tug-of-war between the idea of being inclusive (as expressed in its constitutional documents) and remaining truthful to a very specific concept of cinema. This tale also accounts for how, in 2011, it was clear that the future generation of Spanish film-makers could only be accommodated with difficulty by the hegemonic inner group, and this fact led to the formation of other film cultures outside and in opposition to the institution. De la Iglesia's actions were the catalyst for this development.

In a long interview with film critics Angulo and Santamarina in 2012, de la Iglesia reflected on his term as president two years after his tenure had ended. In April 2009, there was a vacancy at the head of the Academia when the then president Ángeles González-Sinde was made Minister of Culture in the government of José Luis Rodríguez Zapatero (Rocío García, 'De la Iglesia quiere', n.p., and 'No venimos', p. 36). González-Sinde's promotion demonstrated the significant links that existed between the cinema industry, the Academia and government from 2004 to 2011. As Ignasi Guardans pithily put it in 2010, '[t]he Spanish cinema sector carries much weight in the government's decisions' (Belinchón, 'Desde 2002,' n.p.). González-Sinde, a scriptwriter, is also the daughter of the first and highly regarded president of the Academia, and boasts a CV that included film-making studies in the US. By appointing her, Zapatero was selecting a professional highly primed for the job, but also following through with a deliberate policy of allocating cultural posts – such as the Ministry of Culture, and the heads of the Spanish Film Institute and the Cervantes Institute – to makers of culture or renowned cultural administrators, rather than populating them with experts with more theoretical or technical qualifications (lawyers and MBA graduates, for example).[11]

The presidency of the Academia is decided by academicians' votes, regardless of the weight of the party in government. De la Iglesia explains that he was not the candidate of choice of González-Sinde and her team. They did not oppose his candidacy, but the suggestion to run came from industry technicians, in particular the key make-up artist José Quetglás (Bafta and Ariel Best Make-up and Hair in 2007 for his work on *Pan's Labyrinth*). His election was celebrated as the coming of a new era in which the Academia would become more open to Spain's audiences, and, as de la Iglesia put it, 'function as a nexus between different film professional departments that never agreed'. He went on: 'we lacked a direct relationship with distributors and exhibitors and had to create it' (de la Iglesia in Angulo and Santamarina, p. 313). This pragmatic and commercially hands-on perspective meant that a clash with the more classically culturalist and elitist perspective that González-Sinde brought to her new post was inevitable.

Backstabbing

Spain was at the time 'one of the world's biggest piracy offenders with an estimated 350 million illegal film downloads in 2008, costing the Spanish industry around $1bn in lost revenue, according to the country's anti-piracy association, FAP' (Chris Evans,

'Spain: All Peer-to-Peer Activity', p. 20). The Ministry of Culture, backed by the demands of associations of content creators such as the Academia, wanted drastic action against piracy. A *Ley de Economía Sostenible*/Sustainable Economy Law, popularly known as *Ley Antidescargas* (and also, unfairly, as *Ley Sinde*), was therefore developed.[12] This proposed law was controversial from the outset and the 'Ley Sinde' appellation reflected the widely held view that this was the minister's personal project (Lindo, 'La ley (del silencio)', n.p.). A response was needed to the problem of piracy, but de la Iglesia and others considered the proposals disproportionate, since they threatened to end all peer-to-peer activity, and would therefore punish all Spain's internet end-users. De la Iglesia agreed to negotiate with stakeholders and associations of internet users. He advocated changes in the industry that were not to the taste of the Academia, such as simultaneous multi-platform release:

> The best way to tackle the growing number of illegal downloads is for filmmakers to do their films in HD and offer them for download on the same day as their cinema release for as little money as possible, like iTunes currently does ... The problem is that the Spanish industry doesn't know how to exploit the internet as a business yet. (Cited in Chris Evans, 'Spain: All Peer-to-Peer Activity', p. 20)

In arguing that Spanish cinema needed to wake up to the power of the internet, and warning that the Academia was lobbying for a law that would prop up an outdated business model, de la Iglesia angered producers like Gerardo Herrero. He also broke ranks from the institution and particularly its fourth article of faith – that the theatrical and DVD exploitation of films is paramount. However, he could no longer remain neutral when, in its attempt to combat illegal downloading, the law intended to curb the activities of peer-to-peer sites (Chris Evans, 'Spain: All Peer-to-Peer Activity'). In January 2011, when a revised and more widely accepted version of the law was being drafted, the main parties, with the support of the Catalan nationalist CiU (Convergència i Unió), decided on a different version, sidestepping all verbal agreements and negotiations. De la Iglesia felt that he had been left out in the cold, and several academicians, including vice-president Icíar Bollaín and former president Gerardo Herrero, declared that he no longer represented the Academia's views (cited in Hermoso, 'Icíar Bollaín', n.p.). He resigned in January 2011.

In a final act as president, de la Iglesia presided over the Goya award ceremony and used his address to criticise the Academia as well as the Ministry of Culture, and to highlight his alignment with those who were unhappy with the law. 'The rules of the game have changed,' admonished de la Iglesia. He reminded an audience composed of Academia members and government officials that those who felt that the law was designed to punish them, and who had been 'othered' by the media discourse with the label *internautas*, were in fact Spanish citizens and, crucially, potential Spanish cinema spectators.[13] 'Audiences we have lost. They don't go to the cinema because they are in front of a computer screen,' he added (de la Iglesia, 'Discurso íntegro', n.p.).

The media chose to look the other way. Jesús Ruiz Mantilla's article for *El País* made it clear that the main attraction of the Gala was not de la Iglesia's impassioned speech about the sustainability of the Academia's model of film culture. The value of the event for him was dramatic. Since the setting was an opera theatre, he compared the events with famous operas, but kept his distance from the proceedings with scorn and puns about clowns (Ruíz Mantilla, 'Entre Puccini', n.p.).

It is precisely in such moments when the Galas are disrupted by elements that contradict the hegemonic film culture – by a president who has been elected to represent their interests, but holds views that clash with their idea of cinema – that we can see glimpses of other film cultures and their challenges. By January 2011, the Academia had a reputation for being inward-looking (*endogámica*) and out of touch with audiences (Angulo and Santamarina, p. 312). Almodóvar showed the way to rogue film professionals; de la Iglesia followed. De la Iglesia's course – from the popular auteur, to the influential director/producer chosen by his peers to lead them, to his resignation – has the purpose, not so much of reviewing his changing fortunes, but of explaining that behind the seemingly immovable and residual cultures of the Academia, we can sometimes detect forces that have the power to renew the institution and with it Spanish cinema. An institution that began by building Spanish cinema's cultural credibility transnationally in the 1980s and 90s was, by 2011, increasingly perceived as distant from those whom it purported to serve, and was in dire need of change. It was also seen by some critics as capable of vindictiveness against those who did not toe the line. Carlos Boyero wrote in his review of the 2014 Goyas that the way de la Iglesia was treated on that occasion left a bitter taste:

> Leaving Álex de la Iglesia out [of the nominations from the Best Film Goya, 2014] stinks of treachery, of punishment to the imprudent, terrible child who dared express his thoughts out loud at a Goya Award Ceremony and went against the collective beliefs of his trade. (n.p.)

I argued in the Introduction that the power of the hegemonic is strong. While fronting the Academia, de la Iglesia wrote and shot *The Last Circus*, by his own admission his most Spanish political film (see Angulo and Santamarina, pp. 284–90). He presents it to these scholars as a working through in the Freudian sense. Two clowns are forced to club each other to death in the diegesis by a sadistic Francoist military. In the end, it transpired that both de la Iglesia and González-Sinde had been used to score political points. The politicians bypassed one and kept the other out of the final discussions of the law (Lindo, n.p.). The infamous *Ley de Economía Sostenible* was passed on 24 January 2011, after having been rejected by the Spanish lower chamber in December 2010. Then it was hastily withdrawn by the Socialist Party in retreat during December 2011, only to be passed by the PP. It is now known as *Ley Sinde-Wert*.

5

There Is No Such Thing as a Weak Enemy

The Goyas don't have the right to monopolize the image of the films made in this country.

(Miñarro, p. 63)

The Academia ... is not the space where cinema lives.

(José Luis Guerín cited in Belinchón *et al.*, 'Cine español', n.p.)

The film-makers quoted here express the same sentiment: the Academia and the Goyas neither produce nor represent that which is most valuable in Spanish cinema. These film-makers stand for a type of aesthetic and thematic experimentation that they claim would put Spanish cinema on a par with contemporary transnational art cinema trends, trends the Academia and the Goyas cannot account for. At the same time, for these film-makers, the box-office successes from the popular auteurs examined in the previous chapter are beside the point. The industry may depend on Santiago Segura for internal revenue and to bolster a national industry, but for international critical capital, entirely different players are needed.

I mentioned in the Introduction Elsaesser's claim that, in European countries, the film-making landscape is usually composed of three camps: art and auteur cinema, commercial productions facing Hollywood, and, as he explains, 'another player, the avant-garde cinema whose film-makers, however, have almost always refused the label national cinema, because they saw themselves as both international and anti-Hollywood' (Elsaesser, p. 42). This chapter deals with this third player. Directors and producers such as Mercedes Álvarez, José Luis Guerín, Isaki Lacuesta, Lluís Miñarro, Javier Rebollo, Marc Recha, Jaime Rosales, Ariadna Pujol and others developed, from the 1990s, critically acclaimed careers and films, bypassing the channels of approval of academicism and refusing to make the Academia's ideal films, films they consider the result of compromises they are unwilling to make.

This chapter examines these independent/avant-garde practices, focusing in particular on the period towards the end of this study, 2007–11. I then trace back their aesthetic ancestries and describe the film culture they have cultivated in opposition to the hegemonic film culture and, for the most part, to the Academia. I will do so by discussing a disruptive moment when members of this group and the Academia crossed paths. This disruptive moment is connected directly to the ambiguous relationship of the independent/avant-garde sector and those mechanisms of national validation of quality, the Goyas.[1]

As we saw in the Introduction, the Academia sought to become the certifier of value in cinema in the Spanish state and in its nations without a state, Catalonia and the Basque Country. For a section of the field, the Academia achieved the authority on the hegemonic film culture made in Spain and made in Spanish, Catalan, Basque and Galician. This is attested by the fact that, as I argued in the Introduction, when the voice of Spanish cinema is invoked by the press, nationally and internationally, it is often the words of the president of the Academia that are quoted. Moreover, the films endorsed by the Goyas often enjoy a second life of theatrical exhibition and a special DVD release, which indicates that audiences trust the value judgments articulated through these awards.

However, critics and film-makers in the independent/avant-garde camp do not acknowledge the Academia's authority as a certifier of value. This was particularly evident between 2007 and 2011 when the independent/avant-garde film-makers and practitioners asserted themselves as the true certifiers of value through opinions and articles expressed and published particularly in the cinephile journal *Cahiers du Cinéma España*, which was launched in May 2007 (and became *Caimán Cuadernos de Cine* in December 2011). This magazine, together with the cultural supplement of the Barcelona daily *La Vanguardia*, was the main critical platform of the independent/avant-garde sector. Other trusted certifiers of value in the period of study were the prestigious international festival juries, including, within Spain, FiCXixón (Festival Internacional de Cine de Gijón/International Film Festival of Gijón), particularly under the direction of José Luis Cienfuegos, and the juries of Donostia Zinemaldia (Festival de Cine de San Sebastián/San Sebastian International Film Festival). Even more crucial were the endorsements of juries and programmers at festivals outside Spain: Cannes, Berlin, Karlovy Vary, Locarno, Rotterdam and Sundance. For the avant-garde, true value resides in the judgments of these authorities rather than in national prizes.

These fundamental differences over criteria of quality mattered a great deal, because it was not simply a question of 'agreeing to disagree', as we shall see. This challenge to the academicism of the Academia is not to be taken lightly: if the Academia's mandate as the main certifier of value in the cultural field was put in jeopardy by the cinephiles, its reason for existing in the first place was at stake.

A SEVERE CASE OF CINEPHILE ANXIETY

As a form of introducing the independent/avant-garde camp and the brand of Spanish film culture it encouraged, I will start by relating something that happened in the world of Spanish cinema in the final months of 2009 that sent shivers down the spines of the stakeholders of hegemonic film culture. This chapter takes as its starting point this moment of crisis, because it brought to mainstream media attention the existence of this third player. Prior to October 2009, this player had mostly inhabited the fringes in cinephile periodicals and at film festivals, as well as also coming together for specialised film events at museums and the Filmotecas, but without troubling the mainstream media.

Álex de la Iglesia's tenure as president of the Academia had begun a few months earlier, in June 2009. Ignasi Guardans, also newly appointed as head of the Spanish

Film Institute, announced in October a new Order changing the conditions of eligibility for state subsidies for film projects. The proposed change meant that, among other things, only films with a budget of over €600,000 ($815,000) could qualify for the complementary state subsidy based on how a feature film performs at the box office.[2]

Guardans's move requires some contextualisation. Although the economic crisis arrived in late 2008, the entire scope of its catastrophic consequences for Spain and its cinema were not yet known. Perhaps sensing an impending economic shake-up, the minister of culture, Ángeles González-Sinde, appointed Guardans – an expert in intellectual property, media and international law, and former Euro-Parliamentarian for the Catalan nationalist party CiU – to head the Spanish Film Institute and manage the cinema coffers. Guardans had been chosen for his expertise on the transnational contexts in which audiovisual industries operate (García and Belinchón, 'La ministra de cultura', n.p.). This appointment was welcomed by those in the industry who were more concerned with sustainability and who wanted to see Spanish cinema less dependent on subsidies. Guardans was seen by some as supportive of an industry model based on public/private financing, with Spain's broadcasters as partners in production, an arrangement that had in fact been inscribed as law since 1999 and was also spelled out in the Cinema Law of 2007 (see Triana-Toribio, 'Residual Film Cultures', pp. 65–81). Among these was Rafael Alvero of the exhibitors' association FECE (Federación de Cines de España), who declared his despair at the situation where 150 films had been made in 2006, but the local film market share actually dropped to single figures for most of 2007. His hopes were pinned on the correct development of this law, which would mean fewer films with larger budgets, and safer bets at the box office (cited in Wallerstein, p. 2). Conversely, Guardans's appointment seemed to go against the grain of the hegemonic film culture belief, shared by independent/avant-garde film culture, that film is a cultural good and it is the state's responsibility and duty both to fund it and to protect cultural diversity through cinema.

Guardans was tasked with developing this new Cinema Law. His declared mission was to strengthen Spanish cinema's industrial framework with austerity measures that would satisfy the film production subsidiaries of the television channels keen to finance box-office-friendly films. His aim was to slim down the annual Spanish film output to fewer, more profitable films with wider circulation (see Chris Evans, 'Carlos Cuatros' [sic], n.p.; Ríos Pérez, n.p.), in preparation for what already looked likely to be, from the vantage point of 2009, a bleak future.[3] He had also been very open about which side of the films-as-culture versus films-as-industry debate he was on. His expressed opinions about the need for films and film-makers to rise above party politics delighted the more conservative media, who have always condemned Spanish cinema for supporting left-wing and liberal agendas ('Guardans', n.p.). His desired model for Spanish cinema was one in which film-makers would be less dependent on state protection and work more effectively with solvent producers and television companies than was the case at the time of his appointment.[4] He issued the proposal for the Order to 'consolidate' output, restricting state help to more ambitious projects, those likely to recoup the state investment via national and international box-office sales.

As soon as the proposal was announced, a group of more than two hundred film industry professionals came together to fight it. They created the Colectivo Cineastas contra la Orden (Film-makers' Collective against the Order – henceforth Collective) to air their grievances before Guardans (Belinchón, 'Cineastas contra la Orden', n.p.). The Collective argued that this change worked against the spirit of the Cinema Law, which had been written by cinephile critics and civil servants such as Fernando Lara and passed by the PSOE in its 2004–8 term of government. The Cinema Law professedly encouraged new work and diversity, something that is stated in its preamble (*Ley del Cine 55/2007*, p. 2).

Guardans dismissed their concerns about the changes in eligibility, arguing that they were mere 'cinephile anxieties' (Diego Galán, 'Enemigos', n.p.; Rocío García, 'Los cineastas', n.p.), so the Collective turned to higher powers in the form of the Spanish Audiencia Nacional and the European Union in Brussels. Cinephile critics and professionals everywhere rallied around the defence of 'small' or 'humble' films, as supportive critics called them in *Cahiers du Cinéma España*.[5] The Collective's appeal brought the Spanish film industry to a halt when it was upheld by the EU (Belinchón and García, n.p.). No scheduled film shoot could go ahead without the security of state film subsidies in a country where, as Fernando Evole put it, 'we have no cinema industry to speak of ... just hundreds of producers jumping through hoops to be eligible for [state] funding' (Wallerstein, p. 2).[6] Brussels had made it impossible for any subsidies to be awarded until modifications were made to the ICAA's draft of the Order.

Since the Academia is supposed to be a wide tent for everyone and a mediator between the ICAA and the industry, its president could not be seen to side with any of the factions. What is more, de la Iglesia had clearly promised to be a president who acted as an interlocutor between different sectors of the industry and with audiences (Angulo and Santamarina, p. 313). His goodwill notwithstanding, in his press declarations de la Iglesia ended up sounding very much like an outnumbered parent among warring siblings, making fruitless pleas for everyone to be patient and not to fight with each other (Rocío García, 'Los cineastas', n.p.).

The Collective's demands were simple: to continue to be supported by the state in making these 'small' or 'humble' films for non-commercial circuits or for non-profitable commercial exploitation. They issued a manifesto stressing that legislating against small films would destroy cultural diversity, undermine cultural exception and amount to giving up on the idea that cinema could be a cultural good, integral to Spain's future. The manifesto stressed that it also meant giving up on some of the films that have always been certified as of high quality:

> The type of cinema that this draft of the Order seeks to eliminate is that which is made with fewer than two million euros' investment from a producer (sometimes much less). It is the cinema made by small and medium-size production companies, employing a vast number of technicians and it is a cinema with added value. This is the cinema that represents Spanish culture in dozens of festivals, that is being exported and sells well abroad, and the cinema that attracts prestige year after year throughout the world. It is the cinema that plays to full houses in festivals, at universities, in museums, at embassies and in Instituto Cervantes sites. ('Manifiesto', n.p.)

The films defended by the Collective were not necessarily intended for traditional industrial distribution and exhibition channels, but might travel internationally, and still, in their view, had to be made.

Influential critics in the dailies joined those of *Cahiers du Cinéma España*. 'It is the state's duty to support a self-sustaining audiovisual industry as much as those taking aesthetic risks, those two positions should not be incompatible,' declared an editorial from *El País* ('Patinazo de cine', p. 32), and Luis Martínez from *El Mundo* expressed a similar sentiment to the *Cahiers* critics (Heredero and Reviriego, 'Nueva Orden', p. 58). While mainstream critics wanted to have their cake and eat it, those from *Cahiers du Cinéma España* were more biased, arguing that not supporting these films would be suicidal for a future self-sustaining industry, since they were the sandboxes in which budding film-makers could learn their craft. Without these sandboxes, Spanish cinema had no chance of a generational replacement, argued critics such as Carlos F. Heredero ('Hacia una nueva', pp. 6–8). Indeed, the Collective included film-makers who might potentially be incorporated into the commercial mainstream in years to come, as had been the promise with Julio Medem, or indeed of Almodóvar back in the 1970s, although Heredero would never put his name in the same category.

If de la Iglesia was outnumbered, Guardans was overruled. As the critic Diego Galán observed, in dismissing the cinephile defenders of 'small' films, Guardans had failed to remember the Spanish proverb: there is no such thing as a weak enemy (Diego Galán, 'Enemigos pequeños', n.p.). In spite of the powerful interests backing Guardans, and pressing on with the changes I have outlined, the head of the ICAA was forced to resign in 2010 by González-Sinde (García and Belinchón, 'La ministra de Cultura', n.p.). Some producers and distributors were candid about having pinned their hopes on Guardans's strategies for industrial correction and consolidation, such as the Order that so angered the independents. As I have explained elsewhere (Triana-Toribio, 'Residual Film Cultures', pp. 65–81), there was dismay in the industry when he resigned, but those who despaired wanted to remain unnamed, something that attests to the power of Guardans's 'weak enemy':

> This was a bolt out of the blue. 'With the new film fund in place and attracting big projects like Juan Antonio Bayona's *The Impossible* [2012], starring Ewan McGregor, and Juan Carlos Fresnadillo's *Intruders* [2011], starring Clive Owen, we thought finally the industry was moving in the right direction,' one leading producer told *ScreenDaily*. 'Now we don't know what to expect under another new director general. I just hope we don't revert back to supporting small-budget local cultural films only.' (Chris Evans 'Carlos Cuatros' [*sic*], n.p.)

The few who put their heads above the parapet at the end of 2009 summed up the interests of the commercial cinema, of the cinema industry and, it has to be said, of the bulk of the Academia. The producer, director and influential academician Gerardo Herrero delivered a withering assessment of the Collective: '[They] are only interested in milking the system for all it's worth and about making films that interest no one' (Rocío García, 'Los cineastas, n.p.). Another influential member of the Academia, who wishes to remain anonymous, admitted to me that those films were driving audiences out of cinemas.

The purpose of this chapter is not to cast value judgments or to evaluate the debates surrounding the viability of these small films by independent film-makers. What interests me is how the formation of the Collective in 2009 as a group of clearly identified individuals enables more situated arguments about the ideas that underpin their support of an artisanal mode of production.

THE CINEPHILE HABITUS

What had been up to 2009 a series of separate independent film professionals within and outside the Academia, but who had not for the most part sought visibility, could now be identified as a lobby group. Coming together to protest against Guardans, they usefully – for the film scholar – put all their names together on a single list, something they would normally resist. Independent/avant-garde creators, as well as wanting to be free from commercial and industrial shackles, in general avoid being pinned down as a group or movement, seeking instead to maintain separation from each other (Belinchón, 'Hago otro cine', n.p.).

The two hundred or more signatories of the 2009 manifesto represented several generations of film industry professionals (directors, scriptwriters, art directors, actors, producers, etc.), festival programmers, critics, film and communication studies students and academics. There were EOC alumni ranging from the *auteur maudit* Cecilia Bartolomé, whose career in the 1970s remains in the margins, to the respected and well-known Josefina Molina, and the influential and famous producer and director Fernando Trueba, past president of the Academia (1988) and Oscar winner in 1994 for *Belle Époque*. There were other members of the Trueba film-making clan – younger brother David (director of *Soldiers of Salamis* [2003]) and son Jonás, who was then preparing his first film.[7] Other signatories were the Catalan transnational director-producer Miñarro (producer of the Argentine auteur Lisardo Alonso, the Portuguese/France-based Manoel de Oliveira, the Catalans José Luis Guerín and Albert Serra, and Thailand's auteur and Palme d'Or winner, Apichatpong Weerasethakul).[8] More Catalan film-makers of different generations and traditions such Ventura Pons, Judith Colell (who became vice-president of the Academia in 2011) and Isaki Lacuesta also put their names to the document. And the list included other Madrid-based independents such as Pablo Llorca (working since the late 1980s) and the younger Javier Rebollo, the director identified by the press as the spokesperson for the group. While there were different generations in the Collective, the perception was that the group was led by its youngest members – like Rebollo, who was born in 1969.[9]

The belief that films that are the experimental, personal projects of their auteurs and sustain cultural diversity should be supported by the state is at the heart of European and, indeed, Spanish film legislation. In actual fact, in spite of the protests of the Collective, these guarantees continued to appear in Guardans's *Orden*; in a long interview, Guardans explained that the only new condition was that these films had to prove their identity as art cinema: 'films that undertake a creative risk are going to be helped as much or even more as before' (Heredero and Reviriego, 'Entrevista: Ignasi Guardans', p. 63).

Nowadays, the availability of digital technology has supposedly democratised film-making, allowing both budding and mature film-makers to take aesthetic risks at reduced costs, and to distribute their films independently through online platforms, such as PLAT TV, created in 2009 by Beatriz Navas and Víctor Berlin (see <plat.tv/que-es-plat>). However, the reaction of the Collective showed that they were still very wedded to the theatrical release of their films, and one of their main concerns was that the *Orden* might mean that the new, alternative modes of distribution could become the only ones available for 'small' or 'humble' films. If we historicise the presence of the state as a safety net for experimental film-making, we can see that the Collective felt that a specific idea of cinema was under threat, an idea that in Europe had been in place since the *nouvelle vague*. For the Collective, working on small personal projects was an essential part of a film-maker's training, in the same way that attending a film school was. Expecting the state to bear the lion's share of the financial burden for aesthetically risky films, including the burden of theatrical distribution, has a long history that can be traced back to a time when Spanish cinema was aspiring to be 'European': to the 1950s and particularly the 1955 Salamanca conference.

When, in the early 1960s, Francoist film legislator García Escudero wanted young Spanish film-makers to make Spanish films count as a New European cinema and represent their nation at festivals, as 'a cinema of reality, a cinema of individuality and a cinema of freedom' (García Escudero, p. 103), he asked the young men in question what they needed to achieve this. As we saw in Chapter 1, they demanded that he put in place ring-fenced subsidies for projects that would not be part of the mainstream through the creation of a specific funding mechanism: the Special Interest Award (*Premio de Interés Especial*).[10] The assumption of the Academia generation that the state should be the main film producer, particularly of films that took aesthetic risks, was established with García Escudero's example, which became the backbone of the Miró Law of 1983. The Film Law of 2007, in turn, harks back to that earlier text.

As well as appropriating ideas from the past about the way in which aesthetic risk should be funded, the Collective look to history for their understanding of what constitutes aesthetic risk in the first place. Carlos Losilla, Belén Vidal and others have identified many in the Collective as aesthetic inheritors of the European and Spanish/Catalan avant-garde of the past (Belén Vidal, 'The Cinephilic Citation', n.p.).[11] The younger leaders of the Collective see themselves – and are seen by critics and academics – as the true keepers of the flame of the cinephiles of the 1950s–60s, 'reclaim[ing] the [Escuela de Barcelona's] avant-garde torch of formal innovation, setting themselves as the counter cinematic alternative to today's mainstream cinema' (Ledesma, p. 260). Indeed, a number of them trained with Escuela de Barcelona member Pere Portabella at Barcelona's Universidad Pompeu Fabra (Quintana, Personal interview).

The cinematic ideal of the Academia founders in their early years, and that of the Collective's leaders in the early twenty-first century, is by and large the same: the period between 1958 and 1968, which represents the golden years of European art cinema and the birth of cinephilia, *sensu stricto* (de Valck and Hagener, p. 11). Consequently, the Collective want access to comparable financial systems to those enjoyed by their predecessors to make *their* 'cinema of reality, cinema of individuality and cinema of freedom' (ibid.). But as a result, their manifesto also has a particular claim on the attention of the academicians, and explains why they are far from a weak enemy. In the membership of the Collective, many academicians can see their younger selves, clinging to principles they held dear before the realities of the industry forced them to accept compromise.

I traced in Chapter 1 the processes that gave the founders of the Academia their habitus – their disposition or 'feel for the game'. These are central to understanding a generation of film professionals that created such instruments as the Miró Law.[12] These same processes made them come together as a group to bring forth the Spanish cinema of democracy, to defend the art and auteur cinema model I have called the hegemonic model, but also the avant-garde model as the point of initiation into film-making. On this basis, it could be expected that, out of those budding experimental film-makers, the next generation would emerge.

The Collective, particularly its younger and more activist members, have a comparable shared habitus and had been integrated into comparable modes of film-making through film schools such as the Catalan Escola Superior de Cinema i Audiovisuals de Catalunya (ESCAC), the MA of Documentary at the Barcelona Pompeu Fabra, and ECAM (Escuela de Cinematografía y del Audiovisual de la Comunidad de Madrid). At the same time, they write or contribute to debates in *Cahiers du Cinéma España* and in the cultural supplement of the Barcelona daily *La Vanguardia*, as we saw earlier, thus echoing the practices of the young cinephiles of the 1950s and 60s, who wrote about legislation and state funding, as well as on aesthetic themes, in *Objetivo*, *Nuestro Cine*, *Nuevo Fotogramas* and *Contracampo*. Young and old shared a suspicion of commercial mainstream genre cinema (both national and Hollywood), particularly of comedy and melodrama. The difference, as we have seen throughout this study, is that the old guard did manage to make their personal films – the realist, literary and political works that became hegemonic (first with Saura and Camus, then with the younger social cinema of León de Aranoa and Bollaín). They benefited from state subsidies, and the Academia consolidated their success with its prizes.[13] Members of the Collective can be forgiven for feeling that they had been undermined by the withdrawal of state money, when they had come to expect it as a natural inheritance in film-making.

AVANT-GARDE VS. THE NATIONAL CINEMA

Paradoxically perhaps, for a sector with such an expectation of, and dependency on, a state subsidy system, the film-makers in the independent/avant-garde camp do not feel a strong attachment to the nation. Elsaesser explains that it is in the nature of European avant-garde film culture 'to have almost always refused the label national cinema' and to position themselves 'as both international and anti-Hollywood' (p. 42). Like the avant-gardists of the Escuela de Barcelona in the 1960s, the avant-gardists of the first decade of the twenty-first century were also wary of the national label. There is plenty of evidence of this stance in *Cahiers du Cinéma España* since 2007, but particularly around the time when the Collective mobilised against the *Orden*. Talking to *Cahiers du Cinéma España* in 2009, Lacuesta sidestepped questions on whether his films were indebted to national traditions by arguing that it was more important to talk about aesthetic issues: 'Don't you think that the idea of a national cinema is old news?' (p. 10). Rebollo, in the same piece, categorically denied being part of any Spanish film-making tradition. A more conciliatory Lacuesta explained that he admired many Spanish film-makers, such as Edgar Neville, Buñuel and José Val del Omar, but no more so than others of different nationalities. He also pointed out that in Barcelona there has been a connection with the art cinema tradition of the Escuela de Barcelona and with Guerín, removing himself from identification with the idea of Spain as a territory to which he belongs and hinting instead at allegiances to Catalonia (ibid.).

In their conversation, Lacuesta and Rebollo wish not so much for total divorce from the national (they do reluctantly admit to some continuity) but to distance themselves from what Heredero calls in the same issue of the magazine 'the traditional formulas of Spanish production', by which he meant, in 2009, social realism, commercial mainstream comedies, thrillers, melodramas and horror films (see 'Hacia una nueva', pp. 6–8). Part of their strategy of cinephilic internationalism and their disavowal of the Spanish national cinema's themes and topics is a clear rejection of the kind of responsibility with the representation of reality that the Academia cherished: social realism and the direct engagement with the politics of memory that was encouraged, particularly between 2004 and 2011. Pedro Aguilera, for instance, discussing his film *Naufragio* (2010), about a sub-Saharan migrant, declared: 'I have tried to distance myself radically from the cinema of social realism, to tell a story with a marked symbolic and surrealist atmosphere, with African voodoo references' (cited in Reviriego and Yáñez, p. 22). This practice put independent/avant-garde film-makers beyond the remit of the Academia, which, as I have been arguing, looks to target a general audience and appeal to middlebrow taste, aiming, as James English puts it, 'to bring cultural workers and their products under tighter supervision and discipline' with their Goya categories and other modes of guidance for film-makers (p. 37).

This failure to fit the received model is a deliberate strategy by the Collective's younger film-makers, a strategy that, for many, includes refusing to make films that can be labelled according to the Academia's preferred categories. As Quintana explained in an interview in 2013, 'documentary' became a loose label for work that was simply unclassifiable, because film-makers such as Álvarez, Guerín, Lacuesta and Serra, for example, did not want to define films in the 'feature', 'short' or 'fiction' boxes, or to use generic labels such as 'drama' or 'comedy' (Personal interview, n.p.). Taxonomies are useful for institutions and for awards, but these are not docile film-makers and neither are their films. Even the labels 'documentary' or 'essay film' are far from accurate in some cases, as Quintana argued (ibid.).

Rejecting the national goes hand in hand with embracing the non-national. Heredero explains in the same issue of the magazine that the avant-garde cinema 'expresses itself in happy and uninhibited intercourse [*concubinato*] with other foreign film traditions', or, to use less sexist language, with international cinema ('Hacia una nueva', p. 6). The independent avant-garde expresses its transnationalism through what Vidal has characterised as 'cinephilic citations' from a range of cinemas and origins – from references to Hollywood's John Ford in *Innisfree* (José Luis Guerín, 1990) to Lacuesta's *La noche que no acaba*/*All Night Long* (2010), which weaves a tapestry of documentary footage, citations from 1950s Hollywood Technicolor films and images of Ava Gardner's stay in Tossa de Mar while shooting *Pandora and the Flying Dutchman* (Albert Lewin, 1951). In *Las variaciones Marker/The Marker Variations* (2007), meanwhile, Lacuesta enters into a dialogue both formal and thematic with the key French avant-garde film-maker (Belén Vidal, 'The Cinephilic Citation', n.p.). So, for these film-makers, the models are rarely national and the film cultures their films usually engage are European. 'The directors who have best captured the cities in their films are Godard and Tati, although I am also interested in the spaces of new architecture filmed by Antonioni,' declared director Álvarez (cited in Reviriego and Yáñez, p. 22).

There are further reasons behind this rejection of 'the national' that need explaining. In my Introduction, and particularly in Chapters 1 and 2, I showed how hegemonic Spanish cinema culture and the Academia emerged from a culture of resistance to Francoism, and how cultural production was co-opted into the service of the political process of democratisation, particularly in the 1990s but also beyond that decade. In Chapter 2, I demonstrated how the Goyas have become, for the right-wing PP, the symbol of the cultural strategies of the Socialist Party during the 1980s, something which has led to politicised clashes between the film industry and the government when the PP is in power. In turn, these clashes have resulted in very negative press in daily newspapers and a co-optation into the political fight of actors and film-makers who either side with one political party or the other, or who find themselves sometimes caught in the crossfire. This has, in turn, led to a disenchantment and disengagement. Much of the independent/avant-garde camp is made up of film-makers who refuse to be dragged into the fight. Their experimentation and concentration on the aesthetic possibilities of film were also strategies for trying to stay outside party politics.

MOMENTS OF DISRUPTION AND ANTI-INSTITUTIONALISM: THE CASE OF *LA SOLEDAD* (2007)

> Prizes have been useful ... not just to the bureaucrats of culture but also to those who accrue advantage or profit as they distance themselves from culture's bureaucratic epicentres. With the rise of the prize bureaucracy comes also the rise of the anti-institutionalism (or 'independent') position and the prize-bashing rhetoric that attends it. (English, p. 41)

In the Guardans dispute in 2009, prominent academician Gerardo Herrero charged the Collective, and by extension the independent/avant-garde sector, with making films of dubious interest. Such charges are fair if one takes into account only the taste of mainstream audiences and economic indicators, but they do not hold up when one considers what the programmers of international film festivals looked for in a Spanish film in the first decade of the twenty-first century. These small films (besides some by Almodóvar, Amenábar and Isabel Coixet) were the only Spanish output that appealed to film festival programmers (see Quintana, 'Entre el genio', p. 21); therefore, as Heredero explains, this cinema, which does not fit into the 'tired and televisual' patterns that dominate Spanish film-making, is the only one that puts the Spanish film industry on the global art cinema map (Heredero, 'Hacia una nueva', p. 7). As evidence, Quintana cites examples such as Albert Serra's *Honor de cavellería/Quixotic*

(2006) (winner of the FIPRESCI prize at the Viennale in 2006 and shown in Mar del Plata in 2007); Serra's *El cant dels ocells/Birdsong* (2008), which went to Cannes and Mar del Plata in 2008; and *Petit indi/Little Indi* (2009) by Marc Recha, selected for Locarno and Seminci in Valladolid in 2009. In addition, *Tiro en la cabeza/A Shot in the Head* (Jaime Rosales, 2008) was shown to great acclaim at San Sebastian in 2008, and *Solitary Fragments*, also by Rosales, was selected for Un Certain Regard at Cannes in 2007. However, there were no Spanish films in official competition at Cannes in 2007 or 2008.

In 2010, Fernando Lara argued that Spain's absence from festivals such as Cannes was due to the Spanish industry's failure to produce cinema that mattered:

> I have been able to ascertain personally that the selection team of most major festivals think that we lack originality; we don't take [aesthetic] risks and [do not make] innovative contributions. When they see Spanish films, more often than not, they dismiss them as 'conventional', 'derivative' and 'televisual'. ('Ni propios ni extraños', p. 69)

According to Lara, the exceptions to that rule were those independent/avant-garde films, more often Catalan productions than from Madrid or elsewhere in Spain. By 2010, Spanish cinema was far removed from the main trends of European art cinema. 'We were exotic only once: when Francoism made us the exception in a context of occidental democracies' (ibid.). Therefore, when Herrero levels accusations of parochialism against the Collective, he represents the biases of the national industry, but not the view of the cinephile press and festival juries, either national or international.

Although experimental Catalan films perform well at international festivals, according to Lluís Miñarro, 'It is very unlikely that the minority cinema or the most aesthetically challenging cinema will win Goyas' (p. 63). So what has happened on the rare occasion when they do? What is being rewarded? What is being ignored? In 2008, Jaime Rosales's *Solitary Fragments* was awarded three Goyas: Best Film, Best Director and Best New Actor. In the main category, *Solitary Fragments* was competing against *Siete mesas de billar francés/Seven Billiard Tables* (Gracia Querejeta, 2007), *Las 13 rosas/The Thirteen Roses* (Emilio Martínez Lázaro, 2007) and *The Orphanage*.

There are a number of clues to suggest that giving the three main Goyas to *Solitary Fragments* was not business as usual. Displayed on the cover of a special edition of the Academia's monthly magazine devoted to the twenty-second Gala was a smiling, tuxedo-ed Rosales holding up his trophy, along with a leading article entitled 'A Night of Surprises'. We also know that insiders in the press room during the award ceremony reacted with general astonishment ('Una noche de sorpresas', p. 5). We can guess the reasons why this was a surprise by looking at the previous two years' choices.

The twentieth award ceremony of 2006 seemed to confirm the triumph of the 'genre film with aspirations'. *La vida secreta de las palabras/The Secret Life of Words* (2005), like much of Isabel Coixet's work, imitates the aesthetic of US independent cinema and draws on transnational stars such as Sarah Polley and Tim Robbins, supplementing this formula with elements of melodrama. The favourite finalists in the twenty-first ceremony, *Volver* and *Pan's Labyrinth*, were genre films poised to deliver big box-office success, nationally and internationally, making €10,243,082 and

	Best Film	**Best Director**	**Best Original Screenplay**	**Best Adapted Screenplay**
2008	*La soledad* (dir. Jaime Rosales)	Jaime Rosales for *La soledad*	Sergio Gutiérrez Sánchez for *El orfanato*	Félix Viscarret for *Bajo las estrellas*
2007	*Volver* (dir. Pedro Almodóvar)	Pedro Almodóvar for *Volver*	Guillermo del Toro for *El laberinto del fauno/Pan's Labyrinth*	
2006	*La vida secreta de las palabras* (dir. Isabel Coixet)	Isabel Coixet for *La vida secreta de las palabras*	Isabel Coixet for *La vida secreta de las palabras*	Mateo Gíl and Marcelo Piñeyro for *El método*

€8,896,195 respectively. They were also relatively popular with mainstream critics: a perfect combination for the Goyas. Both were backed by a powerful distributor: Warner Bros. Entertainment España S.L.[14] Both were directed by heavyweights in the international arena: Guillermo del Toro and Pedro Almodóvar. With such precedents in the two previous years, the smart money was on *The Orphanage* to sweep the categories at the ceremony in 2008. It was the film that confirmed the consolidation of genre cinema, particularly horror, in the Spanish film industry, which had seen heavy investment by producers such as Filmax, and the international success of Jaume Balagueró and Paco Plaza's *[Rec]* (2007) and Nacho Vigalondo's *Cronocrímenes/ Timecrimes* (2007), bought by Hollywood before it even premiered in Spain (see Roma, p. 31; Lázaro-Reboll, *Spanish Horror Films*). *The Orphanage* also came with the endorsement of Guillermo del Toro as 'godfather' (Roma, p. 31). Given these features and pedigree, *The Orphanage* might have been expected to beat a film like *Solitary Fragments*, which was formally innovative and had not been seen by many.

On the night, Bayona received the award for Best New Director, while Rosales received the more significant Goya for Best Director. The main award of the night, Best Film, went to *Solitary Fragments*, along with one of the performance awards as well. Three Goyas confirmed that the academicians were keen, at least on this occasion, to endorse formal experimentation and aesthetic risk. The distance between Rosales and Bayona was clear, since the remaining Goyas won by *The Orphanage* were in the less prestigious 'technical categories' such as artistic direction, special effects and sound.

Solitary Fragments did not receive any 'technical Goyas'. What the academicians were commending instead were cinephilic values from a director who declared his admiration for and influence by canonical European art cinema – Godard, Antonioni and Pasolini, among others – and whose production company is named after Ingmar Bergman's *Wild Strawberries* (1957). Divided into four chapters, *Fragments* portrays moments in the lives of women and men, from the mundane to life-changing decisions and events. It is tempting to summarise the plot around Adela (Sonia Almarcha), one of the main characters, but the truth is that it is an ensemble film, where different solitudes are framed. Adela and her baby son, Miguelito, move to Madrid from a village, leaving behind her ageing father (Juan Margallo) and Miguelito's father (Goya winner José Luis Torrijo). In Madrid, Adela shares a flat with Inés (Miriam Correa) and

Carlos (Lluís Villanueva), and works as a Trade Fair employee. Inés's family enters the story. Her mother, Antonia (Petra Martínez), runs a small local shop and worries about her other daughters, Nieves (Nuria Mencía), who undergoes an operation on a cancerous tumor, and Helena (María Bazán), who plans to finance her holiday apartment on the Mediterranean coast with her mother's funds, angering Inés.

The acting is understated and restrained, even in scenes of pathos, with a subject matter typical of melodrama (the illness and death of a parent, a lover or a child). The cast list is equally low-key, with no big Spanish stars. Goya winner José Luis Torrijo was making his screen debut, while the rest of the actors are known either for supporting roles or for their work onstage. Mencía and Correa have worked on television and had supporting roles in feature films. Martínez and Margallo, who have also appeared in supporting roles in films such as *Bad Education* (Almodóvar), are known mainly as stage actors and award-winning theatre directors. Crucially, they are also members of key independent theatre groups Tábano and TEM (Teatro Estudio de Madrid), which were on the receiving end of Francoist censorship in the 1970s. Margallo's presence further cements the connections between *Solitary Fragments* and Spanish traditions of visual and scenic arts of the highest prestige. Margallo played the fugitive soldier in *The Spirit of the Beehive*, in which he was the symbol of resistance against Francoism, befriending the girl protagonist Ana.

As we saw in Chapter 1, *The Spirit of the Beehive* is the paradigmatic Spanish art film. By alluding to it through its casting of Margallo, *Solitary Fragments* simultaneously distances itself from the mainstream and declares it allegiance to the tradition of prestige. It does this as well via its formal style, telling its story through the use of split-screen, long takes and static compositions without recourse to establishing shots. The lack of music on the soundtrack, the eccentric framing and the enigmatic use of off-screen space all serve to strongly differentiate the film from *The Orphanage*, as well as from the main winners of 2007, *Volver* and *Pan's Labyrinth*. The artless costume and art design (no costumes were designed specifically for the actors, the make-up and hair are natural) also distance *Solitary Fragments* from these other three films, all of which rely on skilled and complex art design, wardrobe and make-up, as well as costly special effects. Due to the flourishing of horror film-making bolstered by companies such as Filmax, Spain had become, in the early 2000s, an important training ground for experts in special effects and was developing a solid cadre of award-winning art and costume designers, such as Paco Delgado (who designed costumes for *Les Misérables* [Tom Hooper, 2012] and *Biutiful* [Alejandro González Iñárritu, 2010], and for a number of other widely acclaimed films).

Given these marked differences from previous winners, and from its direct competition in 2008, the Academia's choice of *Solitary Fragments* is therefore intriguing. Why would a lobby which is protectionist of the Spanish film industry and its professionals select a 'small' film when the industry relies so much on large ones? Perhaps the answer can be detected in two key events of 2007. Firstly, at a time when Spanish films were seldom selected for Cannes, this most prestigious of festivals picked *Solitary Fragments* for its Un Certain Regard section, as I noted earlier. The same year saw the introduction of the new Film Law, which committed to defending cultural diversity in the face of market forces that seemed to be inundating Spanish cinema with larger productions and safe box-office films. For an Academia sensitive about international, and especially French, esteem, and about its historical mission, both these facts would dispose it well to Rosales's film.

Moreover, a few months before the Gala of 2008, the Academia had selected *The Orphanage* to represent Spain at the Oscars, much to the acclaim of critics such as Sergi Sánchez, who saw this as an enlightened choice. Sánchez felt that the Academia usually only sent films that represented 'the conventions of Spanish cinema: social cinema with a message and revisionist historical cinema', films which were meaningful nationally but were not the type of cinema needed to compete abroad. 'Let us copy from here and there,' he wrote, 'let us show that we can make competent genre cinema' (p. 11). In the same article, Sánchez predicted that *The Orphanage* was going to triumph at the Goyas. It did not, and what we witnessed instead was the Academia's cinephile anxieties. The awards made to *Solitary Fragments* must be seen, then, as a sort of recalibration, a correcting of a potential bias towards the commercial. After the success of *Volver* and *Pan's Labyrinth* in 2007, one might have expected further success for a genre-inspired cinema in 2008, but in fact the opposite was the case: the success of genre cinema in the previous year made the success of *Solitary Fragments* more, not less, predictable.

A final point about the independent avant-garde cinema is that it cultivates anti-institutionalism and stresses its independence from the Academia's bureaucracy, all the while knowing full well that it relies on that bureaucracy. I started this chapter with the words of José Luis Guerín, a film-maker who did not sign the Collective's manifesto, although his producer Miñarro did. Guerín's declarations about the Academia in 2011 – in the midst of the clash between the president of the Academia and the Ministry of Culture that I discussed in the previous chapter – are worth quoting in full:

> These disagreements are more industrial than about film-making. For me the conflict lies elsewhere. The conflicts of the Academia may be very important but I don't think they are about cinema. The Academia is very important vis-à-vis production, but respectfully, it's not the space where cinema lives. I have great respect for those colleagues who deal with these issues because I could not deal with them, but I don't think the Academia is where film-makers meet. (Guerín cited in Belinchón *et al.*, 'Cine español', n.p.)

Guerín's relationship with the Academia, like Almodóvar's, provides an example of a film-maker who has succeeded in staying marginal to an institution that has awarded few prizes to him. His only win has been the Goya for Best Documentary Film in 2001 with *En construcción/Work in Progress* (2001), a much acclaimed film, which was also given that year's Special Jury Prize at the International Film Festival of San Sebastian and the National Cinema Prize. Such prizes make for a good springboard to the national film industry. Yet Guerín is a key example of those 'who accrue advantage or profit as they distance themselves from culture's bureaucratic epicentres' (English, p. 41). Such independent film-makers can remain anti-institutional and only mobilise when their funding sources are put under threat. They can maintain the position that films and film-making are not, in their view, what matter to the Academia. They can even engage in prize-bashing rhetoric and defend their ideas from the inside, from the most prestigious publications: Miñarro's words quoted at the beginning of this chapter come from *Cahiers du Cinéma España*. The Academia has to take it, precisely because, as I explained in the first chapter, it declares inclusivity and pluralism in its mission statement. More importantly, without the independent avant-garde player, Spanish cinema loses its place among the world cinemas that matter. Guerín's work, always at the cusp of documentary and fiction, for instance, is clearly related to Érice's techniques in *El sol del membrillo/The Quince Tree Sun* (1992) (Caputo, n.p.). Like Guerín, Érice is not a prolific film-maker, but one with impeccable European influences (see Danks, n.p.), who is often cited as influential to major art cinema film-makers.

In this chapter, we have seen how, in the period of study, the Academia's aspiration to be a unified professional body representing the entirety of Spain's film industry remained an aspiration. The hegemonic film culture has always concentrated on strengthening commercial cinema and supporting a national industry in the face of foreign competition, particularly from Hollywood. This position is clear in their support of the Miró Law and subsequent legislation, including the Film Law of 2007. As we have seen throughout this book, it is in the nature of the Academia, some of whose most powerful members are key players in the industry, to favour larger projects with Goyas and other forms of recognition. In the final chapter, I will trace what happens when the focus shifts to the transnational industrial context in which Spanish cinema has to perform.

6
Transatlantic Academia

This chapter focuses on the Academia's transnational strategies. Between 1986 and 2011, the Spanish Film Academy was mostly concerned with its own formation as a national institution, and with the creation and support of national awards and ceremonies, such as the Goyas and the Galas. Despite this emphasis on the 'inside', the Academia has also engaged in transnational projection towards Latin America, assuming from its inception a position as the geopolitical centre of film cultures in Spanish as well as of the film cultures within Spain. It has done this automatically, instinctively. In recent years, however, the challenges to this position have mounted up, as I aim to show here.

Whether the Academia admits it or not, the outside has defined it and affected its decisions. We have seen evidence of this throughout this book, and particularly in the last chapter, where I showed how Spanish avant-garde film culture is motivated by themes and styles that are transnational, and that travel through the international festival circuit. The directors I discussed in Chapter 5 have developed strategies similar to those of other transnational auteurs (see, for instance, Barrow, pp. 137–54; Martin), and that has led them to keep the Academia – with its mostly industrial internal concerns that some of those film festival auteurs would regard as petty – at arm's length. But the Academia is also affected by the international circuit of value formation. When Cannes recognises Spanish cinema, the Academia follows: we saw this with the recalibration that took place with the Goya success of *Solitary Fragments* in 2007 after the film had been selected for Cannes. And, as we will see, this was not the only time Cannes has served as a beacon. But the most evident manner in which the outside has defined the Academia is the way in which it takes as its model AMPAS, the Hollywood Academy. This emulation has posed interesting challenges to the Academia, as can be seen in its adaptation of the Best Film award, which became the *Goya a la Mejor Película Extranjera de Habla Hispana*.

WHAT HOLLYWOOD WANTS ... AND WHAT IT GETS

The Oscar for Best Foreign-Language Film award dates from 1956. Before this, films in languages other than English and from nations other than the US had at times been presented honorary awards without undergoing a process of nomination and voting, as Robert Osborne explains. From the twenty-ninth Oscar ceremony onwards, however, international films not principally in English could be 'nominated and voted along with other awards' (p. 140). In this manner, AMPAS normalised the recognition of excellence in film-making beyond Hollywood and beyond the English language.

In introducing this award, AMPAS made itself the arbiter of film-making around the world, an imperialist move that has been studied in depth by film scholars. As the Oscars became the hegemonic prizes, the foreign-film award grew in prestige and importance and became a key element in deciding what mattered and what did not in world cinema. In the same way as film festivals and other instruments that parcel out cinema for audience consumption, the foreign-film award worked to categorise and ghettoise world cinema as a single unit, 'disregarding its diversity and complexity', as Stephanie Dennison and Song Hwee Lim argue (p. 7). One key concern of those who, like Dennison and Lim, have studied the power dynamics involved in the categorisation of the rest by the English-speaking West has been to reveal how this mapping of otherness favours films that offer an alternative to Hollywood. This means that, traditionally, films that differentiate themselves by not following Hollywood's most popular generic patterns are the ones that count as 'world' or, in AMPAS parlance, 'foreign'.

When it established the Best Foreign-Language Film award, AMPAS set up a selection system by which recognised partners in each film-making country could put forward a film each year for the consideration of members. In Spain, the Academia has been this recognised partner since 1986. Up until 2001, the film selected for the consideration of AMPAS was voted for by all Academia members, as was the case with the Goyas (see Santamarina, 'Academia', p. 28). From 2001, as the Academia website explains, in the first round all the members vote for their favourite from a list of eligible films, after which a notary selects the top three and, in a second voting round, the academicians choose the one to be sent to AMPAS.[1] The final choice is publicly announced in September prior to the Oscars ceremony. Every year since its formation, the Academia has submitted a film, and, at the time of writing, three of these have won the Oscar: *Belle Époque*, *All About My Mother* and *The Sea Inside*.

It is worth remembering that the Academia, during the period of this study, was principally preoccupied with the monitoring of internal film cultures by establishing awards of excellence for the guidance of internal consumers. Through the 'Goya effect' (Brunet, pp. 4–6), mediating between films and audiences and giving the Goya winners a second theatrical life, the Academia has to a large extent succeeded in guiding the taste of audiences in Spain. But sending a selection to satisfy the taste of others – of the Hollywood academicians – requires another type of knowledge. What can we learn from the assumptions the Academia has made about the tastes of the Hollywood Academy? Besides casting doubts on whether the academicians know enough about American culture, what we learn from the lively debates about what will or will not please AMPAS is that the Academia's choices have been surprising at times, and on occasions symptomatic of generational change or of changes in the industry.

As Ángel Fernández-Santos explained in an article in 1996 entitled 'A Coherent Contradiction', members of the Academia use different criteria when selecting films for the Goyas and for the Oscars. He declared, revealingly, that the motives for selection are strategic and indeed predetermined: for the Goyas, the academicians were not simply selecting their favourite film, but often one that is convenient to vote for because it has been made by friends (the critic confesses that this is sadly often the case), while for the Oscars, those strategic interests were less of a concern. According to Fernández-Santos, with the foreign-language Oscar, guesswork is more important than networks – that is, selections are made to satisfy what are believed to be the tastes of the academicians in Hollywood ('Una coherente contradiccíon', p. 40). How this knowledge is arrived at is not fully explained in the article.

Fernández-Santos explains that, in an informal conversation with a group of academicians, only two films were discussed as possible candidates that year: *Bwana* (Imanol Uribe, 1996) and de la Iglesia's *The Day of the Beast. Bwana* is a drama/thriller about a working-class couple (played by Andrés Pajares, known for his work in Saura's *¡Ay, Carmela!*, and María Barranco, who was brought to international fame in Almodóvar's *Women on the Verge of a Nervous Breakdown*). One afternoon they find on the beach two men, Ombasi and Yambo, washed up on the shore trying to reach Europe from Africa. The film deals with the subject of illegal immigration and racism in Spain, a country experiencing increased migration in the 1990s, and where multiculturalism had been more an aspiration than a reality. Fernández-Santos, an academician himself, felt that *Bwana* dealt with universal themes – racism and immigration – that would resonate with members of the Academy. For the critic and his fellow academicians, *The Day of the Beast*, on the other hand, was a bit too 'local' and, at the same time, too indebted to Hollywood. The film is a horror/comedy about a Basque Catholic priest who goes to Madrid to prevent the rise of the devil on Christmas Eve, 1995. Hugely popular in Spain, both with audiences and critics, the film's outlandish plot cloaks a deep criticism of the media, and of the neoliberal economic policies and their effects in the capital city and in the country more widely (see Buse, Triana-Toribio and Willis, pp. 54–75). In the end, the Academia sent *Bwana* to Hollywood.

The main arguments Fernández-Santos cites in defence of the Academia's choice are vague and impressionistic: that a drama with some comedic elements will go down better than a horror comedy, that AMPAS favours films that deal with 'present-day concerns' (such as illegal immigration) over films that do not (disregarding *The Day of the Beast*'s engagement with contemporary politics). What is not stated but latent in this article is the perception that *The Day of the Beast* – and indeed de la Iglesia's work in general – is too reliant on Hollywood models. As Buse, Triana-Toribio and Willis point out, there are allusions to *Elmer Gantry* (Richard Brooks, 1960) in the title credit sequence, and the film's diegesis 'cites heavily from the iconography of the satanic horror movie which had become a very popular cycle in the early to mid-1970s following the worldwide success of *Rosemary's Baby* (Roman Polansky, 1968)' (p. 61). Fernández-Santos does not explain this in detail, but argues that the subject matter seemed too close to Hollywood: 'it concerns itself with a theme that has been frequently the subject matter of Hollywood films' ('Una coherente contradiccíon', p. 40). In short, there is in *The Day of the Beast* too much Hollywood to be sent to Hollywood.

Fernández-Santos may well have been right in suggesting that the Hollywood Academy would not be interested in awarding the 'foreign' Oscar to what some regard as an imitation of Hollywood. This is a widely shared assumption, and one that was explained in 2015 by Wendy Mitchell of *Screen International*, just at the time when the long shortlist for the foreign Oscar was announced. Her thoughts clearly chime with what Fernández-Santos had expressed in 1996:

Of course, the wonderful thing about most of those 83 foreign language films is that they aren't trying to emulate US indies or studio blockbusters (America is doing just fine making those itself, thanks very much). They are introducing audiences to new approaches, new voices, or people and places they wouldn't otherwise see on screen (even if universal themes emerge). It's the foreign films that don't have a strong sense of place or identity that feel more pointless. To make a generic cop drama is no way to make a mark on the global scene. (n.p.)

Whether generic or not, *Bwana* did not even make it to the shortlist that year, and we will never know whether the Academia guessed rightly that *The Day of the Beast* would not have fared any better. Judging by how it was misread by some US academic critics as retrograde and conservative when it was clearly a progressive film that expressed prescient suspicions about the economic corruption of Spanish elites, perhaps the academicians were right to hold it back (see Buse, Triana-Toribio and Willis, pp. 55–60).

The success of *The Sea Inside* in 2005 was interpreted as evidence that AMPAS looks for films that 'aren't trying to emulate US indies or studio blockbusters' and which can claim universal themes rather than being too local. But internal priorities, as we saw in Chapter 3 on Almodóvar and the Academia, sometimes trump such pragmatism. So, in 2003, *Talk to Her*, winner of the Golden Globe for Best Foreign-Language Film, was passed over for *Mondays in the Sun* as the film selected for AMPAS consideration. The main factors that this timid realist film had in its favour were that it starred Javier Bardem and dealt with the problem of unemployment in Spain. Crucially, it was made at a time when the conservative PP was in power, and the reviews of this film show how it could be used to embarrass the government for its neoliberal policies that had contributed to the destruction of industrial jobs. AMPAS ignored the Academia's choice (Spain was not in fact shortlisted), and the Best Foreign-Language Film award went to the German film *Nirgendwo in Afrika/Nowhere in Africa* (Caroline Link, 2001). As we saw in Chapter 3, this was also the year when *Talk to Her* won the Best Original Screenplay award.

A decade after Fernández-Santos's reflections on what the Spanish Academy thinks Hollywood Academy wants, Sergi Sánchez, writing in *Fotogramas*, tried to explain the Academia's decision of 2007. This time the Academia had changed its 'painfully conservative' strategy (in Sánchez's words), a change inspired, in his view, by the success of *Pan's Labyrinth* in several categories at the Oscars (a success that has to be tempered with the fact that the foreign-film award that year went to *The Lives of Others* [Florian Henckel von Donnersmack, 2006]). The Academia changed its strategy and went for the 'genre but with aspirations' of Bayona's *The Orphanage*, with its clear debt to Hollywood (and which was discussed in the Introduction). Here the rule about sending 'Hollywood back to Hollywood' was openly ignored. This is because what seemed to be criteria dictated by knowledge about Hollywood were in fact guided by internal priorities: Spain's box-office returns for Spanish films had been dire in 2006, and *The Orphanage* was performing well. Sánchez suggested that shortlisting this film for the foreign-language Oscar would encourage audiences even more.

TAINTED LOVE: GOOD THINGS COME FROM BAD PRIZES

As well as generating debates inside the Academia, the Best Foreign-Language Film award was the inspiration for a Goya category. As Ana Arrieta, director of the Academia between 1996 and 2008 and a custodian of knowledge about the institution's early life, explained in an interview, 'nobody contacted Hollywood to obtain the submission criteria; no one spoke English in those days. We just wanted to create something similar to what Hollywood had' (n.p.). In the first year of the Goyas, the Academia introduced a category to mirror the foreign-language film Oscar, but adapted it to refer to Spanish spoken outside Spain, mainly in Latin America. The award became *Goya a la Mejor Película Extranjera de Habla Hispana*/Best Spanish-Language Foreign Film, which then was renamed *Mejor Película Hispanoamericana*/Best Hispano-American Film in 2007.

The terms Hispanic and Hispano-American were not understood as synonymous with Latin American in this case, as they sometimes can be. At the start, the prize regulations ensured that Brazilian productions were excluded, since the films must have as 'main or basic' language one of the official languages of Spain or the Spanish-speaking countries (including Catalan, Basque and also Quechua or Aymara, but not Portuguese). Theatrical release in Spain was not a condition, but theatrical release and screening for seven consecutive days in the country of production was. A further rule stipulated that the film be put forward for consideration by the Academia members through the country's own Academia (as is the case in Chile, Mexico and Argentina) or through a comparable professional body (for instance, in the case of Cuba) (see Academia, *Bases*, pp. 12–13). In 2013, after the period covered in this study, the prize was amended and the language criterion relaxed to include Portuguese. The new rules are only territorial and now the prize can be awarded to Brazilian and Portuguese films. Such amplification does not respond to any specific threat, but simply to the much tougher competitive conditions for production and exhibition that non-Hollywood audiovisual products face and which has led to greater integration in the industry.

In its desire to emulate AMPAS and the Oscars as closely as possible, the Academia did in fact the opposite of Hollywood. Instead of choosing from among what is *not* in their national language, the language criterion dictated that only the official national languages should be considered. It may seem a very short step from promoting Spanish films to promoting films in Spanish, but the impulse here is certainly not the same as the one behind the foreign-language Oscar. It is worth interrogating this 'natural' impulse of the Spanish Academia to position itself at the centre of film-making in Spanish in 1986, thus assuming from Europe the role of its arbiter.

Such an action indicates a not-so-residual Eurocentric and imperialist mindset in Spanish cultural institutions such as the Academia that sees Latin American countries as former colonies first and foremost. This default colonialist and paternalistic attitude is part of what Néstor García-Canclini calls the 'persistence of the *legados coloniales* [colonial legacies]' (p. 83) and is certainly at work in the Goya award for the Best Spanish-Language Foreign Film. Colonial legacies, according to García-Canclini, are 'the narrations forged during the colonial epoch and which government officials, journalists and writers still use' (ibid.). Phrases such as *mercado cultural natural* (natural cultural market), *encuentro intercultural* (intercultural meeting) and *idioma compartido* (shared language) hide the fact that, as García-Canclini puts it:

> It was not an encounter as if two societies got together in the middle of the Atlantic for a pleasant exchange, but a history of battles and impositions. Deconstructive criticism is still necessary whilst the images destined to mask violence and domination persist in international cultural fairs, school books and the discourse of the Iberoamerican governmental meetings where the enthusiasm for businesses in 'common' eschews the conflict from the memory's imaginaries. (ibid., p. 88)

By placing itself at the centre of film-making in Spanish, the Academia brushes under the carpet these histories of violence and domination, while indulging in what Ella Shohat and Robert Stam characterise in *Unthinking Eurocentrism* as a persistent Eurocentrism naturalised as common sense (p. 1).

A recent study by Silvia Rodríguez Maeso and Marta Araújo defines Eurocentrism as 'a paradigm for interpreting (past, present and future) reality that uncritically establishes the idea of European and Western historical progress/achievement and its political and ethical superiority, based on scientific rationality and the construction of the rule of law' (p. 1). The critique of the discourse of Eurocentrism in the early 1990s by Shohat and Stam, and continued by scholars such as Rodríguez Maeso and Araújo, has transformed postcolonial studies of media, but the critique needs to be constantly restated in film, audiovisual and media studies. These writers brought our attention to the situatedness of interventions by Europe or the West into global film festivals, awards systems and funding pools. These interventions are not made on an even playing field, for, as Shohat and Stam establish at several junctures, Hollywood and AMPAS are Eurocentric in privileging Europe-originated cultural production.

During a series of interviews I conducted with various Spanish film academicians and other key stakeholders in 2013/14, when I asked if they felt there was anything Eurocentric at work in establishing a foreign film in Spanish award, with the Academia as its privileged arbiters, they seemed puzzled by my question. I put it to them that the Academia was imitating a controversial and imperialist Oscar category, and pointed out that the AMPAS foreign-film category is frequently criticised for reducing all world cinemas to films that happen not to be in English (see, for instance, Mitchell; Lodge). They responded that the Goya category was in fact very beneficial and did much to raise the profile of Latin American cinema, which is of course true. Inspired though it may be by an unthinking Eurocentrism, this bad prize has come to do good things for Latin American film-makers and films.

A PRIZE, COMPROMISE AND CONTRADICTIONS

The Goya for the Best Spanish-Language Foreign Film did not emerge in a political and cultural vacuum, and the Academia's neocolonialist default mode needs to be explained. In the 1980s, the focus of Spain's nascent democratic diplomacy was not Latin America. When the Academia was created, the governing PSOE had thrown its weight behind linking Spain with 'Europeanism and modernity' and consolidating the relationship between Spain and the US (Balfour and Quiroga, p. 292). In the process, the so-called historical and highly problematic links with Latin America, tainted with ideas of responsibility and perhaps even the need for reparation, were neglected (ibid.). Of course, films from Latin America have never made up the largest proportion of the foreign films distributed in Spain. Unsurprisingly, the majority 'foreign' cinema in Spain originates from the US. In fact, in the late 1980s and early 90s, the presence of films from Latin America in Spanish screens dipped. In the three years from 1992 to 1994, only fifteen films from Latin American countries were distributed in Spain (Sánchez and Martialay, p. 90).

Even if it was starting from a low base, then, there were in the late 1980s good economic reasons for reviving old-fashioned and ideologically suspect concepts of the neocolonialist mindset which see Latin America as Spain's *mercado cultural natural*. Even while it was turning towards Europe, the Spanish film industry had a strong rationale for allying itself with other industries in Spanish. Spain's entry into the EU meant that it had to accept new regulations for the circulation of European films within Spain, which posed another possible threat to home-grown productions (see Riambau, 'La década', p. 404). The shared language could help to combat the hegemony of Hollywood, but also to compete against other European films. Supporting Spanish-language productions was not just a commonly held aspiration, but part of a wider survival strategy. For Spain, the late 1980s meant the deregulation of European state-controlled broadcasters, and the early 90s were filled with uncertainty over the looming GATT agreements, in which the US wanted to include audiovisual products. The calls for developing the *mercado cultural natural* were affected by these factors, and further encouraged by the cultural exchanges around the quincentenary of 1492.

Changes took place in Spanish cultural policy discourse – including in the Academia – after 1992. This is a crucial year in the life of Spain's view of Latin America, marking a critical before and after. The commemoration of what was for some the 'discovery of America', and for others the inauspicious and unlucky arrival of Christopher Colombus, brought forth contradictory discourses about Latin America in Spain. As Balfour and Quiroga explain, for the Spanish right and its main representative the PP, the relationship between Spain and Latin America is one in which Spain owes a 'cultural debt to Latin America'. For the right, this debt means that, on cultural matters, Spain should lead and all Latin America, without exception, follow (p. 324).

The left-wing discourse departs from a position of colonial guilt and thus avoidance of the past which manifested itself at the start as a preference to concentrate on links with Europe and the US during the transition to democracy. The Academia shared this position, particularly at its inception, since, as we saw in the first and second chapters, its founding members were either card-carrying Socialist Party members or known sympathisers who had taken part in the anti-Francoist movement. Equally, the Academia, as we saw in Chapters 1 and 4, had Europe on its horizon not only in the awards it created and in the film legislation it lobbied for (such as the Miró Law, which was modelled on the French film legislation), but also in the auteurist models of European cinema it espoused.

However, once the Europe-first strategy and the avoidance of Latin America had run its course, the discourse on the left changed, as politicians and academicians alike became increasingly aware of the risks of paternalism and more attuned to ideas of reciprocity and mutual respect and dependence, at least on paper. This attitude that departs from guilt and paternalism, but tends towards ideas of mutual collaboration, explains the trajectory of the Goya for Best Spanish-Language Foreign Film, which has undergone a number of tweaks and changes during its short existence. These changes are as good as an admission of uncertainty, or even unease, about its purpose. As I mentioned at the start, the name and the criteria changed in 2007, removing the word 'foreign' from the rubric, and introducing the term 'Hispano-Americano'. Then the criteria changed again in 2013 to include Brazilian and other Portuguese-language films. Indicatively, other prizes were created, widening the pool of 'foreign' films in which the Academia tries to locate excellence. In addition, in 1993, a Goya for the Best European Film was introduced, sending out the message loud and clear that the Academia was not simply preoccupied with locating quality in Hispano America (its ex-colonies), but also in countries with which it had no colonial past (and no guilt).

The right of the Academia to pass judgment on all Hispano-American film has not gone unchallenged by other institutions. In 2000, the actions of the Academia Mexicana de Artes y Ciencias Cinematográficas (AMACC) spoke louder than words. This Academia, with a longer history than its Spanish counterpart, established the *Ariel de Oro a la Mejor Película Iberoamericana*/Golden Ariel to the Best Ibero-American Film award, boldly staking a claim for their academicism in deciding what is excellent in films in Spanish. The Mexican film industry is traditionally one of the strongest in the continent, with its vitality partly derived from its proximity to Hollywood, so it is not exempt from cinematic power dynamics within the Americas. Nevertheless, it is clear that as Spain becomes more aware of its geopolitical and cultural vulnerability as just one country among many that speaks Spanish – and more recently a country in economic crisis facing booming Latin American economies – we may witness more adjustments to this award.

The Academia's attitude towards Latin American cinema is greatly affected by the long-standing practice of co-production, particularly with Mexico and Argentina, and by the constant transatlantic traffic of film professionals and films since the 1930s. Although the co-production as a form of financing films jointly by Spain and Latin America had been more or less abandoned in the 1980s, the practice was resuscitated after 1992, and intensified as the Council of Europe established Eurimages, a funding pool to help the co-production, distribution and exhibition of European cinema (see Otero, pp. 17–27). By 2007, Jennifer Green, Spain and Portugal correspondent for *Screen International*, reported that while Spanish producers were focused principally on European territories, nevertheless 'Spain has long been the first port of call for Latin American productions seeking financing and entry to Europe' (p. 2). Indeed, many founding Academia members were already engaged in co-productions with Latin America. Gerardo Herrero, president of the Academia in 1994, was involved in key Latin American films as producer of, among others, Francisco Lombardi's *La boca del lobo/In the Mouth of the Wolf* (Peru/Spain, 1988) and Juan Carlos Tabío and Tomás Gutiérrez Alea's *Guantanamera* (Cuba/Spain, 1995) (Herrero, p. 87). Other academicians were born in Latin America and moved to Spain or worked in both. Lima-born, multi-Goya winner Fernando Fernán Gómez and Amparo Rivelles, who worked in the 1970s in Argentina, I have already discussed as paragons of Spanish acting in Chapter 2. Key Academia members through the period of study had transatlantic careers in an industry with porous borders.

It is through industrial and professional concerns that I want to explore the uses of the Goya for the Best Hispano-American Film. The award helped build the Goya as a brand beyond the confines of the nation and secured distribution of the films in Spain. But more importantly, and in a retroactive loop, it was perceived as helping Latin American professionals gain access to European cinema. As Stephanie Dennison explains, it has always been widely believed that co-productions have this effect: '[f]or Latin American film-makers and producers, the main impetus for collaborating with producers from Spain ... is to increase a film's chances of entering both/either the Spanish TV market, and/or the European cinema circuit' (p. 14). European prizes, whether awarded by international film festivals or national institutions such as the Academia, are alternative vehicles that may lead to this Holy Grail of access to Europe. In the words of the Chilean director Matías Bize, winner in 2010 for his film *La vida de los peces/Fish Life* (2010), this is the allure of the Goya for the Best Hispano-American Film:

> For us the Goya is crucial. I think myself lucky. You may not be aware of the importance of the Goya, but it opens many doors, it helps with distribution of the film in other countries, it even launches the film in Spain. For Hispano America, it's a fundamental award, one which you access after a long selection process. (Belinchón, 'Entrevista a Matías Bize', n.p.)

On a smaller scale than AMPAS's foreign-language Oscar, *Fish Life*'s Goya turned the spotlight on the film and its director, but also on Chile as a film-making nation, with articles in national newspapers and interviews with Bize. When the film was premiered, four months later in April 2011, the so-called 'Goya effect' (Brunet, pp. 4–6) took over and it was reviewed (always mentioning the award) in *Fotogramas* (Vall, n.p.), *Cahiers du Cinéma España* (Pena, p. 33) and other monthly film magazines.

The prize may issue from a bad place – from a Eurocentric attitude and imperialist mindset – but in a crowded market in which producers, distributors and film-makers are seeking any slight advantage, such awards are invaluable. Liz Czach has noted the 'critical capital' at stake in such prizes, and how 'the value that a film accrues through its success in the festival circuit' (p. 82) is displayed prominently on posters and publicity material, becoming indispensable to the overall promotion and distribution of a film (see also Elsaesser, p. 87). The Goya has become a coveted badge of honour, as Bize confirms in his testimonial about the prize.

IDEAL LATIN AMERICA

When the Academia awards a Goya to a Spanish film, it is holding up that film as a model to emulate. Does the Hispano-American Goya perform the same function? The answer must be no, but a qualified no. The process of selection of films at their origin is similar to Spain's selection process for the Oscars (and, since 2000, for the Mexican Ariel). Each academy or equivalent institution, in selecting for the Spanish

Academia, chooses what is 'best' within the annual output according to their own criteria. The academicians in Spain do not envisage that, by picking a winner, they are holding up a model of film-making, certainly not for a whole continent of disparate film-making cultures. Even so, the academicians' choices still reveal much about their ideal of Hispano-American cinema. Over the three decades of the prize, there have been two clear periods, the break between the two marked by generational change:

1. From 1986 until 2004/5, the auteurist generation at the heart of the Academia chose winners from its corresponding generation in Latin America.
   Their counterparts in Latin America, born mainly in the 1940s and early 50s, trained or were exiled in Europe in many cases, making the links and interactions between these two groups strong. Many of the films selected are politically committed, condemning dictatorships in the manner of Luis Puenzo's *La historia oficial/The Official History*, foreign-language Oscar winner of 1986. A favourite of the academicians was three-time winner Argentinian Eduardo Mignogna (1940–2006), with fellow Argentinian Carlos Sorin a clear second.
2. A second period begins around 2005 with the Uruguayan film *Whisky* (Juan Pablo Rebella and Pablo Stoll, 2004) (both directors born in 1974). In May 2004, *Whisky* had won the FIPRESCI and Un Certain Regard awards at Cannes. From 2005, all winners, with the exception of Alejandro Doria's *Las manos/The Hands* (2006) in 2007, were from the new generation of film-makers, mainly born after 1970. Interestingly, and leaving aside *Whisky*, these post-2005 choices do not signal a preference in the Academia for the Latin American arthouse 'festival film', a recognisable product resulting from global cinephilic taste and transnational production strategies (see Galt and Schoonover's *Global Art Cinema*). Rather than victories for the typical festival films of Lisardo Alonso, Lucrecia Martel, Josué Méndez or Carlos Reygadas, the Academia's choices correspond in this period to the Latin American middlebrow – for instance, *La buena vida/The Good Life* (Andrés Wood, 2008), or *Fish Life*.

In terms of the countries selected, we could argue that for the Academia, at the time of writing, Hispano-American mostly means Argentinian, since Argentinian films won in 1986, 1992, 1993, 1996, 1997, 1998, 2000, 2001, 2003, 2005, 2006, 2007, 2009, 2010, 2012 and 2015, taking sixteen out of twenty-nine prizes. It is tempting to see this affinity with Argentinian films as related to the fact that these stories emanate from professionals working in Argentina, a predominantly white European nation with lifestyles and concerns closer to those of Spaniards. Argentina is notorious among the Latin American nations, because its native population was decimated through war and other forms of state violence during the eighteenth and nineteenth centuries. However, there is a counterargument to the idea that affinity in taste and interests may be affecting the academicians' choices. In most Latin American countries, the social groups most likely to access film-making come from the middle class, and are thus, invariably, of European white ancestry – even in countries where the proportion of indigenous population is larger (Peru, for instance, with 31 per cent in 2014).

CHALLENGES FOR THE ACADEMIA: THE CROSSOVER LATIN AMERICAN FILM AT THE GOYAS

This primacy of Argentinian cinema for the Academia was strongly in evidence in 2010. In this year, a crossover took place, and a film that was nominated for Best Hispano-American Film was also nominated in multiple main Goya categories. It was a co-production with Argentina: *El secreto de sus ojos/The Secret in Their Eyes* (Juan José Campanella, 2009). *The Secret* was nominated for Best Film, Best Director, Best Adapted Screenplay (Campanella and Eduardo Sacheri), Best Leading Actor, Best New Actress (for Soledad Villamil, although her career spanned two decades in Argentina) and Best Music (Federico Jusid). Villamil and Jusid won and so did the film in the Best Hispano-American Film category. *The Secret in Their Eyes* went on to become Argentina's entry for the foreign-language Oscar in 2010, a prize that it also won. In addition, the film reaped multiple awards from its own national academy (Campanella, Sacheri, Villamil and Jusid were selected again) and received the Mexican Academy's Golden Ariel for the Best Ibero-American Film. The film itself was something of a crossover, which may have been the secret to its success. It is a good example of what Spanish critics approvingly call an ambitious genre film – or genre film with aspirations – which we discussed in the Introduction and at other junctures in this book: a thriller, the film has clear resonances with the dictatorship and the 'dirty war' in Argentina between 1974 and 1983.

Crossover films are revealing of change and challenge traditional categories. For example, *Pan's Labyrinth*, which I discussed in the Introduction, fitted the political agenda of the Socialist Party by addressing historical memory, but it was also a genre film, drawing heavily on the conventions of fantasy and horror, and through this capturing large audiences. This Spanish co-production with Mexico also threw up interesting challenges for the classificatory bodies of national industries' awards in Spain, Mexico and the US. It was Mexico's entry for the foreign-language Oscar (which it did not win), but it was also nominated for Oscars in Best Cinematography, Art Direction and Make-up, winning them all. As we saw earlier, the Goyas for Best Original Screenplay and Cinematography went to the Mexicans del Toro and Navarro.

The degree of overlap and the contradictions in award-giving that these cases reveal to a very significant extent with the film industries of Argentina, and to a lesser extent with the Mexican industry, were to be expected. Moreover, as co-productions became the norm through the first decade of the millennium, this type of crossover between nominations for the main awards and the Goya for the Best Hispano-American Film increased. Nor is this a phenomenon exclusive to Spanish-language film industries. As cinema becomes less fenced in by national borders, the sustainability of 'foreign' awards – be they Spanish, Mexican or from the US – becomes more questionable.

As I noted earlier, there are English-language industry voices arguing strongly that 'Cinema is never "foreign".' In the lead-up to the foreign-language Oscar in 2014, Wendy Mitchell reiterated that

> [i]t is worth arguing for the umpteenth time that some of these films are among the best of the year, not just the best of the year *not* in the English language. It would be great to see the

Academy take more risks by nominating international films across categories, not just ring-fencing them. (n.p.).

Are there similar voices within the Academia calling on it to nominate Latin American films across categories even in the cases when these are not co-productions with Spain? The possibility is contemplated in the rules of the Spanish-language prize, and perhaps there will soon be a demand for cinema in Spanish and Portuguese no longer to be thought of as 'foreign'.

HISPANIC TRANSNATIONAL COLLABORATIVE NETWORKS

The Best Hispano-American Film award is also a symptom of the increased dialogue among the industries in Spanish-speaking countries and their institutions.
The Spanish and Mexican academies nominate films to compete for each other's awards, and the Argentinian and Chilean academies put forward films for consideration. This exchange is a facet of more meaningful collaboration among the academies, alongside other national bodies such as the national film institutes, as part of what Deborah Shaw calls a transnational collaborative network ('Deconstructing', p. 63).

From the early 1990s, it became clear that Spanish institutions were keen to renew links with other Spanish-speaking film industries. The Academia's official magazine, *Academia*, published in April 1995 its tenth issue, entitled *Latinoamérica años 90*. It featured on its cover a still from *Caballos salvajes/Wild Horses* (1995) by Marcelo Piñeyro, a road movie set in Patagonia starring the Argentine/Spanish actor Héctor Alterio, as well as Argentinian actor Leonardo Sbraglia, who has a substantial career in Spain. The issue contains articles by some of the best-known film professionals and critics at the time from Argentina (Diego Batlle, Adolfo Aristarain, Alberto Lecchi, Cecilia Roth), Bolivia (Jorge San Jinés), Chile (Ricardo Larraín), Colombia (Sergio Cabrera), Cuba (Jesús Díaz, Julio García Espinosa, Juan Carlos Tabío), Mexico (Guillermo del Toro, Carlos Monsiváis, María Novaro, Arturo Ripstein), Peru (Miguel Barreda, Giovanna Pollarolo), Spain (Ángel Amigo, Antonio Banderas, Agustín Díaz Yánes, Gerardo Herrero, Joaquín Jordà) and Venezuela (Roman Chalbaud).
These articles and short comment pieces, as well as attesting to the long history of excellent film-making and the potential still untapped in the region, lamented the mutual lack of knowledge of each others' cinema traditions, the difficulties in financing in any territory and the obstacles to distribution among Latin American screens. It has always been difficult for, say, Peruvians to see Mexican, Bolivian or even Spanish films in their theatres, since film traffic is mediated by the US, even among Spanish-speaking countries. As Giovanna Pollarolo put it, for a Latin American film to premiere in another Latin American country, it was still contingent on the film succeeding first in the US, by winning an Oscar, or being distributed by one of the majors (p. 67).

The writers repeatedly emphasised the need to capitalise on the shared language and cultural ties. A very candid article by Ángel Amigo declared that 'the commercial relationship between Spain and Latin-America is practically non-existent at present', and he explained that there was no specific cultural policy from the Spanish Film Institute regulating the relationships with Latin America, as well as no legal framework for them (pp. 84–5). The tone of the issue is sombre, with the writers lamenting the waste of a potential 'natural' market of over 300 million Spanish speakers. The Goya award to the Best Foreign Film in a Hispanic Language, as it was known then, was not mentioned as a mechanism that could secure more visibility for films in Spanish, but this is hardly surprising, since the Goyas themselves were in their infancy, and the 'Goya effect' (Brunet, p. 4) had not yet taken hold. And yet, producer Herrero – a key academician, once president and founder of Tornasol Films, one of Spain's main companies, which has a history of successful work in Latin America – argued already that the Goyas, used creatively and boldly, could contribute greatly to the marketing and publicity of films in Spanish (p. 87).

This *Latinoamérica años 90* issue of 1995 was timely and, with the benefit of hindsight, clearly part of a more extensive conversation taking place about the need for change. In its editorial entitled 'Un futuro común'/'Common Future', the Academia pledged its support for new developments:

> If Spain and the Latin countries share – as is the case – cultural codes, histories and feelings, if we are exporting ways and experiences of political cooperation, the time has come to acknowledge that this cooperation must reach the cultural market. Governments must understand – on both sides of the Atlantic – that film-making is yet another industrial reality and our market must be organized as a veritable common market, so that a film from Venezuela, or Mexico or Argentina, is considered (by audiences) in the same way as a Spanish film. And vice versa, of course.
>
> Establishing whatever it takes to achieve this goal – co-productions, global distribution, screen quotas – is a challenge and a necessity. Something to which this Academia can contribute. (p. 9)

In the following year, the first Summit of the Americas took place in Venezuela, a meeting of Spanish and Latin American heads of state where audiovisual industry matters took up much of the discussion. At the summit, the directors of Spanish and Latin American Film Institutes signed agreements that led in 1997 to the birth of Programa Ibermedia, an initiative inspired by the European Eurimages fund and which soon became the main funding pool for Latin American co-production (Programaibermedia.com). Ibermedia is a platform designed to 'incentivize co-production of fiction and documentary films' in a community of nineteen countries: Argentina, Bolivia, Brazil, Colombia, Costa Rica, Chile, Cuba, Dominican Republic, Ecuador, Guatemala, Mexico, Panama, Paraguay, Peru, Portugal, Puerto Rico, Spain, Uruguay and Venezuela (ibid.). Its declared mission is to 'create a Latin American audiovisual space' through, among other initiatives, subsidies open to 'all the film independent producers of the member countries' (ibid.).

As a key lobby for Spain's independent producers, the Academia has been a beneficiary of Ibermedia, the extent of which has been attested by a number of studies (see Falicov, pp. 67–88; Villazana). Conversely, the Goyas have contributed to the positive impact that Ibermedia claims to have in this new Latin American audiovisual space: *Historias mínimas/Intimate Stories* (2002), *Whisky* and *The Secret in Their Eyes* were all funded in part by Ibermedia. Of the other 'necessary' steps that the Academia declared itself ready to contribute to in 1995, awarding prizes to Ibermedia projects was one that it took on most willingly. In contrast, the collaboration among Spanish and Latin American academies did not go far beyond producing the lists of nominees for each others' Best Hispano-American or Ibero-American Film awards. In fact, the Academia seemed more interested in developing its ties with other European academies, as seen in the *encuentro de academias* (meeting of academies) that Spain hosted in Madrid after the Network of Film Academies meeting at the Karlovy Vary Film Festival in 2007 (Academia, 'La sede', p. 15). Stronger links started to be forged in 2011, during Enrique González Macho's first term as president of the Academia (2011) (see Lara, Personal interview, n.p.), but this did not take place until the end of my period of study. On 25 February 2013, academician José Garasino campaigned for the meeting of the academies of Latin America and Spain and the establishment of the Federación de Academias Iberoamericanas (see 'Se creó', n.p.) Sadly, Garasino died soon after the initial encounter.

The perception is strong that the future of the Academia depends on strengthening these links with the other Spanish-speaking film cultures of the world. Alongside this, the institution needs to negotiate its relationships with other film cultures that use not only Spanish but Catalan, Basque, Galician or Bable as their language but which are situated within the peninsular territory.

As I argued in the Introduction, the creation of the Academia sought a consensus and, by and large, has been working towards being an inclusive body, but there are challenges ahead, such as negotiating the relationship with Spanish cinema's second but crucial industrial base in Barcelona. The Catalan film industry created its own academy and its own response to the Goyas in 2002: the Acadèmia del Cinema Català and the Gaudí Awards. The Spanish Academia itself was the initiative of a Catalan man (Alfredo Matas) and the Goyas' trophy was designed by Berrocal, who was inspired by a sculpture by the Catalan sculptor Benlliure (see Vergés, n.p.). These two academies are situated side by side in Passeig de Colom in Barcelona and their relationship is one of collaboration, but the fact is that the good intentions of hosting the Goyas alternately in Madrid and Barcelona never took hold and hardly any film in Catalan has won a major Goya – one exception is the Catalan director Agustí Villaronga, who won the Best Film and the Best Director awards for *Pa negre/Black Bread* (2010) in 2011. Internal and transnational challenges lie ahead for the institution.

If this study covers the period between 1986 and 2011, it is because the change of government in 2011 brought momentous changes to Spanish cinema, changes that affected all film cultures. The PP brought in severe cuts to funding at the start of their term in power. As Paul Hamilos reported in *The Observer* in 2013, senior figures in the Spanish film industry perceived in these measures a form of revenge or vendetta on the part of the Spanish government (n.p.). The VAT (Value Added Tax, equivalent to the US/Canada's GST) for cultural consumption was raised to 21 per cent, making going to the cinema prohibitively expensive. Due to these new conditions (discussed further in the Epilogue to this book), the future of the film industry may well rest on its transatlantic connections, as Paul Julian Smith argues in the article by Hamilos (n.p.).

It will be in the Academia's interest to become part of the transnational instruments and navigate the future of Spanish-language film-making as a partner, albeit one with a long prestigious history and much talent to contribute. The Academia will continue to forge links with other film academies in Latin America, in the same way as Spanish producers, big and small, will continue to be aware that their survival depends greatly on negotiating and harnessing the financing power of supranational funding bodies such as Ibermedia.

We must accept the Academia's nature as a professional organisation with members who are powerful players in the industry. Therefore, whatever shape its transnational strategy takes after the period of study, it will always retain a core of nationalist protectionism of the commercial and industrial interests of its membership. The only difference is likely to be that the national industry whose interests are defended will not solely be Spain's, but will also include those of other Latin American territories with which Spain teams as production partner.

Epilogue

This book has shown how a generation of professionals prepared the Spanish film industry for what they assumed would be its, and their, dual role in democracy: to provide, in order of importance, culture, education and entertainment to Spanish audiences, while acting as a beacon to the world of what the newly democratic nation could achieve culturally. I have concentrated on one instrument they crafted to deliver these aims: the Academia.

Both the institution and its effects have guided my exploration into what worked and what did not work, into which film-makers and films found fertile ground in the conditions created by new and improved funding mechanisms, newly created or repurposed awards and other types of support, and which ones did not. I have explained how 'desirable' films received prizes, and I have also shown how undesirable fare was screened out when it was deemed unsuited for audiences in a newly democratic country, finally joining Europe in every sense. In short, I have looked inside and outside the Academia to see the form that film cultures took.

Some of the key members of the Academia are very powerful and influential in the industry and have the ears of politicians, but the Academia itself is not a wealthy institution, which makes it vulnerable. A non-profit organisation, it is financed principally by membership fees, supplemented by contributions from partners and the state. Many of its best plans in the period of study had to be abandoned, such as the collaboration between the Academia and film historians and other academics, or the publication of the more scholarly periodical *Cuadernos de la Academia*, which president Borau championed during his tenure. Some annual internal prizes have effectively become biannual due to financial constraints.

Whatever the financial restrictions of the past, academicians are no doubt feeling nostalgic for those days. The Academia was born in the early years of a Spanish Socialist government that was strongly committed to investment in cultural projects, an outlook that enjoyed a brief return with the PSOE administration of 2004–11. The international financial and banking crisis, which hit Spain harder than others, meant that members of the Academia waited anxiously for the outcome of the general election of 20 November 2011 and how it would affect the Spanish film industry. The election was of course won decisively by the right-wing Partido Popular, which is why my study ends in 2011. The election result and what followed marked the end of an era, as the incoming party made clear it would be championing austerity and the shrinking of the state, including – indeed especially – support for culture.

Even before an election result unfavourable to state support of arts and culture, the Academia knew what was coming. In June 2011, a letter from the then president Enrique González Macho let it be known that the Academia was preparing for a change in fortune:

> La Academia is the visible head of an industrial sector facing an uncertain future alongside Europe's and Spain's economy. It is this uncertainty that tells me we must steer a firm course through the storm, sail our ship through the hurricane of change and above all, regain pride in a profession which has been very much maligned in recent years, mostly unfairly and for reasons not connected with how we perform our professional roles. (González Macho, 'Carta del Presidente', p. 44)

By December 2011, with the PP returned with a majority government, González Macho was admitting his 'disquiet' at the election results, but the truth is that the Academia had already been battening down the hatches for the effects of this foretold hurricane on the horizon. González Macho did not put it in so many words in his June statement, but the Academia had to anticipate that loss of power by the Socialists spelled bad news for a certain kind of film culture, given the PP's well-publicised animosity towards the Spanish cinema industry, in particular the Academia and what it represented (García, 'González Macho reconoce', n.p.).

The June 2011 issue of the Academia's main publication, *Revista Academia*, had been entirely devoted to the industry, with interviews with several stakeholders keen to analyse the state of play, including the then recently appointed new Spanish Film Institute/ICAA director Carlos Cuadros. The issue is marked by a combination of soul-searching and self-justification: an assessment and acknowledgment of the current terrain, but a reassertion of the cinema as cultural and economic goods. Around the same time, the Academia commissioned the document 'El estado de la cuestión' ('State of Affairs') by Fernando Lara, former Spanish Film Institute director, and a respected and acclaimed film critic and festival director with a deep knowledge of European and Spanish film contexts. After a thorough discussion with many groups – including production and distribution companies of all sizes, pioneers working with new platforms, and traditional bricks-and-mortar multiplex and cinema theatre owners – and working with the latest figures from the public administration, Lara came up with fifteen points of action for the nation's cinema. Among these was the need for public money both from central government and from the different autonomous regions to support the industry, without which the agendas of cultural diversity would not be met. Otherwise, cinema would increasingly mean Hollywood films and nothing else. This demand for money is put into the context of the dire situation of the economic crisis, but it has to be observed that the amount of debt and corruption unearthed during the subsequent years was not yet known.

Lara's recommendations were largely ignored by the new administration. In its first few months, the PP government proceeded to bring in its harshest and most unpopular measures; it became clear that culture in general and cinema in particular were in for rough treatment. The most notorious measure was the halving of the state funding for cinema between 2012 and 2014, and the increase of the VAT applied to cultural activities, including cinema, to 21 per cent. This deliberate strategy of slashing public spending, not by reducing it but by attacking what the government calls 'a culture of state funding', is entirely politically motivated (Hamilos, n.p.).

The Academia has had to enter into the fray to fight for the survival of a certain idea of Spanish cinema. As the most visible representative of the industry, it has become the sparring partner for the party of government, and the war of attrition between the two has seen some Punch and Judy moments. As Mar Binimelis, Miguel Fernández Labayén and Josetxo Cerdán explain (p. 1), matters came to a head when the Minister of Finance and Public Administration, Cristóbal Montoro, stated that "'los problemas del cine español no tienen que ver sólo con las subvenciones, también con la calidad'" ("'Spanish cinema's problems are not simply connected to state funding but to quality'" (Belinchón, 'Cristóbal Montoro', n.p.).

By making his declaration on a popular public radio station, Montoro had thrown down the gauntlet to the Academia, which had no choice but to pick it up (see Belinchón, 'Cristóbal Montoro'). It did so with a humorous open letter from the Board of Directors to the minister, which was posted on the Academia website, and widely publicised in the national press and film magazines such as *Fotogramas*. In it they defended the quality of Spain's cinema, and invited Montoro to 'take it easy' (*que se relaje*) and watch a Spanish film – or any film, for that matter. They warned him that as a minister, he had a 'best before' date, like yogurt. And quoting the poet Antonio Machado, the letter made poignant comments on life's quick pace, implying that culture is eternal, unlike the PP's tenure in power. In sum, *Ars longa vita brevis* was the Academia's retort to Montoro (see Academia, 'Carta abierta', n.p.).

Between 2011 and 2015, the conditions for Spanish cinema in general have changed dramatically and this kind of firefighting, whether light-hearted or not, has become routine. In my opinion, it may prevent the Academia from concentrating on the many challenges ahead. For instance, it will need to reflect critically and genuinely on its historical Madrid-centrism. It will be the task of future film scholars and critics to examine how the Academia has struggled to position itself at the centre of a network of institutions in a country where territories vie for national status, such as the Basque Country and Catalonia.

The Academia has an outpost in Catalonia, but now Catalonia, the second centre of Spain's film industry, has two film academies. In 2002, the region created its alternative to the Academia and the Goyas: the Acadèmia del Cinema Català and the Gaudí Awards. The general perception within the institution was that, by 2011, the many Catalan film academicians (around 290, 30 per cent of the Academia's membership) were at the heart of the institution. But that had not always been the case. Rosa Vergés, who won a Goya for Best New Director with *Boom, Boom* in 1991, remembers a time when the power base was unambiguously Castilian and there was little hope of change. 'Many of us here in Catalonia worked to contest this concentration: the actor Ovidi Montllor, the director of cinematography Josep M. Civit, the film-maker Ventura Pons and myself, among them' (Vergés, n.p.).

Their efforts came to fruition between 1994 and 1998, in the period when Borau was elected as president, and when Fernando Guillén and Vergés became vice-presidents. Part of this group's mandate was to open a site in Barcelona. This became a reality in 1994, and its representatives in Barcelona argue that the relationship between the centre and the periphery became more fluid for a while and Catalan membership grew.

In the words of Vergés, it became difficult on occasion to differentiate between 'them and us', and this has become a truism, as film-making becomes an increasingly globalised and transnational undertaking. However, the efforts of the cinema made in Barcelona to be relevant to Madrid institutions, not simply the Academia, is characterised by a constant tussle. Sometimes there are victories, such as securing a site in Barcelona in the first place and holding the Gala ceremony in the city in 2000, but nothing can be taken for granted.

It has generally been understood that among the trio that presides over the Academia, there should be at least one Catalan professional. For instance, in 2011, when González Macho put forward his group, the first and second vice-presidents were the Basque actor Marta Etura and the Catalan film-maker Judith Colell. The current trio, Antonio Resines, Gracia Querejeta and Edmon Roch, more than fulfils that requirement, as Roch also sits on the Board of Directors of the Acadèmia del Cinema Català. But their predecessors, de la Iglesia, Bollaín and Emilio Pina, had not followed this unwritten rule, and there may be a time in the future when Catalan interests are not represented in the presiding trio again.

As I explained in Chapter 5, a sizable part of the independent/avant-garde sector is based in Barcelona, and Catalan film-making cannot be liminal to the Madrid industry, though the Goyas have clearly sidelined film-making in Catalan in the past: the first film in the language to win a Goya for Best Film was *Black Bread*, and that only happened at the twenty-fifth Gala in 2011. It beggars belief that Catalan cinema had to wait a quarter of a century for this recognition.

It is not just the centre/periphery dynamic that begs attention. For many film professionals, the Academia has become simply too dominant or hegemonic, too entangled with the institutions and political parties created during the transition, even if they are so often at daggers drawn with one of those parties. A tangible representation of this fact is what I was often told in hushed, humorous tones: that the Academia site in Madrid shares its toilets with the main headquarters of the PP in Calle de Génova, which are situated next door. Talk about too close for comfort!

It is therefore little wonder that groups of emerging film-makers, producers and other film professionals, alongside critics and academics, now want to work together while seeking to put some distance between themselves and the sites of hegemonic power – or at least to redirect the conversation away from political confrontation and to emphasise what Spanish cinema contributes to Spain's economy and culture and to discuss its future. During September 2014, there were encouraging noises about the organisation of a Congreso del Cine Español, something akin to a Salamanca conference for the 2.0 generation. Academician Gerardo Herrero rightly argued that without the government being on board with this, little could be achieved (García and Belinchón, 'Entusiasmos', n.p.).

The challenges to the Academia come from groups that belong to emerging film cultures that have grown, or are endeavouring to grow, outside it, usually trying to avoid the distraction that comes with direct political interactions with the main two parties, but not ignoring the need to fight for the rights of film professionals. One such group is CIMA (Asociación de Mujeres Cineastas y de Medios Audiovisuales/Association of Women in Film-making and Audiovisual Media), with over 300 members. CIMA has been battling since 2009 against the dearth of women in all branches of the film-making professions, and their exclusion from decision-making bodies. One consequence of the climate of fear that comes with austerity and cuts is that hard-fought-for rights and measures to tackle inequality are put to one side: such issues, we are told, must wait for more affluent times. CIMA, in contrast, insists that no one should use the draconian cuts to the industry as an excuse not to tackle the status quo in a country where only 8 per cent of the directors are women.

Another emergent organisation to watch is La Unión de Cineastas (The Film-makers Coalition) with a membership of over 200 film professionals, from film-makers to academics. La Unión wants to find 'new avenues for Spanish cinema', and fight to reposition Spanish cinema 'as a fundamental cultural element in our society of the twenty-first century' (see Unión de Cineastas, n.p.). This group meets to engage with legislation, and to discuss the critical moment for Spanish cinema when an entire younger generation has been let down with regards to funding and access to the profession. These independent film professionals have to find imaginative solutions to pursue their careers in film-making and do so by resorting to low-cost strategies and digital platforms, but they keep demanding to be heard. They are, after all, the future of Spanish cinema.

As for Spanish cinema's past, it keeps raising its head in most unexpected ways. As I write this epilogue, the newly appointed Minister of Education, Culture and Sports, Íñigo Méndez de Vigo y Montojo, 9th Baron of Claret, has declared himself a fan of Spanish cinema (see Palomo and Marcos, n.p.), but the Spanish cinema he prefers is that of the 1960s and early 70s shown in the TVE1 programme *Cine de barrio/Neighbourhood Cinema*. This is precisely the Spanish cinema made by those successful commercial producers and directors who did not get an invitation to the lunch at O'Pazo, where the idea of the Academia was born; precisely the cinema that the Academia sought to consign to oblivion. With these calculated if humorous words, the Baron in one sentence brushed aside three decades of Spanish cinema, while showing that, for some at least, the debates of the 1980s live on.

Will it be up to the Academia to continue to harness and negotiate the forces of film-making and their relationship with the Spanish state, with Europe and with the world in the future? It seems likely. But from the vantage point of 2015, it is clear that the emergent groups will play a larger role in what lies ahead for Spain's film industry, and this is something that the Academia cannot ignore if the story of Spanish Film Cultures, and the Academia, is to be continued ...

Notes

INTRODUCTION

1. A brief history of each of these academies is included in their websites: <http://www.academiadecine.org.ar>; <http://www.academiamexicanadecine.org.mx>; <http://www.bafta.org/about/>; <http://www.academie-cinema.org>; <http://www.deutsche-filmakademie.de>.
2. The hugely popular local comedy *Ocho apellidos vascos/A Spanish Affair* (Emilio Martínez Lázaro, 2014) falls outside the timeframe of my analysis, but confirms my affirmation. *A Spanish Affair* was the Spanish box-office smash of 2014, and indeed of all time: within one month of its release in March it had attracted more spectators than any film screened in Spain barring *Avatar* (James Cameron, 2009). It won three Goyas in acting categories, but what is crucially important none of the most prestigious awards: Best Film/Best Director/Best Screenplay (see Buse and Triana-Toribio).

I THE HOUSE IS BUILT OF THE STONES THAT WERE AVAILABLE

1. This title is inspired by a line in Bertolt Brecht's poem 'Bad Times'.
2. Definition of the Academia. Available at: <www.academiadecine.com/la_academia/historia.php?id_s=1&i_ss=26>.
3. These terms echo the vocabulary of the preamble to Spain's constitution, which had just been passed by the first democratic government in 1977.
4. See, for instance, Kowalsky, pp. 188–208.
5. For a discussion, see, for instance, Riambau ('La década', pp. 399–447); Triana-Toribio (*Spanish National Cinema*, pp. 109–11); Faulkner (*A History*, pp. 160–96).
6. At the time, the influential film critic Fernando Lara elaborated on the areas that the new legislation could improve ('La hora', pp. 42–3).
7. Pierre Bourdieu coined the term 'habitus' to express a series of predispositions and inclinations that are connected to class, agency and education among other factors. It is explained as a 'feel for the game'.
8. See also: <www.mcu.es/cine/MC/FE/FondosFilm/ColeccEsp/EscuelaCine.html>.
9. Jordà, by his membership of the Escuela de Barcelona and his legacy, is connected to the Catalan avant-garde cinephiles of the 1990s onwards, who are discussed in Chapter 5. See Riambau and Torreiro on Jordà, pp. 80–9.

10. Ibid., p. 95.

11. Scholarship on The Salamanca Conversations is extensive. Beyond those quoted in this chapter, other sources worth mentioning are the documentary *De Salamanca a ninguna parte/Salamanca to Nowhere* (Chema de la Peña, 2002), and Faulkner (*A Cinema*, pp. 1–24).

12. See: <http://www.mecd.gob.es/cultura-mecd/areas-cultura/cine/promocion/premios.html>.

13. Censorship rules appear in several studies. See, for instance, Torres, *Spanish Cinema* (which the ICCA published in English as part of a campaign to disseminate knowledge about Spanish cinema abroad).

14. Pedro Lazaga told Montero: 'I twist and turn the scripts I write to give this message: that if we are not happy it is because we don't want to be. Beauty, happiness, that is my world' ('Una manera', p. 10).

15. The inheritors of this model have adopted their elders' modes of representation and aesthetic strategies, pursuing a *cine social* or *cine comprometido* that is still concerned with the representation of reality and addressing social issues. Examples are Icíar Bollaín and Fernando León de Aranoa.

16. The director talks about his frustrations with the censorship apparatus in a classic study by Antonio Castro published in 1974, pp. 315–23.

17. In the early 1970s, Dibildos and Iquino became a producer/director team of a type of film called *la tercera vía* (the third way). *La tercera vía* intended to capitalise on the changing tastes and mores of Spanish cinema's middle-class audiences (see Monterde, 'Tercera Vía', pp. 848–9). Faulkner's must-read analysis of this much derided trend (in *A History*, pp. 119–58) demonstrates the sham modernity those films offered. The state commended them with prizes, but letters to film magazines at the time reveal that audiences were highly critical of the old-fashioned style and morality of these films. In a series of letters about the melodrama *Aborto criminal/Criminal Abortion* (Ignacio F. Iquino, 1973), Davin Wottle argues: 'I understand anyone's reluctance to use space discussing the value of this film, but those who should be ashamed are those who gave it a "special interest" award' (p. 9).

18. Preamble to the Royal Decree 3071/77 of 11 November 1977, *Boletín Oficial del Estado* (*Official State Gazette*), 1 December 1977.

19. The crudeness or explicitness of the representation of violence is a trait of this auteurist generation, taking to extremes neorealism's imperative of bearing witness to the harshness of rural life. Representing Spain's rural past in the early Franco era was intended as a reminder that the 'modern' Spain of the 1960s was built on repression and the state brutality of the rural working classes. Backwardness, feudal conditions, lack of education and fanatic religious fervour were the targets of these middle-class, urban film-makers, who often sought to emulate Buñuel's *Las Hurdes/Land without Bread* (1933), but who were also influenced by the increased explicitness in depictions of film violence elsewhere (Sam Peckinpah was widely admired at the time). These portraits played well with festival audiences. José Luis Gómez won the Best Actor award playing the title role in Ricardo Franco's *Pascual Duarte* (1976) in Cannes in 1976.

20. See Pérez Millán, pp. 125–54.

21. See: <http://elpais.com/diario/1980/04/16/cultura/324684001_850215.html>.

22. There is a wealth of material on this legislation. In my effort to guide readers to both Spanish and English sources, here are some of the most informative: Hopewell, *Out of the Past*, pp. 225–42; Triana-Toribio, *Spanish National Cinema*, pp. 108–32; Ansola González, pp. 102–21; Losilla, 'Legislación', pp. 33–43.

23. See, for instance, Matas quoted by Múñoz Suay in 'Columna-Bis', p. 11.

24. 'A pact was brokered; once we became a group Alfredo disappeared' (Villalba cited in Sánchez Salas and Sánchez Salas, p. 67). Despite (or because of) Matas's disappearance, his name is invoked as the force behind the Academia and the Goyas. In 2013, the weekly magazine *El País Semanal* argued in an article about the prizes that recent developments – such as transnational stars nominated for awards and films in English, and in French in competition – might have seemed unattainable when the Academia was created, but were 'probably exactly what Alfredo Matas had in mind' (Socías, p. 39).

25. *Cuadernos de la Academia* was envisaged by José Luis Borau, president of the Academia (1994–8), as a scholarly publication for the study of film, and destined to open the Academia publications to film researchers and critics (Peláez Paz, p. 100).

26. In recent years, scholars have succeeded in moving the debate about this legislation beyond the blanket accusations and finding value in what independent producers contributed to Spanish cinema (see particularly Faulkner, *A History*, pp. 162–96).

27. This form of financing was first envisaged for Spanish cinema in 1993/4. The 1994 Law was influenced by the GATT agreement discussions in Europe. The uncertainty about whether European audiovisual products would be exempted from this trade agreement with the US weighed heavily on Spanish producers. They lobbied the then Minister of Culture, Carmen Alborch, for protection. The result was a decree for funding cinema from the profits of television channels. It was not implemented at the time. When, in 1999, the PP in government made use of it, private, state and regional television channels all became producers for Spanish cinema (see Yáñez).

2 AND THE WINNER IS …

1. See 'Muere García Escudero', n.p.
2. Besides the institutional ones, there were yearly prizes from publications such as *Fotogramas*, which awarded the *Placa de San Juan Bosco* from 1951. These were awarded in several categories and based on readers' votes. They were renamed the *Fotogramas de Plata* in December 1970. See Monterde, 'Continuismo', p. 239.
3. See: <http://www.academiadecine.com/la_academia/historia.php?id_s=1&id_ss=26>.
4. See: <http://www.academiadecine.com/premios/premios_gonzalezsinde .php?id_s=2&id_ss=31>.
5. This prize was awarded annually during the time of this study; it became biannual after that (thanks to Fernando Lara, a jury member, for this information, October 2014).
6. See Antonio Santamarina, 'Muñoz Suay', p. 100. See also: <http://www.academiadecine .com/premios/premio_munozsuay.php?id_s=2&id_ss=32>.
7. See: <http://www.academiadecine.com/publicaciones/cuadernos.php?pagina=2&id _s=3&id_ss=39>.
8. See: <http://www.academiadecine.com/publicaciones/otras.php?id_s=3&id_ss=48>.
9. See: <http://www.academiadecine.com/premios/segundo_chomon.php?id_s=2&id_ss=33>.
10. James English talks about 'Nobel envy' (p. 64) as the impulse that prompted the proliferation of prizes in the arts and sciences.
11. 'Nothing would disgust me more [than an Oscar],' said Buñuel. 'I wouldn't have it in my home.' English uses Buñuel as a prime example of what he calls 'the symbolic efficacy of refusal' (p. 221).

12. As Bowskill reminds us, there had been a Francoist prize of the same name.
13. Lázaro-Reboll links the use of the 'Goya' brand to cultural strategies during the early years of the Socialist government (1982–92) that were geared to connect the Socialist cultural project with the eighteenth-century Spanish Enlightenment (*Facing Monstrosity*, pp. 2–3).
14. Faulkner gives a sympathetic and nuanced treatment to several films that resulted from the Miró legislation, rescuing them from negative criticism (*A History*, pp. 185–9).
15. On 'good' films, see Miró, pp. 38–46. 'Good' films for her would be made when higher budgets translated seamlessly into higher quality. By the time *Voyage to Nowhere* was made in 1986, Miró's successor at the head of the Spanish Film Institute, Fernando Méndez-Leite, followed her policies. Miro's Law had been implemented in 1984, but 1986 was the year since its implementation when the fewest films were made in Spain. Those few films had higher budgets than the films of preceding years.
16. From May 1984, committees awarded state funding to independent producers and directors. See, among others, Losilla ('Legislación', pp. 33–43).
17. On how the style created through these committees' decisions became conventionalised and canonical from the mid- to the late 1980s, see particularly Losilla ('Legislación', pp. 33–43) and Hopewell ('"Art"', pp. 113–22).
18. Muñoz Suay quotes the actor in 'De los cómicos', p. 6.
19. *La venganza de Don Mendo* is one of Spain's most frequently performed plays.
20. On this prestigious literary adaptation, see Brasil Campos, pp. 176–7.
21. The auteurist generation's prejudice against TV re-emerges when it is argued that contemporary actors are not as good as the old ones due to their television training. When the Academia celebrated its twenty-fifth anniversary, *El País* film critic Elsa Fernández-Santos wrote: 'To be sure, Spanish cinema looks more than ever like a luxurious shop window of international stars (the names of … Bardem, and Cruz suffice), but it is also a shop window of aspiring stars, far removed from those smoke-filled café counters from where actors emerged who never stood on a red carpet or knew about photo calls' ('25 aniversario', n.p.).
22. Scholarship on *¡Ay, Carmela!* is extensive. Beyond those quoted in this chapter, other publications highlight the film's national and international validation. See Hopewell ('"Art"', pp. 113–22); MacDonald, pp. 47–59; Thompson, pp. 147–63.
23. *La Santa Compaña* is a legendary procession of dead souls popular in the Spanish Atlantic regions.
24. See Granado, pp. 18–19, on the trophy's history.

3 BEING DIFFERENT: ALMODÓVAR AND THE ACADEMIA

1. Almodóvar's speech at the 2010 Gala is available on YouTube at: <http://www.youtube.com/watch?v=6Xc-iCbmlLo>.
2. I quote from the translation of this interview in Francia and Pérez Perucha, pp. 2–8. The original can be found in *Filmoteca Española* and it is worth consulting, since Willoquet-Maricondi's translation contains errors.
3. The films that he calls *cine costumbrista* in the early 1980s are comedies by directors based in Madrid, such as Fernando Colomo's *Tigres de papel/Paper Tigers* (1977), José Luis Cuerda's *Pares y nones* (1982) and Fernando Trueba's *Ópera prima/Opera Prima* (1980), and the

comedies of Francesc Bellmunt (based in Barcelona) such as *L'orgia/The Orgy* (1978). These are out-of-time comedies, with a clear debt to Woody Allen's solipsistic style and where women are stock characters, peripheral to the action. Their protagonists are immature heterosexual men with 'a vaguely progressive past' (Torreiro, p. 297) who, getting on in years, are still trying to be part of an emergent cultural scene but have 'many cultural hang ups' (ibid.). These men are ignored in Almodóvar's early films, which are more interested in the emergent cultural scene, particularly in its women and gay men, not in ageing interlopers.

4. See YouTube at: <http://www.youtube.com/watch?v=tdYEvvMvhyM>.
5. See: <http://www.cinematheque.fr/fr/dans-salles/hommages-retrospectives/fiche -cycle/jess-franco,174.html>.

4 ROGUE MALES, 'BAD' FILMS AND 'BAD' LOYALTIES: SANTIAGO SEGURA AND ÁLEX DE LA IGLESIA

1. Source: ICAA database. Available at: <https://icaa.mecd.es/Datos_tecnicos_Peliculas.aspx>.
2. The fact that Spanish cinema had attracted 11 per cent fewer spectators and made losses of over 2 per cent compared with the previous year was discussed under apocalyptic headlines in Spain's main newspapers.
3. See: <http://www.imdb.com/title/tt1417108/>.
4. These comedies were, and remain, the chief experience of Spanish cinema for many Spaniards of an older generation, something that is confirmed by the popularity of the television programme *Cine de barrio/Neighbourhood Cinema* (TVE1), which has been showing them since 1995.
5. Several points of contact between the comedies of Italy and Spain in the 1960s were discussed by critics such as Fernando Méndez-Leite in his *Historia del cine español*. Subsequent critics have explored connection in themes, style and even the frequency of co-production between the two countries.
6. The symbiotic relationship between Spain's cinema and its television has become more important since 1999, as the television channels (public and private) support the national film production. Five per cent of their annual profits (6 per cent in the case of public television) is invested into financing Spanish cinema as prescribed by Spanish law.
7. In the 1960s and 70s, there were only two state television channels; therefore, audiences' familiarity with actors of Leblanc's generation is hardly comparable with the status of television celebrities when several private television channels, as well as a number of state-owned ones, are competing for attention.
8. On the 11 March 2004, suicide bombers linked to Al-Qaeda detonated several devices in commuter trains killing 191 and injuring more than 1,700. This tragedy has become a key historical and political milestone for Spain.
9. In *Brain Drain 1*, a young Spanish man follows his girlfriend to the UK, where she is attending university. It is supposedly set in Oxford, but not much effort is made at the level of *mise en scène* to disguise what is evidently the Universidad Laboral de Gijón in Spain. Placards and banners in Spanish are visible on screen.
10. Produced by national and international producers: Tornasol Films, Oxford Crimes, Telecinco Cinema from Spain, La Fabrique 2 from France and the backing of Warner Bros., among others.

11. In the same vein, writer César Antonio Molina preceded her at the helm of the Ministry of Culture. In 2005, the Socialist Party administration appointed as head of the Spanish Film Institute the respected critic Fernando Lara, former director of the Seminci/International Film Week of Valladolid, one of Spain's longest-standing and most prestigious film events. González-Sinde replaced Lara with Ignasi Guardans in 2009.
12. Including, among other strategies, that a commission in the Ministry of Culture be legally authorised to block or close down web pages, blogs or other types of internet pages where films can be downloaded. Such intervention does not need to be sanctioned by a judge. This power was considered an infringement of liberties. At no point were the responsibilities of the Internet Service Providers around piracy and illegal downloading discussed.
13. *Internautas* should be translated as the neutral 'web users', but in the context of the debate it came to mean 'web users engaging in illegal downloading'.

5 THERE IS NO SUCH THING AS A WEAK ENEMY

1. While many authors have taken an interest in the avant-garde, at the time of writing my knowledge about it benefited most from the work of, and conversations with, Ángel Quintana and Belén Vidal. I want to thank them for their contribution to this chapter, for which they shared unpublished work with me. Crucially, Eduardo Ledesma, Vidal and Diana Cullell also allowed me access to their Escuela de Barcelona film collections.
2. For full details of the demands of the Cineastas contra la Orden, see: <http://cineastas contralaorden.blogaliza.org>.
3. See, for instance, Ríos Pérez, n.p.
4. As I have argued elsewhere, as well as intervening in the eligibility of projects for state subsidies, Guardans aimed to rationalise the complex and expensive proliferation of film festivals in Spain, another area in which he collided head on with the interests of both hegemonic and avant-garde film cultures (Triana-Toribio, 'FICXixón', pp. 217–36; Triana-Toribio, 'Residual Film Cultures', pp. 65–81).
5. Articles and debates were published in *Cahiers du Cinéma España*, in December 2009.
6. Evole was at the time of this 'crisis' the general director of the third biggest cinema chain in Spain, Yelmo Cineplex. This declaration comes from the year before the Collective's actions but still accounts for the context in which they took place.
7. Jonás Trueba released *Los ilusos/The Wishful Thinkers* in 2013.
8. At the time of writing, Miñarro had made *Familystrip* (2009), *Blow Horn* (2009) and *Stella cadente/Falling Star* (2014).
9. See: <http://cineastascontralaorden.blogaliza.org/quienes-somos>.
10. A significant aspect of García Escudero's plans for Spanish cinema, not often discussed, is that he envisaged a system by which Spanish cinema would be self-supporting after a series of seed grants or start-up projects (*Cine español*, pp. 81–3).
11. See *Journal of Spanish Cultural Studies* vol. 15 no. 3, 2014, an issue dedicated to the study of Spanish independent film-makers.
12. Bourdieu's 'habitus' and 'class habitus' are notoriously capacious concepts. For the purposes of this study, I have used Randal Johnson's observation that it 'is often described as a "feel for the game"', which comes with class, agency and education (p. 5).

13. Judging by the launch issue of *Cahiers du Cinéma España*, in May 2007, older film-makers still mattered for the independent/avant-garde film-makers, whether it was those who refused compromise to the mainstream such as Basilio Martín Patino (1930–), Víctor Érice (1940–) and the Argentinian director of *La hora de los hornos/The Hour of the Furnaces* (1968), Fernando Solanas (1936–), or the more commercially inclined (see Heredero, 'Miradas hacia el futuro', pp. 11, 28, 32).
14. Data from the 'Catálogo de cine'. Available at: <http://www.mecd.gob.es/catalogodecine/2014/presentacion.html>.

6 TRANSATLANTIC ACADEMIA

1. See, for example, Academia, 'Premios: los Oscar', n.p.

Bibliography

Please see Note on referencing and translations on p. viii for details.

Academia de las Artes y las Ciencias Cinematográficas de España, 'Premios: los Oscar', Academiadecine.com. Available at: <www.academiadecine.com/premios/ otros. php?id_s=2&id_ss=46>. Accessed 12 August 2015.
——, 'Un futuro común: editorial', *Academia: revista del cine español* no. 10, April 1995, p. 9.
——, 'La sede de la Academia acogerá un encuentro de las academias europeas', *Academia: noticias del cine español (Boletín)* no. 137, August/September 2007.
——, 'Bases de los Premios Anuales de la Academia de las Artes y las Ciencias Cinematográficas', candidatos para las votaciones (Madrid: Academia de las Artes y las Ciencias Cinematográficas, 2008), pp. 6–13.
——, 'Premiados en festivales internacionales', *Academia: revista del cine español* no. 180, July 2011, p. 6.
——, 'Carta abierta al Ministro de Hacienda y Administraciones Públicas', 11 October 2013. Available at: <http://actualidad.academiadecine.com/noticias/detalle.php?id_noticia=1083>. Accessed 12 August 2015.
'Actualidad: un caso alarmante: prohibición en toda España de "La prima Angélica"', *Nuevo Fotogramas*, 19 June 1974, p. 17.
Alonso, Agustín G., 'Almodóvar y la Academia de Cine, un "amour fou"', RTVE.es, 15 February 2010. Available at: <www.rtve.es/noticias/20100215/almodovar-academia-cine-amour-fou/ 318106.shtml>. Accessed 12 August 2015.
Alonso, Juanjo, 'Los Goya, del "No a la guerra" a la defensa del juez Garzón', Libertaddigital.com. Available at: <www.libertaddigital.com/espana/2013-02-18/los-goya-del-no-a-la-guerra-a-la -defensa-del-juez-garzon-1276482557>. Accessed 12 August 2015.
Álvarez Monzoncillo, José María and Juan Menor Sendra, 'La estructura del audiovisual en la Transición', in Manuel Palacio (ed.), *Las imágenes del cambio: medios audiovisuales en las transiciones a la democracia* (Madrid: Biblioteca nueva, 2013), pp. 15–34.
Amigo, Ángel, 'Allí no es más difícil', *Academia: revista del cine español* no. 10, April 1995, pp. 84–5.
Angulo, Jesús and Antonio Santamarina, *Álex de la Iglesia: la pasión de rodar* (Donostia-San Sebastián: Euskadiko Filmategia/Filmoteca Vasca).
Ansola González, Txomín, 'El decreto Miró: una propuesta ambiciosa pero fallida para impulsar el cine español en los 80', *Archivos de la Filmoteca* no. 48, 2004, pp. 102–21.

Arrieta, Ana, Personal interview with Nuria Triana-Toribio, Madrid, 19 March 2014.

Balfour, Sebastian and Alejandro Quiroga, *España reinventada: nación e identidad desde la Transición* (Barcelona: Península, 2007).

Bardem, Juan Antonio, *Y todavía sigue: memorias de un hombre de cine* (Madrid: Ediciones B, 2002).

Barrenetxea Marañón, Igor and Magdalena Garrido Caballero, '*¡Ay, Carmela!*', in Lorenzo J. Torres Hortelano (ed.), *Directory of World Cinema: Spain* (Bristol: Intellect, 2011), pp. 127–8.

Barrow, Sarah, 'Transnational Film Financing and Contemporary Peruvian Cinema: The Case of Josué Méndez', in Stephanie Dennison (ed.), *Contemporary Hispanic Cinema: Interrogating the Transnational in Spanish and Latin American Film* (Woodbridge, Suffolk: Tamesis, 2013), pp. 137–54.

'Bases para el premio'. Available at: <http://premiosgoya.academiadecine.com/descargas/ bases28goya.pdf>. Accessed 10 January 2016.

Beck, Jay and Vicente Rodríguez Ortega, 'Introduction', in Jay Beck and Vicente Rodríguez Ortega (eds), *Contemporary Spanish Cinema and Genre* (Manchester: Manchester University Press, 2008), pp. 3–8.

Belinchón, Gregorio, 'Cineastas contra la Orden impugnan ante la Audiencia Nacional', Cultura.elpais.com, 23 December 2009. Available at: <http://cultura.elpais.com/cultura/ 2009/12/23/actualidad/1261522804_850215.html>. Accessed 11 August 2015.

———, 'Desde 2002 hay una campaña orquestada contra el cine español', Cultura.elpais.com, 23 November 2010. Available at: <http://elpais.com/diario/2010/11/23/cultura/ 1290466802_850215.html>. Accessed 12 August 2015.

———, 'Entrevista a Matías Bize: "Para nosotros el Goya es fundamental"', Cultura.elpais.com, 1 April 2011. Available at: <www.elpais.com/articulo/cine/Goya/fundamental/elpepucin/ 20110401elpepicin_11/Tes>. Accessed 12 August 2015.

———, 'Muere el actor Tony Leblanc', Cultura.elpais.com, 24 November 2012. Available at: <http://cultura.elpais.com/cultura/2012/11/24/actualidad/1353778294_858774.html>. Accessed 12 August 2015.

———, 'Cristóbal Montoro carga contra el cine español', Cultura.elpais.com, 8 October 2013. Available at: <http://cultura.elpais.com/cultura/2013/10/08/actualidad/ 1381261922 _490006.html>. Accessed 12 August 2015.

———, 'Hago otro cine … luego existo', Cultura.elpais.com, 7 November 2013. Available at: <http://cultura.elpais.com/cultura/2013/11/07/actualidad/1383860563_955814.html>. Accessed 12 August 2015.

—— and R. García, 'Conmoción en el mundo del cine por la decisión de Bruselas de bloquear las ayudas a rodajes', Cultura.elpais.com, 25 November 2009. Available at: <http://cultura .elpais.com/cultura/2009/11/25/actualidad/1259103601_850215.html>. Accessed 12 August 2015.

———, Rocío García, Elsa Fernández-Santos and Borja Hermoso, 'Cine español, el teatro del conflicto', Cultura.elpais.com, 12 February 2011. Available at: <http://elpais.com/diario/ 2011/02/12/cultura/1297465201_850215.html>. Accessed 12 August 2015.

Bentley, Bernard P. E., *A Companion to Spanish Cinema* (Woodbridge, Suffolk: Tamesis, 2008).

Bergfelder, Tim, 'National, Transnational or Supranational Cinema? Rethinking European Film Studies', *Media, Culture and Society* vol. 27 no. 3, 2005, pp. 315–31.

Binimelis, Mar, Miguel Fernández Labayen and Josetxo Cerdán, 'In and Out: The Transnational Circulation of Spanish Cinema in Digital Media', *Journal of Spanish Cultural Studies* vol. 16 no. 1, 2015, pp. 1–18.

'Board of Governors'. Available at: <http://www.oscars.org/academy/history-organization/governors.html>. Accessed 12 August 2015.

Bolaño, Roberto, *Llamadas telefónicas* (Barcelona: Anagrama, 1997).

Bourdieu, Pierre, *Distinction: A Social Critique of the Judgement of Taste*, trans. by Richard Nice (Cambridge, MA: Harvard University Press, 1984).

———, 'The Production of Belief: Contribution to an Economy of Symbolic Goods', *The Field of Cultural Production*, ed. and intro. by Randal Johnson (Cambridge: Polity, 1993 [2012]), pp. 261–93.

Bowskill, Sarah, 'Politics and Literary Prizes: A Case Study of Spanish America and the Premio Cervantes', *Hispanic Review* vol. 80 no. 2, Spring 2012, pp. 289–311.

'Box Office: Data, Spain', *Screen International* no. 1688, 1–7 May 2009, p. 26.

Boyero, Carlos, 'Premios razonables en una fiesta sin gracia', Cultura.elpais.com, 10 February 2014. Available at: <http://cultura.elpais.com/cultura/2014/02/10/actualidad/1392064303_764409.html>. Accessed 12 August 2015.

Brannon Donoghue, Courtney, 'Sony and Local-Language Productions: Conglomerate Hollywood's Strategy of Flexible Localization for the Global Film Market', *Cinema Journal* vol. 53 no. 4, 2014, pp. 3–27.

Brasil Campos, Vanessa, 'The Nail/El Clavo', in Lorenzo J. Torres Hortelano (ed.), *Directory of World Cinema: Spain* (Bristol: Intellect, 2011), pp. 176–7.

Brunet, Pau, 'El efecto Goya', *Academia: revista del cine español* no. 164, February 2010, pp. 4–6.

Buse, Peter and Nuria Triana-Toribio, '*Ocho apellidos vascos* and the Comedy of Minor Differences', *Romance Quarterly* vol. 62 no. 4, 2015, pp. 1–13.

—— and Andrew Willis, *The Cinema of Álex de la Iglesia* (Manchester: Manchester University Press, 2007).

Cadalso, José, *Cartas marruecas: noches lúgubres* (Madrid: Cátedra, 1981 [1775]).

Cahiers du Cinéma España, 'Dialogar, filmar, vivir ... coloquio con Isaki Lacuesta y Javier Rebollo', *Cahiers du Cinéma España* no. 27, October 2009, pp. 10–11.

Caldwell, John Thornton, *Production Culture: Industrial Reflexivity and Critical Practice in Film and Television* (Durham, NC: Duke University Press, 2008).

Cambra, Pilar, 'Rogelio Díez: "Ya hay (casi) Ley de Cine"', *Nuevo Fotogramas*, 28 February 1975, pp. 8–9.

Caputo, Rolando, 'Defeating the Irremediable Solitude: An Interview with José Luis Guerín', Sensesofcinema.com, April 2011. Available at: <http://sensesofcinema.com/2011/feature-articles/defeating-the-irremediable-solitude-of-the-guest-an-interview-with-jose-luis-guerin/>. Accessed 12 August 2015.

Carballo Dávila, Antonio, 'La Academia, un ente de difícil gobierno', *Cineinforme* 49 no. 850, February 2011, pp. 7–8.

Castro, Antonio, *El cine español en el banquillo* (Valencia: Fernando Torres, 1974).

Cerdán, Josetxo and Miguel Fernández Labayen, 'Almodóvar and Spanish Patterns of Film Reception', in Kathleen M. Vernon and Marvin D'Lugo (eds), *A Companion to Pedro Almodóvar* (Malden, MA: Wiley-Blackwell, 2013), pp. 129–52.

Combarros Peláez, César, *50 años de la Semana Internacional de Cine de Valladolid (1956–2005): una ventana al mundo* (Valladolid: Semana Internacional de Cine de Valladolid, 2005).

Corrigan, Timothy, *A Cinema without Walls: Movies and Culture after Vietnam* (New York and London: Routledge, 1991).

Cowie, Peter, 'Introduction: A Family Affair: Uniting the Talents of Europe', in Peter Cowie and Pascal Edelmann (eds), *Projections 15 + The European Film Academy* (London: Faber and Faber/European Film Academy, 2007), pp. xvii–xxxii.

Crespo, Irene, 'Santiago Segura "El 3D esta muy bien para la escatologia y el porno"', *Cinemanía* no. 186, 2011, pp. 84–7.

Crofts, Stephen, 'Concepts of National Cinema', in John Hill and Pamela Church Gibson (eds), *World Cinema: Critical Approaches* (Oxford: Oxford University Press, 2000), pp. 1–10.

Czach, Liz, 'Film Festivals, Programming and the Building of a National Cinema', *The Moving Image* vol. 4 no. 1, 2004, pp. 74–88.

Danks, Adrian, 'Great Directors: Victor Erice', Sensesofcinema.com, March 2003. Available at: <http://sensesofcinema.com/2003/great-directors/erice/>. Accessed 12 August 2015.

De la Iglesia, Álex, 'Vindicación de la camiseta', *El País*, 7 July 2007, p. 45.

——, 'Carta a *El País* de un cineasta del país', Cultura.elpais.com, 6 February 2008. Available at: <http://elpais.com/diario/2008/02/06/opinion/1202252411_850215.html>. Accessed 12 August 2015.

——, 'Discurso íntegro de Álex de la Iglesia en la entrega de los Goya', Cultura.elpais.com, 13 February 2011. Available at: <http://cultura.elpais.com/cultura/2011/02/13/actualidad/1297551609_850215.html>. Accessed 12 August 2015.

Dennison, Stephanie and Song Hwee Lim, 'Situating World Cinema as a Theoretical Problem', in Stephanie Dennison and Song Hwee Lim (eds), *Remapping World Cinema: Identity, Culture and Politics in Film* (London: Wallflower, 2006), pp. 1–15.

De Valck, Marijke and Malte Hagener, 'Down with Cinephilia? Long Live Cinephilia?', in Marijke De Valck and Malte Hagener (eds), *Cinephilia: Movies, Love and Memory* (Amsterdam: Amsterdam University Press, 2005), pp. 11–24.

Díaz López, Marina, 'El Deseo's "Itinerary": Almodóvar and the Spanish Film Industry', in Marvin D'Lugo and Kathleen M. Vernon (eds), *A Companion to Pedro Almodóvar* (Malden, MA: Wiley-Blackwell, 2013), pp. 107–28.

D'Lugo, Marvin, 'Lo que se espera de España', *Academia: revista del cine español* no. 15, 1996, pp. 39–44.

——, *Guide to the Cinema of Spain* (Westport, CT: Greenwood Press, 1997).

——, *Pedro Almodóvar* (Urbana: University of Illinois Press, 2006).

——, 'Carlos Saura', in Jo Labanyi and Tatjana Pavlović (eds), *A Companion to Spanish Cinema* (Malden, MA: Wiley-Blackwell, 2013), pp. 124–30.

Echevarría, Ignacio, 'Patinazo de cine: Bruselas paraliza la orden que fijaba los nuevos criterios para la subvención del cine español', *El País*, 29 November 2009, p. 32.

——, 'La CT: un cambio de paradigma', in Carlos Acevedo *et al.*, *CT o la Cultura de la Transición: crítica a 35 años de cultura española* (Madrid: Debolsillo, 2012), pp. 25–36.

Elsaesser, Thomas, *European Cinema: Face to Face with Hollywood* (Amsterdam: Amsterdam University Press, 2005).

English, James F., *The Economy of Prestige, Prizes, Awards and the Circulation of Cultural Value* (Cambridge, MA: Harvard University Press, 2005).

Epps, Brad and Despina Kakoudaki, 'Approaching Almodóvar: Thirty Years of Reinvention', in Brad Epps and Despina Kakoudaki, *All about Almodóvar: A Passion for Cinema* (Minneapolis and London: University of Minnesota Press, 2009), pp. 1–34.

Escobar López, Almudena, 'The Accursed Poets', *Little White Lies* no. 36, July/August 2011, pp. 32–5.

Esquirol, Meritxell and Josep Lluís Fecé, 'Un freak en el parque de atracciones: *Torrente el brazo tonto de la ley*', *Archivos de la Filmoteca* vol. 39 no. 10, 2001, pp. 27–39.

Evans, Chris, 'Spain: All Peer-to-Peer Activity May Soon Be Outlawed', *Screen International* no. 1696, 2009, p. 20.

——, 'Giving Audiences What They Want', *Screen International online*, 9 February 2010. Available at: <http://www.screendaily.com/features/territory-focus/giving-audiences-what-they-want/5010529.article>. Accessed 12 August 2015.

——, 'Carlos Cuatros to Replace Ignasi Guardans as ICAA Director', *Screen International online*, 22 October 2010. Available at: <http://www.screendaily.com/news/europe/-carlos-cuatros-to-replace-ignasi-guardans-as-icaa-director/5019720.article>. Accessed 12 August 2015.

Evans, Peter W. (ed.), *Spanish Cinema: The Auteurist Generation* (Oxford: Oxford University Press, 1990).

——, 'Cifesa: Cinema and Authoritarian Aesthetics', in Helen Graham and Jo Labanyi (eds), *Spanish Cultural Studies: An Introduction* (Oxford: Oxford University Press, 1995), p. 215.

Falicov, Tamara L., 'Ibero Latin American Coproductions: Transnational Cinema, Spain's Public Relations Venture or Both?', in Stephanie Dennison (ed.), *Contemporary Hispanic Cinema: Interrogating the Transnational in Spanish and Latin American Film* (Woodbridge, Suffolk: Tamesis, 2013), pp. 67–88.

Falquina, Ángel, 'Carta a Nuevo Fotogramas: a vueltas con los premios', *Nuevo Fotogramas*, 28 February 1975, p. 36.

Farrell, Mary, 'Spain in the New European Union: In Search of a New Role and Identity', in Sebastian Balfour (ed.), *The Politics of Contemporary Spain* (London: Routledge, 2005), pp. 215–34.

Faulkner, Sally, *A Cinema of Contradiction: Spanish Film in the 1960s* (Edinburgh: Edinburgh University Press, 2006).

——, *A History of Spanish Film: Cinema and Society 1910–2010* (London: Bloomsbury, 2013).

Fecé, José Luis and Cristina Pujol, 'La crisis imaginada de un cine sin público', in Luis Alonso García (ed.), *Once miradas sobre la crisis y el cine español* (Madrid: Ocho y Medio, 2003), pp. 147–65.

Fernández Colorado, Luis, 'Los premios', *Cuadernos de la Academia* no. 4, November 1998, pp. 113–22.

Fernández Meneses, Jara, 'Spanish Cinema Legislation 1983–2013', unpublished PhD thesis, University of Kent, 2016.

Fernández-Santos, Ángel, 'Sobre un nuevo cine español', *Nuestro Cine* no. 60, 1967, pp. 11–20.

——, 'Una coherente contradicción', *El País*, 31 October 1996, p. 40.

Fernández-Santos, Elsa, 'Los Goya de "Malamadre"', Cultura.elpais.com, 15 February 2010. Available at: <http://www.elpais.com/cultura/2010/02/14/actualidad/1266102004_850215.html>. Accessed 12 August 2015.

——, '25 aniversario de los Goya', Cultura.elpais.com, 13 February 2011. Available at: <http://www.elpais.com/articulo/cultura/25/aniversario/Goya/elpepucul/20110213elpepucul_1/Tes>. Accessed 12 August 2015.

Francia, Juan Ignacio and Julio Pérez Perucha, 'First Film: Pedro Almodóvar', in Paula Willoquet-Maricondi (ed.), *Pedro Almodóvar: Interviews* (Jackson: University Press of Mississippi, 2004), pp. 4–8.

Galán, Diego, *Venturas y desventuras de la prima Angélica* (Valencia: Fernando Torres, 1974).

——, *Pilar Miró: nadie me enseñó a vivir* (Madrid: Debolsillo, 2007).

——, 'Enemigos pequeños', Cultura.elpais.com, 27 November 2009. Available at: <http://elpais.com/diario/2009/11/27/cine/1259276414_850215.html>. Accessed 12 August 2015.

Galvín, Virginia, 'El Padrino: chicas, intrigas, champán ...', *Vanity Fair* no. 30, February 2011, pp. 106–17.

Galt, Rosalind, *Global Art Cinema: New Theories and Histories*, co-ed. with Karl Schoonover (New York: Oxford University Press, 2010).

García, Rocío, 'De la Iglesia quiere dirigir la Academia', Elpais.com, 19 May 2009. Available at: <http://elpais.com/diario/2009/05/19/cultura/1242684001_850215.html>. Accessed 12 August 2015.

——, 'Los cineastas contra la Orden no tienen ni idea', Cultura.elpais.com, 21 November 2009. Available at: <http://cultura.elpais.com/cultura/2009/11/25/actualidad/1259103603_850215.html>. Accessed 12 August 2015.

——, 'Los hermanos Almodóvar vuelven a la Academia de Cine', Elpais.com, April 2011. Available at: <http://cultura.elpais.com/cultura/2011/04/07/actualidad/1302127210_850215.html>. Accessed 12 August 2015.

——, 'No venimos a romper nada', *El País*, 11 April 2011, p. 36.

——, 'González Macho reconoce que le produce inquietud el cambio ministerial', Elpais.com, 14 December 2011. Available at: <http://cultura.elpais.com/cultura/2011/12/14/actualidad/1323817202_850215.html>. Accessed 12 August 2015.

—— and Gregorio Belinchón, 'La ministra de Cultura destituye a Ignasi Guardans, director del ICAA', Elpais.com, 21 October 2010. Available at: <http://www.elpais.com/articulo/cultura/ministra/Cultura/destituye/Ignasi/Guardans/director/ICAA/elpepucul/20101021elpepucul_11/Tes>. Accessed 12 August 2015.

——, 'Entusiasmos y escepticismos en torno al Congreso del cine español', Elpais.com, 19 September 2014. Available at: <http://cultura.elpais.com/cultura/2014/09/19/actualidad/1411139226_469888.html>. Accessed 12 August 2015.

García, Toni, 'España es un país partido en dos: si uno ríe, el otro llora', Elpais.com, 8 September 2010. Available at: <http://elpais.com/diario/2010/09/08/cultura/1283896801_850215.html>. Accessed 12 August 2015.

García-Canclini, Néstor, *La globalización imaginada* (Buenos Aires: Paidós, 2005 [1999]).

García de León, María Antonia, *Élites discriminadas (sobre el poder de las mujeres)* (Barcelona: Anthropos, 1994).

—— and Teresa Maldonado, *Pedro Almodóvar, la otra España cañí (sociología y crítica cinematográficas)* (Ciudad Real: Diputación de Ciudad Real, 1989).

García Escudero, José María, *Cine español* (Madrid: Rialp, 1962).

García Fernández, Emilio C., *El cine español contemporáneo* (Barcelona: CILEH, 1992).

——, 'Los miembros', *Cuadernos de la Academia* no. 4, 1998, pp. 51–5.

Gómez Bermúdez de Castro, Ramiro, 'Los estatutos', *Cuadernos de la Academia* no. 4, 1998, pp. 21–38.

González Macho, Enrique, 'Carta del Presidente', *Academia: revista del cine español* no. 180, June 2011, p. 44.

Gracia, Jordi, *Estado y cultura: el despertar de una conciencia crítica bajo el franquismo, 1940–1962* (Barcelona: Anagrama, 2006).

Graham, Helen and Jo Labanyi, 'Chronology', in Helen Graham and Jo Labanyi (eds), *Spanish Cultural Studies: An Introduction* (Oxford: Oxford University Press, 1995), pp. 426–42.

Granado, Verónica P., *20 años de Goyas al cine español* (Madrid: Aguilar, 2006).

Green, Jennifer, 'The Game in Spain', *Screen International*, Spain Special: Berlin 2007, February 2007, p. 2.

'Guardans "El cine ha de estar por encima del debate político"', Hoyesarte.com, 28 June 2009. Available at: <www.hoyesarte.com/cine/guardans-qel-cine-ha-de-estar-por-encima-del -debate-politicoq_87630>. Accessed 12 August 2015.

Guarner, J. L., 'La Sex-Comedy a la española o un regalo para Marcuse', *Nuevo Fotogramas* no. 1260, 8 December 1972, pp. 24–6.

Gubern, Roman, *La censura: función política y ordenamiento jurídico bajo el franquismo (1936–1975)* (Barcelona: Ediciones Península, 1981).

——, 'El cine sonoro (1930–1939)', in Roman Gubern *et al.*, *Historia del cine español* (Madrid: Cátedra, 1995), pp. 123–76.

Gunning, Tom, 'The Cinema of Attractions: Early Film, Its Spectator and the Avant-garde', *Wide Angle* vol. 8 nos. 3–4, 1986, pp. 63–77.

Hamilos, Paul, 'Spanish Film-makers Hit Back at "Cultural War" on Funding', *Observer*, 5 October 2013. Available at: <http://www.theguardian.com/world/2013/oct/05/spanish -film-makers-hit-back-at-cultural-war>. Accessed 12 August 2015.

Harbord, Janet, *Film Cultures* (London: Sage, 2002).

Hayward, Susan, *French National Cinema* (London: Routledge, 1993).

Heredero, Carlos F., 'IIEC-EOC', in José Luis Borau (ed.), *Diccionario del cine español* (Madrid: Fundación Autor/Alianza, 1998), pp. 465–7.

——, 'Miradas hacia el futuro', *Cahiers du Cinéma España* no. 1, May 2007, pp. 10–32.

——, 'Hacia una nueva identidad', *Cahiers du Cinéma España* no. 27, October 2009, pp. 6–8.

—— and C. Reviriego, 'Nueva Orden, nueva polémica, *Cahiers du Cinéma España* no. 25, July/August 2009, p. 58.

——, 'Entrevista: Ignasi Guardans, Director General del ICAA', *Cahiers du Cinéma España* no. 29, December 2009, pp. 62–5.

Hermoso, Borja, 'Ceremonia jurásica', Elpais.com, 2 February 2009. Available at: <http://www. elpais.com/articulo/cultura/Ceremonia/jurasica/elpepucul/20090202elpepucul_3/Tes>. Accessed 12 August 2015.

——, 'Icíar Bollaín: De la Iglesia "ha abierto una crisis innecesaria y muy dañina"', Elpais.com, 28 January 2011. Available at: <http://www.elpais.com/articulo/cultura/Iciar/Bollain/Iglesia/ ha/abierto/crisis/innecesaria/danina/elpepucul/20110128 elpepucul_5/Tes>. Accessed 12 August 2015.

——, 'El Goya nuestro de cada año (mea culpa)', Elpais.com, 14 February 2012. Available at: <http://cultura.elpais.com/cultura/2012/02/13/actualidad/1329128942_955094.html>. Accessed 12 August 2015.

Hernández, Marta, *El aparato cinematográfico español* (Madrid: Akal 74, 1976).

—— and Manolo Revuelta, *30 años de cine al alcance de todos los españoles* (Bilbao: Zero, 1976).

Herrero, Gerardo, 'Tan lejos y tan cerca', *Academia: revista del cine español* no. 10, April 1995, pp. 86–7.

Hidalgo, Manuel, 'Acción mutante en el cine español: los nuevos cineastas españoles están aquí', *El Mundo* [Cinelandia], 15 May 1993, p. 1.

Higson, Andrew, 'The Concept of National Cinema', *Screen* vol. 30 no. 4, Autumn 1989, pp. 36–46.

Hopewell, John, *Out of the Past: Spanish Cinema after Franco* (London: BFI, 1986).

———, '"Art and a Lack of Money": The Crisis of the Spanish Film Industry, 1977–1990', *Quarterly Review of Film and Video* vol. 13 no. 4, 1991, pp. 113–22.

Irwin, Robert McKee and Maricruz Castro Ricalde, *Global Mexican Cinema: Its Golden Age* (London: BFI, 2013).

Izquierdo, Laura, 'Lee aquí la única crítica positiva de "Torrente 4"'. Available at: <http://www.rollingstone.es/concerts/view/lee-aqui-la-unica-critica-positiva-de -torrente-4>. Accessed 12 August 2015.

Johnson, Randal, 'Editor's Introduction', in Pierre Bourdieu, *The Field of Cultural Production: Essays on Art and Literature* (Cambridge: Polity, 1993), pp. 1–25.

Jordan, Barry, *Writing and Politics in Franco's Spain* (London: Routledge, 1990).

———, 'Audiences, Film Culture, Public Subsidies: The End of Spanish Cinema?', in Ann Davies (ed.), *Spain on Screen: Developments in Contemporary Spanish Cinema* (London: Palgrave, 2011), pp. 19–40.

Kowalsky, Daniel, 'Rated S: Softcore Pornography and the Spanish Transition to Democracy 1977–82', in Antonio Lázaro-Reboll and Andrew Willis (eds), *Spanish Popular Cinema* (Manchester: Manchester University Press, 2004), pp. 188–208.

Kugelberg, Johan, 'On Punk: An Aesthetic', in Jon Savage and Johan Kugelberg (eds), *Punk: An Aesthetic* (New York: Rizzoli, 2012), pp. 43–143.

Labanyi, Jo, 'Censorship and the Fear of Mass Culture', in Helen Graham and Jo Labanyi (eds), *Spanish Cultural Studies: An Introduction* (Oxford: Oxford University Press, 1995), pp. 207–14.

Lara, Fernando, 'El cine español ante una alternativa democrática', in Enrique Brasó *et al.*, *Siete trabajos de base sobre el cine español* (Valencia: Fernando Torres, 1975), pp. 221–43.

———, 'La hora de la verdad', *Fotogramas*, February, 1984, pp. 42–3.

———, 'Ni propios ni extraños', *Cahiers du Cinéma España* no. 34, May 2010, p. 69.

———, Personal interview with Nuria Triana-Toribio, Madrid, 29 October 2014.

Lázaro-Reboll, Antonio, 'Facing Monstrosity in Goya's *Los Caprichos* (1799)', unpublished PhD thesis, University of Nottingham, 2004.

———, '*Torrente: el brazo tonto de la ley* ye *Torrente 2: Misión en Marbella/Torrente: The Dumb Arm of the Law* and *Torrente 2: Mission in Marbella*', in Alberto Mira (ed.), *The Cinema of Spain and Portugal* (London: Wallflower, 2005), pp. 219–28.

———, *Spanish Horror Films* (Edinburgh: Edinburgh University Press, 2012).

Ledesma, Eduardo, 'Intermediality and Spanish Experimental Cinema: Text and Image Interactions in the Lyrical Films of the Barcelona School', *Journal of Spanish Cultural Studies* vol. 14 no. 3, 2013, pp. 254–74.

Ley del Cine 55/2007, de 28 de Diciembre (Madrid: Academia de las Artes y las Ciencias Cinematográficas, 2007).

Lindo, Elvira, 'La ley (del silencio) de Ángeles González-Sinde', Elpaís.com, 12 November 2011. Available at: <http://elpais.com/diario/2011/11/12/revistasabado/1321052404 _850215.html>. Accessed 12 August 2015.

Lodge, Guy, 'Oscars 2015: What Will Win Best Foreign Langugae Film?', Theguardian.com, 4 February 2015. Available at: <http://www.theguardian.com/film/2015/feb/04/oscars -2015-predictions-best-foreign-language-film>. Accessed 12 August 2015.

Losilla, Carlos, 'Legislación, industria y escritura', in José Hurtado and Francisco Picó (eds), *Escritos sobre el cine español (1937–1987)* (Valencia: Filmoteca Valenciana, 1989), pp. 33–43.

——, 'Fernando Colomo', in José Luis Borau (ed.), *Diccionario del cine español* (Madrid: Fundación Autor/Alianza, 1998), p. 242.

MacDonald, Alice, 'Performing Gender and Nation in *¡Ay, Carmela!*', *Journal of Iberian and Latin American Studies* vol. 4 no. 1, 1998, pp. 47–59.

'Manifiesto'. Available at: <http://cineastascontralaorden.blogaliza.org/manifiesto/>. Accessed 12 August 2015.

Marín Bellón, Federico, 'El "Avatar" del cine español', ABC.es, 15 March 2011. Available at: <http://www.abc.es/20110315/cultura-cine/abci-avatar-cine-espanol-201103150411.html>. Accessed 12 August 2015.

Martin, Deborah, *The Cinema of Lucrecia Martel* (Manchester: Manchester University Press, 2016).

Martin-Márquez, Susan, *Feminist Discourse and Spanish Cinema: Sight Unseen* (Oxford: Oxford University Press, 1999).

Marx, Karl and Friedrich Engels, *The German Ideology*, ed. and intro. by C. J. Arthur (New York: International Publishers, 1970).

Miñarro, Lluís, 'Visión desde el gallinero', *Cahiers du Cinéma España* no. 45, March 2011, p. 63.

Minguet, Joan M. *et al.*, 'Primer debate: la modernidad cinematográfica', in Julio Pérez Perucha, Francisco Javier Gómez Tarín and Agustín Rubio Alcober (eds), *Olas rotas: el cine español de los sesenta y las rupturas de la modernidad* (Madrid: AEHC/Ediciones del Imán, 2009), pp. 407–31.

Ministerio de Educación, Cultura y Deporte, 'Base de datos de películas clasificadas'. Available at: <http://www.mecd.gob.es/cultura-mecd/areas-cultura/cine/mc/cdc/portada.html>. Accessed 12 August 2015.

Mira Nouselles, Alberto, *The A to Z of Spanish Cinema* (Lanham, MD: Rowman and Littlefield, 2010).

Miró, Pilar, 'Ten Years of Spanish Cinema', in Samuel Amell (ed.), *Literature, the Arts and Democracy: Spain in the Eighties* (London: Associated University Presses, 1990), pp. 38–46.

Mitchell, Wendy, 'Cinema Is Never "Foreign"', Screendaily.com, 21 November 2014. Available at: <http://www.screendaily.com/5080272.article?utm_source=newsletter&utm_medium=email7utm_campaign=Newsletter78>. Accessed 12 August 2015.

Monterde, José Enrique, 'Continuismo y disidencia (1951–1962)', in Roman Gubern *et al.*, *Historia del cine español* (Madrid: Cátedra, 1995), pp. 239–93.

——, 'Tercera Vía', in José Luis Borau (ed.), *Diccionario del cine español* (Madrid: Fundación Autor/Alianza, 1998), pp. 848–9.

Montero, Rosa, 'Una manera de fabricar público: Pedro Lazaga', *Nuevo Fotogramas*, 11 April 1975, pp. 8–10.

——, 'Pedro Almodóvar: un chiquito como yo', *El País Semanal*, 28 September 1986, pp. 21–4.

Mortimore, Roger, 'Spain: Out of the Past', *Sight & Sound* vol. 43 no. 4, Autumn 1973/Winter 1974, pp. 119–202.

'Muere García Escudero, figura intelectual de la España del siglo XX', ABC.es, 9 May 2002. Available at: <www.abc.es/hemeroteca/historico-09-05-2002/abc/Cultura/muere-garcia-escudero-figura-intelectual-de-la-españa-del-siglo-xx_97860.html>. Accessed 12 August 2015.

Muñoz Martínez-Mora, Inés, 'Un simulacro de "glamour"', Elpais.com, 14 February 2011.

Available at: <http://www.elpais.com/articulo/cultura/simulacro/glamour/ elpepicul/
20110214elpepucul_1/Tes>. Accessed 12 August 2015.

Muñoz Suay, Ricardo, 'Lágrimas de cocodrilo', *Nuevo Fotogramas*, 14 February 1975, p. 6.

——, 'De los cómicos', *Nuevo Fotogramas*, 28 February 1975, p. 6.

——, 'Réplica', *Nuevo Fotogramas*, 28 February 1975, p. 7.

——, 'Columna-bis: censura ¿nuevas normas? encuesta', *Nuevo Fotogramas*, 14 March 1975,
pp. 10–11.

Nowell-Smith, Geoffrey and Christophe Dupin (eds), *The British Film Institute, the Government
and Film Culture, 1933–2000* (Manchester: Manchester University Press, 2012).

Obelleiro, Paola, 'El galleguismo olvidado de Wenceslao Fernández Flórez', Elpais.com, 4 May
2010. Available at: <http://elpais.com/diario/2010/05/04/galicia/1272968302_850215
.html>. Accessed 12 August 2015.

Ortega, María Luisa, 'Relaciones institucionales y presencia pública', *Cuadernos de la Academia*
no. 4, 1998, pp. 141–53.

Ortiz Villeta, Áurea, 'Fernando Trueba', in José Luis Borau (ed.), *Diccionario del cine español*
(Madrid: Fundación Autor/Alianza, 1998), p. 868.

Osborne, Robert, *85 Years of the Oscars: The Official History of the Academy Awards* (New York and
London: Abbeville Press, 2013).

'Oscars Head Isaacs Calls for More Diversity after Row', *BBC News*, 17 January 2015.
Available at: <www.bbc.co.uk/news/entertainment-arts-30862139>. Accessed 12 August
2015.

Otero, José María, 'El horizonte de las coproducciones', *Cuadernos de la Academia* no. 5, 1999,
pp. 26–7.

Palomo, Miguel Ángel and Natalia Marcos, 'El cine español que le gusta al ministro de Cultura',
Elpais.com, 11 August 2015. Available at: <http://cultura.elpais.com/cultura/2015/08/11/
television/1439318188_455540.html>. Accessed 12 August 2015.

Payán, Miguel Juan, 'Buenafuente presentará los premios Goya', Accioncine.net, 16 November
2009. Available at: <www.accioncine.es/reportajes/noticias/333-buenafuente-presentara
-los-premios-goya.pdf>. Accessed 12 August 2015.

Peláez Paz, Andrés, 'Las publicaciones', *Cuadernos de la Academia* no. 4, 1998, pp. 91–112.

Pena, Jaime, 'La vida de los peces', *Cahiers du Cinéma España* no. 46, June 2011, p. 33.

Pérez Merinero, Carlos and David Pérez Merinero, *Cine español: algunos materiales por derribo*
(Madrid: Editorial Cuadernos para el Diálogo, 1973).

Pérez Millán, Juan Antonio, *Pilar Miró: directora de cine* (Valladolid: Festival de Cine de
Valladolid, 1992).

Perriam, Chris, *Stars and Masculinity in Spanish Cinema* (Oxford: Oxford University Press, 2003).

—— and Nuria Triana-Toribio, 'The Politics of Stardom and Celebrity', in Jo Labanyi and
Tatjana Pavlović (eds), *A Companion to Spanish Cinema* (Malden, MA: Wiley-Blackwell, 2013),
pp. 326–42.

Pita, Elena, 'Pedro Almodóvar: "El cine es cosa de francotiradores"', *La Revista de El Mundo* no. 9,
17 December 1995, pp. 34–40.

Pollarolo, Giovanna, 'Frágiles asideros', *Academia: revista del cine español* no. 10, April 1995,
pp. 60–7.

Povedano, Julián, 'Buenafuente presentará la Gala de los Goya 2010', Elmundo.es, 16 November
2009. Available at: <www.elmundo.es/elmundo/2009/11/16/cultura/1258367507.html>.
Accessed 12 August 2015.

Preston, Paul, 'The Monarchy of Juan Carlos: From Dictator's Dreams to Democratic Realities', in Sebastian Balfour (ed.), *The Politics of Contemporary Spain* (London: Routledge, 2005), pp. 27–38.

Pujol Ozonas, Cristina, *Fans, cinéfilos y cinéfagos: una aproximación a las culturas y los gustos cinematográficos* (Barcelona: Editorial UOC, 2011).

Quintana, Ángel, 'El cine como realidad y el mundo como representación: síntomas de los noventa', *Archivos de la Filmoteca* no. 39, October 2001, pp. 9–25.

——, 'Entre el genio y la marca', *Cahiers du Cinéma España* no. 27, October 2009, pp. 20–1.

——, Personal interview with Nuria Triana-Toribio, Girona, 15 April 2013.

Reviriego, Carlos and Jara Yáñez, 'Pequeño cine en construcción', *Cahiers du Cinéma España* no. 27, October 2009, pp. 22–3.

Riambau, Esteve, 'La década "socialista" (1982–1992)', in Roman Gubern *et al.*, *Historia del cine español* (Madrid: Cátedra, 1995), pp. 339–447.

——, 'Fotogramas', in José Luis Borau (ed.), *Diccionario del cine español* (Madrid: Fundación Autor/Alianza, 1998), p. 373.

——, 'Una institución imprescindible', *Cuadernos de la Academia* no. 4, November 1998, pp. 39–50.

—— and Casimiro Torreiro, *La escuela de Barcelona: el cine de la 'gauche divine'* (Barcelona: Anagrama, 1999).

Ríos Pérez, Sergio, 'Storm Hangs over Spanish Cinema', Cineuropa.org, 28 December 2009. Available at: <http://cineuropa.org/cf.aspx?t=cfocusnewsdetail&l=en&tid=1632&did=116453>. Accessed 12 August 2015.

Rivas, Francisco, 'Entrevista con Pedro Almodóvar: el director de moda', *Magazine Moda 1* no. 2, August/September 1982, pp. 60–3.

Rodríguez Maeso, Silvia and Marta Araújo, 'Eurocentrism, Political Struggles and the Entrenched *Will-to-Ignorance*: An Introduction', in Marta Araújo and Silvia Rodríguez Maeso (eds), *Eurocentrism, Racism and Knowledge: Debates on History and Power in Europe and the Americas* (Houndmills, Hants.: Palgrave Macmillan, 2015), pp. 1–22.

Roma, Sara, 'La cosecha de terror', *Academia: noticias del cine español, especial XXII premios anuales de la Academia* no. 142, February 2008, pp. 30–1.

Romaguera i Ramió, Joaquim, 'Iván Zulueta', in José Luis Borau (ed.), *Diccionario del cine español* (Madrid: Fundación Autor/Alianza, 1998), p. 925.

Romero-Jodar, Andrés, 'Review of Balada Triste de Trompeta/The Last Circus', Academia.edu, 4 September 2013. Available at: <https://www.academia.edu/4422714/Balada_Triste_de_Trompeta_The_Last_Circus_2010_>. Accessed 12 August 2015.

Ruiz Mantilla, Jesús, 'Entre Puccini y Berlanga', Elpais.com, 14 February 2011. Available at: <http://www.elpais.com/articulo/cultura/Puccini/Berlanga/elpepicul/20110214elpepicul_9/Tes>. Accessed 12 August 2015.

Sánchez, Isabel and Julieta Martialay, 'Qué bueno que viniste', *Academia: revista del cine español* no. 10, April 1995, pp. 89–93.

Sánchez, Sergi, 'Cambio ... ¿radical?', *Fotogramas* no. 1969, November 2007, p. 11.

Sánchez Salas, Daniel and Bernardo Sánchez Salas, 'Una cuestión de raccord', *Cuadernos de la Academia* no. 4, November 1998, pp. 63–88.

Santamarina, Antonio, 'Academia de las Artes y las Ciencias Cinematográficas de España', in José Luis Borau (ed.), *Diccionario del cine español* (Madrid: Fundación Autor/Alianza, 1998), pp. 27–8.

——, 'Muñoz Suay: la memoria rescatada', *Cahiers du Cinéma España* no. 1, May 2007, pp. 100–1.

Sartori, Beatrice, 'La generación de la crisis cambia la imagen', *El Mundo* [Cinelandia], 15 May 1993, pp. 3–5.

'Se creó la Federación Iberoamericana de Academias de Cine', Haciendocine.com, 26 February 2013. Available at: <www.haciendocine.com.ar/node/40970>. Accessed 12 August 2015.

Segura, Santiago, 'Un genio en calzoncillos', *El País Semanal*, 13 December 2009, p. 45.

——, 'Monólogo de Santiago Segura en Los Goya 2012', Youtube.com, 20 February 2012. Available at: <http://www.youtube.com/watch?v=KFZmaXDOeMA>. Accessed 11 August 2015.

Shaw, Deborah, *The Three Amigos: The Transnational Filmmaking of Guillermo del Toro, Alejandro González Iñárritu and Alonso Cuarón* (Manchester: Manchester University Press, 2013).

——, 'Deconstructing and Reconstructing "Transnational Cinema"', in Stephanie Dennison (ed.), *Contemporary Hispanic Cinema: Interrogating the Transnational in Spanish and Latin American Film* (Woodbridge, Suffolk: Tamesis, 2013), pp. 47–65.

Shohat, Ella and Robert Stam, *Unthinking Eurocentrism: Multiculturalism and the Media* (New York: Routledge, 1994).

Shone, Tom, 'The Oscars: Who Calls the Shots?', Theguardian.com, 24 February 2011. Available at: <http://www.theguardian.com/film/2011/feb/24/oscars-investigation-power-behind-academy>. Accessed 12 August 2015.

Smith, Paul Julian, *Desire Unlimited: The Cinema of Pedro Almodóvar* (London: Verso, 1994).

——, *Vision Machines: Cinema, Literature and Sexuality in Spain and Cuba, 1983–1993* (London: Verso, 1996).

——, 'Absolute Precision', *Sight & Sound* vol. 8 no. 4, April 1998, pp. 6–9.

——, 'Preface to the Second Edition', *Desire Unlimited: The Cinema of Pedro Almodóvar* (London: Verso, 2000), pp. ix–xi.

——, 'Quality TV? The *Periodistas* Notebook', in *Contemporary Spanish Culture: TV, Fashion, Art and Film* (Cambridge: Polity, 2003), pp. 9–33.

——, 'Resurrecting the Art Movie? Almodóvar's Blue Period', in *Contemporary Spanish Culture: TV, Fashion, Art and Film* (Cambridge: Polity, 2003), pp. 144–68.

——, 'The Sea Inside', *Sight & Sound* vol. 15 no. 3, March 2005, pp. 71–2.

——, 'Family Plots: The Politics of Affect in Spanish Television Drama of the Millennium', in *Spanish Visual Culture: Cinema, Television, Internet* (Manchester: Manchester University Press, 2006), pp. 29–50.

——, 'Women, Windmills and Wedge Heels', *Sight & Sound* vol. 16 no. 6, June 2006, pp. 16–18.

——, 'Pan's Labyrinth', *Film Quarterly* vol. 60 no. 4, Summer 2007, pp. 4–8.

——, 'Pedro Almodóvar', in Jo Labanyi and Tatjana Pavlović (eds), *A Companion to Spanish Cinema* (Malden, MA: Wiley-Blackwell, 2012), pp. 130–5.

Socías, Jordi, 'Un reparto de película', *El País Semanal*, 17 February 2013, pp. 38–44.

Stone, Rob, *Julio Medem* (Manchester: Manchester University Press, 2007).

'Technicolor: postproducción digital en 3D de Torrente 4', *Cineinforme*, November/December 2010, p. 18.

Thompson, Michael, 'Remembering What Didn't Happen in the Civil War: *Beatus Ille* and *¡Ay, Carmela!*', in Alison Ribeiro de Menezes, Roberta Ann Quance and Anne L. Walsh (eds), *Guerra y memoria en la España contemporánea/War and Memory in Contemporary Spain* (Madrid: Verbum, 2009), pp. 147–63.

Torreiro, Casimiro, '¿Una dictadura liberal? (1965–1969)', in Roman Gubern *et al.*, *Historia del cine español* (Madrid: Cátedra, 1995), pp. 295–335.

Torres, Augusto M., *Spanish Cinema: 1896–1983* (Madrid: ICAA/Ministerio de Cultura, 1986).

Trenzado Romero, Manuel, *Cultura de masas y cambio político: el cine español de la transición* (Madrid: Siglo Veintiuno, 1999).

Triana-Toribio, Nuria, 'Ana Mariscal, Franco's Disavowed Star', in Ulrike Sieglohr (ed.), *Heroines without Heroes: Reconstructing Female and National Identities in European Cinema, 1945–51* (London: Cassell, 2000), pp. 185–95.

——, 'A Punk Called Pedro: La Movida in the Films of Pedro Almodóvar', in B. Jordan and R. Morgan-Tamosunas (eds), *Contemporary Spanish Cultural Studies* (London: Arnold, 2000), pp. 274–82.

——, *Spanish National Cinema* (London: Routledge, 2003).

——, 'Santiago Segura: Just When You Thought Spanish Masculinities Were Getting Better ...', *Hispanic Research Journal* vol. 5 no. 2, June 2004, pp. 147–56.

——, 'Auteurism and Commerce in Contemporary Spanish Cinema: *directores mediáticos*', *Screen* vol. 49 no. 3, Autumn 2008, pp. 256–76.

——, 'FICXixón y Seminci: Two Spanish Film Festivals at the End of the Festival Era', *Journal of Spanish Cultural Studies* vol. 12 no. 2, October 2011, pp. 217–36.

——, 'Telecinco Cinema and El Deseo', in Jo Labanyi and Tatjana Pavlović (eds), *A Companion to Spanish Cinema* (Malden, MA: Wiley-Blackwell, 2013), pp. 420–6.

——, 'Residual Film Cultures: Real and Imagined Futures of Spanish Cinema', *Bulletin of Hispanic Studies* vol. 91 no. 1, 2014, pp. 65–81.

'Una noche de sorpresas', *Academia: noticias del cine español, especial XXII premios anuales de la Academia* no. 142, February 2008, p. 5.

Unión de Cineastas, 'Comité de Coordinación'. Available at: <http://uniondecineastas.es/comite -de-coordinacion>. Accessed 12 August 2015.

Vall, Pere, 'Para románticos sin azúcar y fans de las sorpresas', Fotogramas.es. Available at: <http//www.fotogramas.es/Peliculas/La-vida-de-los-peces>. Accessed 12 August 2015.

Vergés, Rosa, Personal interview with Nuria Triana-Toribio, Barcelona, 22 April 2014.

Vernon, Kathleen M. and Barbara Morris, *Post-Franco, Postmodern: The Films of Pedro Almodóvar* (Westport, CT: Greenwood Press, 1995).

Vidal, Belén, 'Memories of Underdevelopment', in Dina Iordanova, David Martin-Jones and Belén Vidal (eds), *Cinema at the Periphery* (Detroit, MI: Wayne State University Press, 2010), pp. 211–31.

——, 'The Cinephilic Citation in the Essay Films by José Luis Guerín and Isaki Lacuesta', Talk delivered at the Centre for the Interdisciplinary Study of Film and the Moving Image, University of Kent, 27 March 2013.

Vidal, Nuria, *El cine de Pedro Almodóvar* (Madrid: ICCA/Ministerio de Cultura, 1988).

Vilarós, Teresa, *El mono del desencanto: una crítica cultural de la transición española (1973–1993)* (Madrid: Siglo Veintiuno, 1998).

Villazana, Libia, *Transnational Financial Structures in the Cinema of Latin America: Programa Ibermedia in Study* (Saarbrucken: Verlag Dr Müller, 2009).

Vincendeau, Ginette, 'Issues in European Cinema', in John Hill and Pamela Church Gibson (eds), *World Cinema: Critical Approaches* (Oxford: Oxford University Press, 2000), pp. 56–64.

Wallerstein, Claire, 'Lost in the Crowd', *Screen International*, Special Issue: Spain, 2008, pp. 2–3.

Wasson, Haidee, *Museum Movies: The Museum of Modern Art and the Birth of Art Cinema* (Berkeley: University of California Press, 2005).

Whittaker, Tom, *The Films of Elías Querejeta: A Producer of Landscapes* (Cardiff: University of Wales Press, 2011).

Wottle, Davin, 'Carta a Mr Belvedere', *Nuevo Fotogramas*, 28 June 1974, p. 9.

Yáñez, Jara, *La aritmética de la creación: entrevistas con productores del cine español contemporáneo* (Alcalá de Henares: Festival de Cine de Alcalá de Henares, 2009).

Index

Spanish films are indexed by their English titles, with a cross-reference from the original version except where this is so close to the English as to be unnecessary. Page numbers in **bold** denote detailed treatment; those in *italic* refer to illustrations. *n* = endnote. *t* = table.

Aída (TV 2005–14) 55, 56
Alborch, Carmen 127n27
All About My Mother (1999)
  1, 55, 69
  awards/nominations 58,
  106
All Night Long (2010) 98–9
Allen, Woody 1, 128–9n3
Almodóvar, Agustín 12, 36,
  57–8, 69, 85
Almodóvar, Pedro 12, 36, 47,
  51, 55, **56–71**, 85, 86,
  89, 94, 99, 108, 128n1
  comments on other film-
  makers 64–5, 128–9n3
  commercial success 61
  domestic reputation 59
  Goya awards/nominations
  48t, 57–8, 61, 75, 100–1,
  101t
  international awards/
  nominations 1, 58, 70
  international reputation
  56, 59, 68, 69–70, 74
  involvement in pop/punk
  music 65–6
  'outsider' status 56, **62–71**
  and queer culture 67–8, 69
  relationship with Academy
  13, 57–9, 61–2, 70–1, 72
  self-promotion/public
  image 65–8
  social/career background
  62–5
Alone (1999) 13
Alonso, Juanjo 53–4
Alonso, Lisardo 95, 114
Álvarez, Mercedes 90, 98, 99
Álvarez Monzoncillo, José
  María 14–15, 18, 33–4
Alvero, Rafael 92
Los amantes del círculo polar
  see *The Lovers of the
  Arctic Circle*
Amenábar, Alejandro 1, 11,
  36, 61, 83t, 85–6, 99

American Pie (1999) 84–5
Amigo, Ángel 116–17
El amor del capitán Brando see
  *The Love of Captain
  Brando*
Andreu, Cristina 74
Angulo, Jesús 87
The Animated Forest (1987)
  48, 48t, **49–50**, *50*, 51,
  52, 73
Antonioni, Michelangelo 20,
  99, 101
Aranda, Vicente 22
Araújo, Marta 110
Arbeloa, Álvaro 81
La ardilla roja see *The Red
  Squirrel*
Argentinian cinema 114–15
Ariel awards (Mexico) 112,
  113, 115
Aristarain, Adolfo 83t, 116
Armendáriz, Montxo 48t
Armiñán, Jaime de 27
Arrizabalaga, José Luis 74
Artiñano, Javier 50
Association of Spanish Film
  Historians 31
¡Atame! see *Tie Me Up, Tie Me
  Down!*
auteurism 24, **75–6**
  'auteurist generation' 15,
  59–60, 63, 128n21
avant-garde cinema *see*
  independent/avant-
  garde cinema
Avatar (2009) 125n2
  (Introduction)
awards *see* Academy Awards;
  Cannes Film Festival;
  Francoism; Goya
  Awards; Venice Film
  Festival
¡Ay, Carmela! (1990) **51–2**,
  73, 107, 128n22
  awards 48–9, 48t, 52, 58
  box-office success 52

Azcona, Rafael 48–9, 48t
Bad Education (2004) 57–8,
  69, 102
Bajo las estrellas (2007) 101t
Balada triste de trompeta see
  The Last Circus
Balagueró, Jaume 101
Balfour, Sebastian 111
La Banda Trapera del Río
  (band) 65
Banderas, Antonio 36, 58, 116
Baquero, Ivana 11
Bardem, Javier 1, 11, 36, 57,
  108, 128n21
Bardem, Juan Antonio 10,
  21, 22, 23, 42
Barranco, María 107
Barreda, Miguel 116
Bartolomé, Cecilia 22, 63, 95
The Basque Ball (2003) 53
Basque separatist movement
  53
Batlle, Diego 116
Bayona, Juan Antonio 1, 36,
  94, 101, 108
Bazán, María 102
Belinchón, Gregorio 81
Belle de jour (1967) 51
Belle Époque (1992) 1, 95, 106
Bellissima (1951) 62
Bellmunt, Francesc 128–9n3
Benlliure, Mariano 118
Bentley, Bernard 37–8
Bergfelder, Tim 10, 73
Bergman, Ingmar 101
Berlin, Víctor 96
Berlusconi, Silvio 56
Berri, Claude 49
Berrocal, Miguel Ortiz 52–3,
  118
Bessy, Maurice 26
Best Hispano-American Film
  (Goya award, formerly
  Best Spanish-Language
  Foreign Film) 105,
  109–19